POLICYMAKING
and
POLITICS
in the Federal District Courts

POLICYMAKING
and
POLITICS
in the Federal District Courts

ROBERT A. CARP
AND
C. K. ROWLAND

THE UNIVERSITY OF TENNESSEE PRESS
KNOXVILLE

PUBLICATION OF THIS BOOK
has been assisted by a grant from the University of Houston.

Copyright © 1983
by The University of Tennessee Press / Knoxville.
Manufactured in the United States of America.
All rights reserved.
First edition.

Clothbound editions of University of Tennessee
Press books are printed on paper designed for
an effective life of at least 300 years, and binding
materials are chosen for strength and durability.

Library of Congress Cataloging in Publication Data

Carp, Robert A., 1943–
    Policymaking and politics in the federal district
courts.

    Bibliography: p.
    Includes index.
    1. Judicial process – United States. 2. District
courts – United States. I. Rowland, C. K., 1943–
II. Title.
KF8775.C37 1983   347.73′22   82-13462
ISBN 0-87049-369-8   347.3072

To the Memory of my Mother, Betty Jean Carp
—R.A.C.

To my Mother Elsie Rowland and my Aunt Polly Coulter
—C.K.R.

Preface

At the outset we feel obliged to set forth our basic beliefs about the causal relationship between judges' background characteristics and their subsequent judicial behavior. A casual observer's reaction to the titles of the various chapters would probably be as follows: "Apparently you believe that if you know the judges's party affiliation, his appointing president, or the locale of his court, then you can tell me how the judge will decide any given case." Or, "Your book gives the impression that 'old-fashioned' things such as evidence, controlling precedents, and the judge's legal training don't make any difference in the way cases are decided." Neither of these assessments could be further from the truth. Both before we began this research and since the project was completed, we have had no cause to doubt what judges and lawyers and traditional public law scholars have told us for years: the best way to predict the outcome of most routine cases is to determine which litigant presents the stronger factual evidence and the best controlling precedents. To say otherwise is to ignore a vast storehouse of empirical and nonempirical knowledge and to cast unjustified doubt upon the competence and integrity of those who administer justice throughout the United States.

We do believe that judges are regularly confronted with cases for which the evidence and controlling precedents are about equally compelling, with issues for which the evidence and case law are conflicting and confusing, and with new types of questions for which there are no controlling precedents or higher court rulings. Judges' personal values, the traditions and practices of their own district or circuit, or the values and attitudes of their particular region then do enter in to the judicial decision-making process. Although such situations may comprise only a minor part of the average judge's caseload, we believe that part is still significant enough to warrant analysis by students of judicial behavior, for in these cases the judge's potential for judicial policymaking is at its maximum.

Acknowledgments

There are many to whom we owe a great deal for their help with this research. Russell R. Wheeler, now assistant director of the Federal Judicial Center, was originally one of the coauthors of this book. Because of the demands of his position at the National Center for State Courts he was unable to continue with the project. Nevertheless, for his countless hours of work during the early phases of the data collection and for his counsel and encouragement since that time, we express considerable gratitude. We also thank Professor Sheldon Goldman, who saved us countless hours of labor by sharing with us background data on many of the judges. To the following of our colleagues who served as readers of the manuscript and who provided us with extremely useful critiques, we offer our sincere thanks: Richard J. Richardson (University of North Carolina), Charles Johnson (Texas A & M University), and Nathan Goldman (University of Texas at Austin).

R.A.C. and C.K.R.

I gratefully acknowledge the Research Enabling Grant provided by the University of Houston in 1979 which gave financial support for data collection during the summer months of that year. To Mrs. Laquita Stidham for her first-rate job of typing the initial draft of the manuscript I also offer my thanks. Finally, I express my gratitude to the members of my family and to a number of very special friends who gave me their love and encouragement during the decade-long period of this research.

R.A.C.

I wish to personally thank the following individuals for their help and useful suggestions: Professors John Nalbandian (University of

Kansas), Roger Marz (Oakland University), William Macauley (Oakland University), and the late Marian Wilson (Oakland University).

C.K.R.

Contents

FIGURES

TABLES

POLICYMAKING
and
POLITICS
in the Federal District Courts

1.

JUDGING AND JUDICIAL POLICYMAKING

INTRODUCTION

Slowly but perceptibly over the past several decades we have become what Jethro Lieberman has called "the litigious society."[1] Daily media accounts mirror the phenomenon: a young woman sues her mother and father for damages due to "failures of parenting"; a college instructor argues in court that a recent merit salary increment is unduly low and hence a violation of his Fourteenth Amendment rights; a graduate of a prominent Ivy League business school sues his alma mater and a former professor because "an investment model learned in the classroom failed to produce the anticipated results." Disputes which at one time were resolved informally between private parties are now more likely to be adjudicated in the public courts. The result has been ever-mounting judicial caseloads and increasing judicial involvement in areas of American life heretofore regarded as "private." These new areas of judicial involvement tend to be relatively free of clear, precise appellate court and legislative guidelines; and as a consequence the opportunity for trial court jurists to write on a clean slate, that is, to make policy, is formidable.

While there are many reasons for our having become a more litigious society, surely a major portion of the responsibility rests with the courts themselves. The great emphasis given to the First and Fourteenth Amendments during the Warren Court era encouraged many to seek judicial relief for grievances that was not attainable from legislative or administrative bodies. Still, the evolution of our litigious society reflects important basic changes in American jurisprudence and in the role of law in the United States. Perhaps the most important change in American jurisprudence has been what some legal scholars have called a shift from contractual to fiduciary jurisprudence.[2] Contractual definitions of the relationship between

1. Lieberman, *Litigious Society*. See also Greenias and Windsor, "Is Judicial Restraint Possible in an Administrative Society?"
2. Lieberman, *Litigious Society*, 21. In this regard Lieberman builds on the work

legal rights and duties are based on relatively specific agreements on rules. Fiduciary legal relationships, on the other hand, are based on relatively subjective standards of duty and trust which define the nature of legal relationships in general, imprecise terms. For example, patients in mental hospitals have acquired the right to expect "a standard of care" commensurate with their general constitutional guarantees, but the specifics of this standard remain ill-defined and subject to judicial interpretations. Likewise, when Congress instructs the Occupational Safety and Health Administration to safeguard the workplace, the proper level of occupational safety becomes a standard for interpretation by bureaucrats and ultimately by the judiciary.

The emergence of new legal questions for which no precise appellate court or legislative guidelines exist gives the jurists more leeway to shape or manipulate specific policy outcomes through application and interpretation of general standards and to interject into their decisions their own values and extralegal cues from the larger political environment. In the parlance of political science, the courts' policymaking role increases relative to their norm-enforcement role because fiduciary jurisprudence requires judges to set policy in the absence of prevailing norms, statutes, or controlling precedents.

Although the role of policymaking has been expanded at all judicial levels, it has been most apparent for federal district judges. The number of civil cases filed in the trial courts increased by more than 300 percent between 1960 and 1980. Still, the importance of this quantitative change pales in comparison with the qualitative alterations in trial litigation. Groups with limited access to legislative and executive policymaking institutions recognized federal district courts as institutions that could translate group demands into public policy.[3] In the recent past the district courts have been battlegrounds of such major public policy questions as abortion, the draft, the war in Vietnam, protection of the environment, and methods of public school integration. Examples of trial judge involvement in new public policy issues abound:

1. When a district court in Ohio ruled that the Environmental Protection Agency was bound by the 1970 Environmental Protection Act and could not rely on the 1899 Refuse Act as the basis for its clean water permit program, the EPA permit program was delayed for over a year. The district judge exer-

---

of Maine, who identified social development with the move from status to contractual definitions of rights and duties. See Maine, *Ancient Law*.

3. For discussion of interest groups in the judicial process, see Vose, "Litigation as a Form of Pressure Group Activity," 20–31. Also see Casper, *Lawyers before the Warren Courts*.

cised his own discretion to interpret ambivalent statutory standards. Moreover, by delaying the EPA's national permit program, he authoritatively allocated values for virtually every American citizen from his Ohio courtroom.

2. When Judge Frank Johnson ruled that conditions in Alabama's state mental hospitals violated patients' constitutional guarantees, he mandated fifty specific policy changes which, in turn, required changes in related budgetary and personnel policy. The district judge translated constitutional standards into policies that affect every public mental patient in the state and, indirectly, every taxpayer. Further, in our common law system, this decision may well influence similar cases throughout the country.

3. In a commentary on the 1981 session of the Texas legislature, the respected *Texas Monthly* (July 1981) observed that a local U.S. district judge, William Wayne Justice, "did more to shape the appropriations bill than any member of the budget committees." Commenting on his many far-reaching decisions on criminal justice, public education, and legislative redistricting, the *Monthly* suggested that were the judge "in the legislature he would never be able to legislate as effectively as he does from the bench."

In each of these examples the judge resolved legal disputes by allocating social values. Whether the decisions were "good" depends of course on one's point of view, but they are important here for two reasons. First, they illustrate current disputes that would not have been on a federal docket only a generation ago; and, second, they exemplify the extent to which district judges exercise discretion and make public policy rather than simply enforcing traditional norms.

If the district courts are political institutions with vast discretion to translate standards into rules and thereby make public policy, a perplexing question is raised: what guides the exercise of this expanded judicial discretion? Do judges exercise discretion in response to legal guidelines and a careful reading of the law, or do personal background and environmental factors enter into the policymaking process? Can differences in the way trial judges reach policy decisions be traced to variations in their political values, attitudes, and decision-making environments?

The conventional answer to these questions has been an unqualified and emphatic no. Traditional legal scholars asserted that judicial decisions were made by fitting mechanically the facts of a given case to the appropriate legal constraints found in precedent, statute, or constitutional law. At the trial court level they accepted the validity of the basic adversary model and its fundamental assumption that fact-law congruence would be achieved through the adversary process. Judges were assumed to be apolitical and able to separate their own values from the judicial decision; thus, extralegal factors were irrelevant.

Most judicial scholars now reject the notion of mechanical jurisprudence, especially when judges are required to make policy in response to new legal questions without precise controlling norms or rules. Indeed, some of the Supreme Court's most prominent jurists have acknowledged the influence of their own personal backgrounds and values on their judicial decisions. In a series of lectures in 1921, Benjamin Cardozo observed that judges often face new or difficult questions and are guided by a "stream of tendency" made up of instincts, traditional beliefs, and acquired convictions to resolve legal questions in the absence of clear legal guidelines.[4] Modern behavioral studies of appellate judges in general, and of U.S. Supreme Court justices in particular, demonstrate convincingly that appellate jurists from like backgrounds respond in the same way to similar extralegal policy influences. Indeed, C. Neal Tate used differences in social and political backgrounds to explain more than 80 percent of the civil liberalism variance among twenty-five Supreme Court justices.[5]

Even a casual perusal of district court decisions suggests that this same "stream of tendency" also guides contemporary federal trial judges. Practicing defense attorneys in any jurisdiction can identify "sympathetic" and "unsympathetic" jurists. Social scientists have likewise found significant linkages between judicial backgrounds and judges' policy propensities. For example, several scholars found that the willingness of district judges to implement national civil rights policies depended on their personal backgrounds and the local political environment.[6]

Although both legal practitioners and social scientists contend that district judges are influenced by extralegal factors, they have not yet fully determined whether the political influences on these judges are systematic or idiosyncratic. Perhaps extralegal effects are limited to a few narrow policy questions (such as school desegregation) under singular circumstances. Or perhaps each judge's "stream of tendency" is unique and purely personal. On the other hand, it seems probable that trial judges with common extralegal back-

4. Cardozo, *Nature of the Judicial Process*, 12–13. See also Cardozo, *Growth of the Law*.

5. Tate, "Personal Attribute Models," 355–56. Also see Ulmer, "Social Backgrounds."

6. Vines, "Federal District Judges and Race Relations Cases"; Giles and Walker, "Judicial Policy-Making and Southern School Desegregation"; Peltason, *58 Lonely Men*.

grounds would respond to the same extralegal cues and that a comparison of judges from like political backgrounds would reveal systematic, similar patterns in their policy decisions. The probability that judges who are similarly situated will respond to the same extralegal cues is buttressed by the nature of judicial recruitment. At a minimum, the process by which district judges are selected suggests that political influences will not be idiosyncratic. Judicial recruitment is a complex process described in detail in several excellent studies.[7] Essentially, the president nominates district judges after consultation with home-state senator(s) and other home-state political leaders from the president's party. After hearings before the Senate Judiciary Committee, nominees are usually confirmed by the Senate. If home-state senator(s) object, however, and invoke senatorial courtesy, the president's nominee is almost always rejected. Not surprisingly, this process has produced a federal bench on which more than 90 percent of the district judges share their appointing president's affiliation. The vast majority also share the basic judicial and political philosophies of their appointing president and home-state senator(s). Judges recruited from the same state share a similar political environment and hear cases in similar judicial settings. Judges from the same party are likely to share a common history of partisan activism.

One would expect the systematic influence of party, appointing president, and local political environment on judicial selection to be reflected in the judges' decisions. That is, Democratic judges ought to behave differently on the bench from their Republican colleagues; the appointees of each president should be somewhat unique in their policy propensities; and jurists from different local environments ought to manifest systematic variations in the way they make judicial policy. Nevertheless, despite the intuitive appeal of these hypotheses, more systematic empirical verification is necessary. We still need additional data to demonstrate the degree to which shared judicial background variables are manifested in common "streams of tendency."

As our review of the literature will indicate, the evidence for a relationship between judicial background variables and subsequent policy decisions is somewhat inconclusive. Although it is fairly strong for appellate court judges, it is weak and inconsistent for trial jurists. On closer examination, however, this apparent anomaly is less perplexing. To interject extralegal influences into their decisions, district judges must have both the inclination and the oppor-

7. See Goldman and Jahnige, *Federal Courts*, 47–77; Chase, *Federal Judges*; Grossman, *Lawyers and Judges*.

tunity to do so. The politics of recruitment almost guarantee that most will have the inclination, but opportunity is a function of organizational as well as environmental and political factors. Although the evolution of fiduciary jurisprudence has expanded the opportunity for district judges to exercise personal discretion by raising new, unprecedented legal questions, trial judges remain limited by their position at the bottom of the federal judicial hierarchy. There, discretion may be constrained by the speed, precision, and consistency with which the appellate courts address new legal questions and issue guidelines for district judges. Since such factors vary from one time period to another, we may expect the exercise of discretion by district judges and the influence of political factors on their decisions to vary accordingly. We have therefore developed a conceptual framework to guide our inquiry which recognizes explicitly the organizational context of district court policy decisions.

CONCEPTUAL FRAMEWORK

Unlike analyses of the Congress and of the Supreme Court, studies of U.S. district courts must account for more than 400 courts and judges in more than 90 districts distributed among 50 states, the District of Columbia, and several territories. Thus the very multiplicity which makes the courts accessible and, therefore, enhances their relevance, also makes these important institutions more difficult to analyze. Moreover, the district courts are organizational anomalies. They are national institutions operating in and constrained by state and local environments. District judges are appointed by federal officials but have strong legal and political ties to the local environment. Also, they are often called upon to administer and interpret state law. Despite their position at the base of the federal judicial hierarchy, trial jurists often find ways to contravene the will of the appeals courts in favor of their own policy propensities. Nevertheless, to a large degree they are still severely constrained by appellate court decisions and guidelines. Thus, the effects of party affiliation, appointing president, and local political environment cannot be explored systematically without recognizing this unique combination of influences which impinge on U.S. district judges.

To understand this complex relationship it is useful to think of the federal district courts as the first tier in an organization which approximates Talcott Parsons's three-tier ideal.[8] Each level in the Par-

---

8. Parsons, *Structure and Process in Modern Societies*, 59–96; also see Goldman and Jahnige, *Federal Courts*, 42–46.

sonian model is structured to facilitate performance of important organizational functions. The institutional level at the top is responsible for articulating the organization's collective purpose, interacting with the larger environment, and setting goals to guide decision making below. The intermediate, or managerial, level functions to translate these guidelines into decision premises that facilitate their application to the organization's specific tasks. This application takes place at the lowest, or technical, level, which bears primary responsibility for generating the organization's product or outputs.

The application of this model to the federal courts is apparent. As the institution topping this hierarchy, the Supreme Court is responsible for setting the basic policy guidelines of the federal judiciary and for preserving the political legitimacy of the courts. The Court must interact with the national social, economic, and political environment by translating inconsistent or even contradictory demands into coherent policies. Within the organization, the Court must promulgate decision criteria and performance standards for the two lower levels. At the managerial level, the appellate courts translate and adapt institutional policy into more precise standards that direct decision making below. In the federal judiciary this policy adaptation is accomplished by reviewing trial court decisions in light of the Supreme Court guidelines and by shaping the lower courts' technical decisions to fit those guidelines. Unlike the Parsonian ideal, however, judicial reviews are undertaken at the initiative of the client at the technical level, that is, the unsuccessful litigant.[9]

We do not, of course, argue that the courts achieve the ideal of Parsons's model. We have used the analogy to help us develop an explanatory theory about the relation between Supreme Court decisions and the subsequent behavior of U.S. trial judges. To the extent that the federal judiciary approximates the Parsonian model, *policy* decisions will be made at the institutional (Supreme Court) level, and the technical (district court) tier will merely apply these policies to routine *norm-enforcement* decisions. On the other hand, to the extent that the institutional and managerial levels fail to guide decision making below, we can anticipate an increase in the amount of

9. In one regard, the transmission of clear cues down the organizational hierarchy is more difficult in the judicial setting than in the ideal setting. Ideally, personnel at the technical level look to unambiguous directives as a welcome means of reducing uncertainty and increasing efficiency, but the policies of judicial recruitment and several innovative studies of lower-court responses to Supreme Court decisions suggest that district judges often welcome ambiguous or contradictory decision premises as an opportunity to circumvent unpopular standards. Certainly, many district judges in the South exploited the ambiguity and imprecision of early desegration opinions by distinguishing local desegregation cases in response to local extralegal pressures and their own personal values.

discretion used by district judges and thus an increase in their policymaking.

In the context of our organizational framework, the discretion exercised by trial judges is a function of the quantity and precision of messages communicated to them by the appellate courts and particularly by the Supreme Court. This view is consistent with the role of information developed by communications theorists, who portray every complex organization as an information network held together by the communication of information among its various levels or components. Organizations that rely on decision premises at the institutional level tend to be cohesive to the extent that policymakers at this level are able to communicate information with minimal distortion of its content. Redundancy, in the language of communications theory, reduces "noise" or extraneous information in communications channels and thus enhances the prospects for clarity and consistency of organizational response. Whatever the goals or purpose of an organization, redundancy, and therefore cohesion, are facilitated when an organization is, in the words of Karl Deutsch, "structured to include the results of its own action in the new information by which it modifies its subsequent behavior."[10]

The introduction of communications theory into the organizational context of the federal judiciary leads us to conceptualize U.S. trial judges as technical-level decision makers who depend on clear, consistent communication of legal guidelines to reduce the noise created by extralegal cues. To the extent that the judiciary approaches Parsons's organizational model, it also promotes the ideal jurisprudence enunciated by the prominent communications theorist Norbert Weiner: "The first duty of . . . the law is to know what it wants. The first duty of the judge is to make clear, unambiguous statements which [expert and layman] will interpret in one way and one way only."[11]

Using the Parsonian model and communications theory, we now suggest in part why the literature has not been able to demonstrate a strong, perpetual link between the political backgrounds and policy decisions of district judges: existing studies tend to ignore the clarity and consistency of the messages trial judges receive from the Supreme Court. During periods of organizational cohesion on the High Court, it sends forth reasonably precise and specific messages, and such clear guidelines restrict the maneuverability of the district judges. However, during times of ideological uncertainty on the Supreme Court, noise is introduced into the communication system.

10. Deutsch, *Nerves of Government*, 77–150.
11. Weiner, *Human Use of Human Beings*.

This in turn increases the amount of discretion open to trial judges to respond to cues from their own political backgrounds and environment. Thus, the relative influence of legal and extralegal factors on the district courts should be a function of the precision and consistency of legal cues from the Supreme Court. Precise cues minimize extralegal effects; imprecise messages maximize them.

If the opportunity for district judges to exercise policy discretion is related to the clarity of Supreme Court communication, then changes in the nature of High Court signals should be manifested in the variability of the voting patterns of trial judges. The contrast between the Warren and the Burger courts offers an obvious test of the proposition. The 1969 transformation marked the end of a liberal court era and the beginning of what Glendon Schubert has termed "the era of Contemporary Conservatism."[12] This ideological shift introduced new legal cues into the judicial communications network and created the need for precise, consistent guidelines to implement these cues at the trial court level. An impressive array of scholars, however, have characterized the lion's share of the Burger Court precedents as ideologically imprecise and inconsistent. They have criticized the unstable Burger Court majority for its lack of clarity in guiding the decision making of U.S. trial judges.[13] While the inconsistency and ambiguity of Burger Court opinions may be overstated in absolute terms, its guidelines are certainly less precise than those formulated by the Warren Court's narrow, but more consistent, liberal majority.

If the effect of extralegal cues on district judges' decisions is heightened by Supreme Court ambiguity, then we would expect such extralegal cues to be particularly strong after the advent of the Burger Court and Contemporary Conservatism in 1969. More precisely, our model would predict that variations in trial judge voting patterns (according to party affiliation, appointing president, and geographic location) should be greater under the Burger Court era than during the Warren Court years. Indeed this is one of the key hypotheses that will occupy us throughout much of the book.

ANALYTIC FRAMEWORK

Besides our conceptualizing of district courts as components in a larger organization held together by an information network, we

---

12. Schubert, *Judicial Policy Making*, 189–213.
13. See Mendelson, "From Warren to Burger"; Wasby, *Continuity and Change;* Goldstein, "Politics of the Burger Court Toward Women"; Walker, "Burger Court and Civil Liberties, 359–90.

must also develop a framework for analyzing individual policy decisions. We are considering here a special case of human judgment. As a concept, judgment has not received the attention from legal scholars that it has from psychologists. Certain psychologists have developed a model of judgment as a two-dimensional process by which humans adapt to uncertain environments and shape the future without severing ties to the past.[14] Judgment allows us to cope with, or adapt to, an uncertain world by providing us the means to go beyond psychological "givens" without sacrificing organization and continuity of behavior. To judge, we exercise discretion by responding to information from the environment and by estimating the probabilities and consequences of alternate decisions.

Given its assumption of uncertainty and its estimates of future outcomes, judgment does not apply in the absence of discretion. Judges actually *judge* only when they exercise discretion in response to uncertainty. When they apply known law to uncontested facts, they administer or enforce norms. District judges make judgments only when they are asked to exercise discretion in the face of uncertain legal guidelines from above.

To analyze this special exercise of human judgment one needs a framework which recognizes its dual nature, that is, what Timothy O'Neill calls "a prudent recognition of the pitfalls of wholesale innovation harnessed to a recognition of the need to adapt to changing circumstances."[15] Most empirical studies of judicial judgment have been guided by one of two general analytic frameworks — organizational and psychometric.[16]

Under the organization framework, judicial decisions are viewed as the product of "work groups" in which prosecutors, judges, defense attorneys, and others interact and cooperate on a regular basis. Variation in outcomes of trials may be explained not by the relative skill of adversaries, the evidence, or controlling law but by differences in organizational structure of characteristics of the work group.[17] Psychometric frameworks, on the other hand, focus attention on the values and psychological factors that influence the decisions of individual judges. Cases are the stimuli, and judges' decisions are the corresponding responses.

It is apparent that the assumptions of each framework make it an

14. Rappaport and Summers, *Human Judgment and Social Interaction.*
15. O'Neill, "Language of Equality," 631.
16. Blumberg, *Criminal Justice;* Heydebrand, "Context of Public Bureaucracies"; Eisenstein and Jacob, *Felony Justice.* The psychometric model is presented in Schubert, *Judicial Mind Revisited.* Its most influential early application was by Pritchett, *Civil Liberties and the Vinson Court.*
17. Eisenstein and Jacob, *Felony Justice.*

inappropriate guide for empirical examination of trial judges' policy decisions. The organizational model is by definition appropriate for routine, norm-enforcement decisions. The psychometric framework assumes a collegial setting in which judges respond nonunanimously to the same case stimuli. Owing in part to the inherent limitations of the organizational and psychometric models, the most influential work on the federal trial courts has rested on analytic frameworks derived from the general systems model borrowed from biology and introduced to political science by David Easton.[18] Richardson and Vines's useful adaptation of the systems model argues that judges have ties to two overlapping subcultures — the legal and the democratic.[19] Judicial policy decisions are made in response to demands from both subcultures. The relative influence of these demands, however, is a function of the type of case, the judge's perception of his role, the clarity of cues from the legal subcultures, and various other factors. According to our organizational view of the district courts, demands originating in the legal subculture will be more important when clear legal guidelines are congruent with the facts presented in a given case. In the absence of precise cues from the legal subsystem, policy decisions are made in response to noise from the democratic subculture rather than to precise guidelines from the legal realm.

Figure 1. **Framework for Analysis of Federal District Court Policy Decisions**

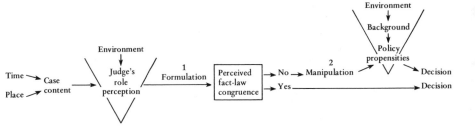

Figure 1 depicts a two-stage decision process in which the judge must first estimate available discretion and then choose between norm-enforcement and policymaking. The process could, of course,

18. Easton, *Framework for Political Analysis.*
19. Richardson and Vines, *Politics of Federal Courts.*

be broken into any number of smaller steps. As in Herbert Simon's general model of problem solving by decision makers, the first step is formulation of the question.[20] Once the problem has been set forth, the decision maker may take the second step — manipulation of alternatives to develop a satisfying solution. In the judicial setting, the formulation of the question requires judges to estimate the amount of discretion available to them and decide how much of this they wish to exercise. To some degree the formulation decision is subjective. Activist judges will find more discretion in a given fact-law situation than will their more restrained colleagues.

THE DATA SOURCES AND RESEARCH METHODS

THE SOURCES OF EVIDENCE

The data for this study have been derived from 27,772 federal district court opinions issued by nearly a thousand judges during forty-four years (1933 through early 1977). The cases were taken from the *Federal Supplement*, the primary outlet for the publication of U.S. trial court opinions. Only those cases were used that fit easily into one of twenty case types which appeared to contain a clear underlying liberal-conservative dimension. They included such cases as state and federal habeas corpus pleas, labor-management disputes, government regulation of the economy controversies, and so on; excluded were cases involving patents, admiralty disputes, and land condemnation hearings. The number of cases not selected was about the same as those included.

For each case, data were also collected on the date of the opinion and on the city, state, district, and circuit wherein the decision was rendered. Not included in the data set were decisions by appellate court judges acting as trial jurists, cases decided by judges outside the districts which they regularly served, decisions handed down by special three-judge courts, and cases decided by judges in the "senior judge" status.

Information was gathered on the political party affiliation, the appointing president, and the year of the appointment of 1,007 judges, although several did not write opinions. The primary sources of this background data were the *Congressional Quarterly Almanac*, *Who's Who in America*, and several of our professional colleagues, whose names are mentioned in the Preface.

20. Simon, *Administrative Behavior.*

We have supplemented the empirical data with anecdotal information gathered from interviews and from unpublished judicial papers. Some of the most useful information derives from the public and private papers of Judge William F. Riley, who was the U.S. judge for the Southern District of Iowa between 1950 and 1956.[21] These approximately 7,000 papers consist of letters and judicial memoranda written by Riley and his political, professional, and judicial associates between 1932 and 1956. Almost half of these papers relate directly to the six-year period of his judicial tenure. A final source of data was provided by the interviews with thirty federal district judges performed for a series of other investigations with which Carp has been associated in the past decade.[22] Material from the Riley papers and from the interviews will provide additional evidence in support of the primary hypotheses we will be testing as well as some anecdotal relief from the empirical data which fill the pages of much of this text.

THE *FEDERAL SUPPLEMENT* AS THE PRIMARY DATA SOURCE

In regard to the policy of West Publishing Company in their publication of the *Federal Supplement*, Professor Allan Vestal tells us, "The attitude of the West Publishing Company . . . seems to be that it will publish any writing which a sitting federal district judge sends into the company. The initiative is with the writing judge. If he does not send in the material, it is not published."[23] Such an observation finds support in an independent analysis of the subject performed by Professor Kenneth Dolbeare and also in a more recent study performed by the Federal Judicial Center.[24] Interviews with personnel at the Judicial Center and with several district judges indicate that occasionally the law clerks, rather than the judge, take the initiative for sending in to West the opinions that they think worthy of publication. Nevertheless the central point remains that West routinely publishes all district court opinions which are sent in to them.

The evidence is overwhelming that most judges, lawyers, and public law scholars regard the *Federal Supplement* as preeminent in the field of publishing district court opinions. (West nurtures this exclusiveness by refusing generally even to acknowledge in its pub-

21. The Riley papers are located in Special Collections, Univ. of Iowa Main Library, Iowa City.
22. See Carp and Wheeler, "Sink or Swim."
23. Vestal, "Reported Opinions of the Federal District Courts," 390.
24. Dolbeare, "Federal District Courts," 377–78; Flanders, *Case Management and Court Management*, 153.

lications the existence of other series of reports.) As the author of numerous studies of the status and contents of the *Supplement*, Vestal tells us, "When the average practitioner considers the actions taken by the federal district courts he thinks of the West publications — first the *Federal Supplement*, and then on a moment's reflection he will probably recall the *Federal Rules Decisions*. These two series are considered generally as the means by which the opinions of the district courts are made available to the legal profession."[25]

The *Supplement* takes on added importance because almost by definition West publishes only those decisions which the judges themselves (or their law clerks) regard as inherently significant and worthy. As Dolbeare says in speaking of the *Supplement*, "At the very least, it would appear that the resultant body of cases would include most of the *major* policy decisions made by federal district judges."[26]

WHAT THE DATA SET REPRESENTS

An argument against performing a study of trial court behavior based on the courts' published opinions is that the final, published opinion of a court tells only a small part of the real story of the case. Because it fails to take into consideration all the nuances of the case and how the judge ruled on the various motions made throughout the trial, it may be thought to be deceptive.[27] The argument is not without merit, but we would respond to it in precisely the same way as did Dolbeare, who relied on *Supplement* opinions in his analysis of federal trial courts and urban public policy: "for what it may be worth in exculpatory terms, we may note that there appears to be no more rigorous way [other than relying on the *Supplement*] to gather data on the outcome of cases, short of a review of transcripts in each court's files — a task whose dimensions foreclose the prospect on more than case study or sampling, rather than comparative, terms. The body of cases actually developed and employed in this inquiry must, therefore, be viewed as an expedient and implications drawn from the following analysis taken as no more than tentative interpretations."[28] Since our sample of cases is more than eighty times larger than Dolbeare's, we are somewhat more bold in support of our subsequent findings, although we are still quite prepared

25. Vestal, "Survey of Federal District Court Opinions," 74.
26. Dolbeare, "Federal District Courts," 378.
27. Chase, *Federal Judges*, 118.
28. Dolbeare, "Federal District Courts and Urban Public Policy," 378.

to concede that the published opinion does not tell "the whole story" of the judicial decision making that went into the case.

A second general critique is about the qualitative nature of our data set. Does it represent a true random sample of *all* cases? a composite of opinions by judges who simply like to see their names in print? the undiluted universe of only the important cases? Such questions are important, and our response to them significantly affects our analyses and generalizations.

First, let us frankly and openly acknowledge the limitations of our data base. Only a small percentage of district court decisions are ever formally published. The vast majority are either not justified in written form at all, or they appear merely as slip opinions or memoranda which accompany a case on appeal. We know very little about the contents or impact of these many unreported opinions, although scholars at the Federal Judicial Center believe that "Findings of fact and conclusions of law are probably the tasks represented most poorly. They are prepared in some form in all nonjury cases, though in some courts the judge may deliver findings and conclusions orally. Judges may differ more widely in their publications habits regarding findings and conclusions than in other types of work."[29] Although evidence suggests that opinions dealing with important issues are more likely to find their way onto the printed page than opinions of a more routine or trivial nature, nevertheless our data base is limited by the absence of published opinions for *all* cases. Our reason for not including the unpublished written and oral decisions is of course that they are virtually unattainable.

The reporting of opinions varies from judge to judge, from region to region, and from one time period to another.[30] The following quotations from three federal district court judges illustrates the variety of factors which help to determine whether or not the judge submits an opinion for publication.

A U.S. judge in Los Angeles told us, "When the judge is first appointed; he comes on the bench convinced he's the wisest judge ever appointed; he really wants to impress everyone; he knows [thinks] every case he gets is important and wants to clarify everything — let the Supreme Court know what the law really is. So he floods West [Publishing Co.]. Then, [about five years into his term] he . . . begins to send in less and less." The California judge then added, "More courts are moving away from — and many have eliminated —

29. Flanders, *Case Management and Court Management*, 153.
30. Flanders, *Case Management and Court Management*, 56–59 and 153; Vestal, "Survey of Federal District Court Opinions." Also see Vestal, "Reported Federal District Court Opinions," and "Publishing District Court Opinions." Also, see Carp and Rowland, "Opinion Writing by Federal District Judges."

written opinions. The Ninth Circuit has for the last six to nine months been moving steadily to bench memoranda, which are not published, rather than written opinions."

A jurist in the District of Columbia observed, "I think a lot of judges — especially new judges like to see their name in print. . . . I remember when I was at a party with the head of West, and he said to my wife: 'Your husband costs us a lot of money.' Well, I thought about that, and I've toned down the number I send in. I think you have to write when it's needed for review in appellate courts." A federal judge in the Fourth Circuit said, "I don't send in many cases. I never have. Now Judge _____, over in the Western District, sends in all his habeas corpus opinions. I think I've sent in one while I've been on the bench. I never send them in unless I think it's going to help another judge." After having read the 27,772 sample cases, we believe that the data set represents the overwhelming majority of the more important, policymaking cases that come before the lower federal judiciary. Perhaps 85 to 90 percent of our sample consist of cases that are somewhat unusual and/or which contain elements that potentially affect parties other than those whose case is being litigated. Dolbeare reached the same conclusion about his smaller sample of cases taken from the *Supplement*. "We have noted a source of probable bias toward the major cases, and the fact that *all* cases which were appealed and decided by a Circuit Court in this period are included reinforces this emphasis on the more important cases. . . . I think it is fair to argue that the cases employed, while not representative of workload, are at least *indicative* of the major policy actions of the District Courts and that they are therefore serviceable for cautious outlining of the primary features of the policy product and impact of these courts."[31]

The remaining 10 to 15 percent of the cases in our sample deal with legal issues which do border on the trivial. For example, a West Virginia jurist took several pages of the *Supplement* to explain why the punishment of a state prisoner for his refusal to bury a dead skunk was not a violation of the prisoner's civil rights. A judge in Pennsylvania agonized at length as to whether the First Amendment protected from a tort action *Time* magazine, which had published a photograph of a man whose fly had become unzipped. Although these less-than-monumental decisions do exist in our data set, two factors minimize their impact on our conclusions. The first is their small number, and the second is that there is no reason to believe that they serve to bias the sample. That is, there is no reason to suppose the Democrats or Eisenhower appointees or southern judges

31. Dolbeare, "Federal District Courts and Urban Public Policy," 378.

are more likely to submit trivial cases for publication than their counterparts with other background characteristics.

THE MAGNITUDE OF THE DATA BASE

Having argued that patterns of policy decisions can be discerned only through the study of a large number of published opinions, we are left with the question: must we bury the reader under an avalanche of almost 28,000 cases? The answer is yes for two reasons. First, the primacy assigned to fact-law congruence by our analytic framework requires the development of useful aggregate estimates of case content. Since each case is in some ways unique, general categories of cases must be defined and each specific case assigned to only one of these. This then becomes an estimate of that case's fact situation and, indirectly, of fact-law congruence and the discretion available to the judge. The accuracy of these estimates is enhanced by the development of the largest feasible number of categories.

Second, a large number of opinions enables us to extend the classification scheme over time and by region. The classification of a civil rights case as a 1961 Mississippi school desegregation decision is a much more detailed estimate of the specific case content than is the classification of "civil rights" with no specification of issue (segregation), time, or place. The expansion of case categories across every district court for forty-four years requires an extraordinary number of cases.

THE BASIC CONTOURS OF THE DATA BASE

From the 27,772 opinions we have developed five general categories and twenty subcategories of case content. (See Appendix A for a more detailed discussion of each of these.) The first general category is that of criminal justice, and from it we developed four more precise sets of cases: (1) U.S. habeas corpus petitions; (2) state habeas corpus pleas; (3) motions made immediately before, during, or after a criminal trial; and (4) conviction for a criminal offense. Decisions favoring the petitioner of the defendant were classified as "liberal." As indicated by Table 1, our data set contains 10,488 criminal justice cases, the most numerous of which involved criminal court motions made immediately before, during, or after trial. Additional analysis indicates that the *Federal Supplement* devotes more space to criminal justice now than in the earlier years of our study: between 1933 and 1953 only 24 percent of our data set repre-

Table 1. Liberal Decisions by Type of Case, 1933-1977

Type of Case	1933-53		1954-68		1969-77		All Years	
	%	n	%	n	%	n	%	n
Criminal Justice								
U.S. habeas corpus pleas	23	412	20	355	31	883	27	1,650
State habeas corpus pleas	12	226	21	1,630	25	1,882	23	3,738
Criminal court motions	30	536	23	1,795	30	2,089	27	4,420
Conviction for a criminal offense	41	179	33	234	39	267	38	680
M	26	—	23	—	28	—	26	—
N	—	1,353	—	4,014	—	5,121	—	10,488
Government and the Economy								
Federal commercial regulation	64	779	68	966	71	851	68	2,596
Environmental protection	59	137	75	131	58	483	61	751
State and local economic regulation	56	162	67	213	74	300	67	675
Rent control, excess profit	59	685	68	139	100	6	61	830
Fair Labor Standards Act	49	1,017	68	651	60	373	57	2,041
M	57	—	68	—	66	—	63	—
N	—	2,780	—	2,100	—	2,013	—	6,893

Support for Labor								
Union vs. company	43	150	49	638	46	440	47	1,228
Union member vs. union	64	11	63	183	47	173	44	367
Employee vs. employer	39	145	40	303	36	302	38	750
M	42	—	49	—	43	—	44	—
N	—	306	—	1,124	—	915	—	2,345
Class Discrimination								
Alien petitions	38	725	39	630	49	153	40	1,508
Indian rights and law	52	75	49	55	46	81	49	211
Voting rights cases	54	26	44	97	49	191	48	314
Racial minority discrimination	56	78	44	426	54	958	51	1,462
14th Amendment and U.S. civil rights cases	21	29	29	344	44	2,207	42	2,580
Women's rights	—	—	—	—	53	256	53	256
M	41	—	39	—	47	—	45	—
N	—	933	—	1,552	—	3,846	—	6,331
First Amendment Cases								
Freedom of expression	40	168	52	259	55	705	52	1,132
Freedom of religion	39	71	35	159	63	353	52	583
M	40	—	45	—	58	—	52	—
N	—	239	—	418	—	1,058	—	1,715

sented criminal justice matters; this jumped to 44 percent between 1954 and 1968 and declined modestly to 40 percent between 1968 and 1977. Only 26 percent of all criminal justice decisions were liberal, that is, favored the defendant.

A second general category, government regulation of the economy, includes five subgroups of cases: (1) federal commercial regulation; (2) environmental protection, pure food and drug, and consumer protection; (3) economic regulation by state and local governments; (4) rent control, excessive profit, and price control; and (5) Fair Labor Standards Act. Judicial victories for the regulator were classified as liberal. This general category comprised 6,893 opinions, in which the government was the victor 63 percent of the time.

The third category is support for labor, which included 2,345 cases in three subcategories: (1) union versus company; (2) union members versus union; and (3) employees versus employer. Decisions coded as liberal were those in favor of labor (and decisions favoring workers in disputes with the labor union hierarchy). Labor won 44 percent of such disputes.

We note here that in subsequent chapters the second and third general categories will often be combined, for reasons of parsimony, into a broader composite of cases, labor and economic regulation. Analysis of this composite reveals that it is receiving less and less space in the *Supplement*. A full 55 percent of our data base for the years before 1954 consisted of economic and labor cases; this percentage dropped to 35 for 1954 to 1968; and for 1968 to 1977 it declined still further to only 23 percent of the total data set.

The fourth category deals with class discrimination and more specifically with six subgroups of cases: (1) alien petitions; (2) Indian rights and law; (3) voting rights cases; (4) racial minority discrimination; (5) Fourteenth Amendment and U.S. civil rights cases; and (6) women's rights. Court decisions favoring the aliens, the Indians, would-be voters, racial minority groups, those seeking to vindicate their Fourteenth Amendment rights, and victims of sex discrimination were defined as liberal. Overall, the liberal position prevailed in 45 percent of the policy cases.

A final category pertains to first amendment freedoms and contains two subcategories: freedom of expression and freedom of religion. If the court supported a broadening of freedom of expression, found that the government had created an unconstitutional establishment of religion, or favored the free exercise of religion, the case was coded as liberal. Fifty-two percent of the decisions were liberal.

In subsequent chapters we shall frequently combine the fourth and fifth categories into one we will call civil rights and liberties.

This combined category accounted for an ever-increasing percentage of *Supplement* opinions. Our data set showed that prior to 1954 and between that year and 1968, only 21 percent of the cases dealt with civil rights and liberties, whereas between 1968 and 1977 this figure almost doubled — to a full 38 percent.

A WORD ABOUT THE DATA ANALYSIS

Despite our frequent use of anecdotal and interview material, our primary goal is to measure quantitatively the effect of extralegal influences on judicial policy decisions. Quantitative studies of the courts pose something of a dilemma for the analyst. On the one hand, some judicial scholars are uncomfortable wth quantitative techniques in general and with statistical measures in particular. Indeed, much legal scholarship is overtly hostile to this approach. On the other hand, the strength of our aggregate data (and our ability to discriminate between liberal and conservative judicial behavior) depends heavily on statistical measures to assess the effects of environmental and background factors on policy decisions.

This dilemma is exacerbated somewhat by the dichotomous nature of the dependent variable. Judicial decisions are yes or no. Obviously the burden of defeat varies according to the punishment, and the value of victory depends on the award, but in the final analysis one side wins and the other side loses. Decisions are also either liberal or conservative. Thus, the outcome of a given case is dichotomous, and our analytic task is to discriminate between liberal and conservative outcomes by measuring the effects on them of environmental and political background variables.

Several alternative strategies recommend themselves to this task. The dichotomous dependent variable is analogous to an interval-level variable and lends itself to a variety of sophisticated and powerful parametric and nonparametric techniques.[32] Yet the temptation to maximize methodological sophistication had to be weighed against the desire to cover the most substantive ground possible. We have sought to achieve a balance by choosing for each chapter the least complex data-analysis technique that is consistent with the substantive goals of that chapter.

In each of the next four chapters we will focus on relationships between liberal outcomes and a single independent variable under a

---

32. For a discussion of least-squares techniques for dichotomous dependent variables by a public law scholar, see Fred Kort, "Regression Analysîs and Discriminant Analysis."

variety of controls. For these chapters we employ simple descriptive statistics or measures of association derived from one-way analysis of variance. In Chapter 6, we will combine the results of the previous four chapters to produce a multivariate model. Our purpose is to discriminate between liberal and conservative outcomes under controls for changes in the nature of Supreme Court communication. To derive a statistical function which discriminates between outcomes and to control for the interaction effects of multiple independent variables, we will apply a combination of discriminant function analysis and logistic regression analysis.

Substantive and sampling considerations caused us to refrain from extensive use of statistical tests of significance. One of these considerations is that with such a sizable data base almost any relationship is statistically significant. To claim that such findings are automatically meaningful would be to beg the question. For the most part the questions that constantly confronted us were: are the relationships *substantively* significant? Do disparities among judge cohorts identify meaningful differences in judicial policy propensities, or do they border on the trivial? We found questions such as these to be the real challenges to our analysis. Our use of statistical significance tests was further limited because these techniques are based on the assumption that the data set represents a random sample of the universe of district court opinions. As noted previously, we do not claim to have a true random sample of the universe of federal district court cases. Indeed, we have intentionally biased our sample to overrepresent *policy* decisions.

2.

THE INFLUENCE OF POLITICAL PARTY AFFILIATION
ON JUDICIAL VOTING PATTERNS

INTRODUCTION AND REVIEW
OF THE LITERATURE

To what degree do the political party affiliations of judges influence their decisions. Although this is now a familiar question, those who reply to it are by no means unanimous in their response. To most judges, lawyers, and members of the courts' "attentive public," the question still rings with genuine impertinence, and their reply to it continues to be something like this: after taking the sacred judicial oath and donning the black robe the judge is no longer a Democrat or a Republican. Such prior orientations are (or at least certainly should be) put aside as the judge enters into a new realm where judicial decisions are the product of precedent, argumentation, and wit rather than such base factors as the judge's background, personality, or political party affiliation. Or, as Donald Jackson quipped in his perceptive book *Judges,* "Most judges would sooner admit to grand larceny than confess a political interest or motivation."[1] Despite the evidence to the contrary, the mechanical jurisprudence myth still retains an impressive number of apologists.

The first major sustained challenge to the mechanical jurisprudence philosophy came of course from the judicial realists, persons such as Jerome Frank, Karl N. Llewellyn, Oliver W. Holmes, Jr., and Morris R. Cohen.[2] For more than half a century the realist school insisted that judges, as the rest of their fellow human beings, are influenced in making adult decisions by the values and attitudes learned from their infancy. Jerome Frank expressed this viewpoint well in his classic *Courts on Trial.* A judge's background, according to Frank, "may have created plus or minus reactions to women, or blonde women, or men with beards, or Southerners, or Italians, or Englishmen, or plumbers, or ministers, or college graduates, or Dem-

---

1. Jackson, *Judges,* 18.
2. For a brief but good summary of the contributions of the legal realist school, see Schubert, *Judicial Behavior,* 9–83.

ocrats. A certain facial twitch or cough or gesture may start up memories, painful or pleasant."[3] To the question of whether judicial decisions are determined at least in part by the judge's partisan affiliation, the response of the realists has been: "Why, of course! Republicans view the world differently from their Democratic colleagues, and this is reflected in the kind of decisions they render. This is natural and inevitable, and those who elect and appoint judges should act accordingly."

The realists must be credited with accuracy in their thrust against the judicial myth, although many questions still remained unanswered in the wake of their well-reasoned assaults on the cult of the robe. Such questions included: to what degree and on what sorts of issues does a judge's partisanship affect his decision making? Does the influence of political party affiliation vary according to region, the tenure of the judge, or from one time period to another? Questions such as these have been the grist of the judicial behavioralist mill that began to grind during the latter half of the 1940s.[4]

The results of the behavioralist studies are highly tentative and a bit inconclusive, although it does appear that of all the background variables measured, political party affiliation is the best predictor of judicial behavior. Stuart Nagel, for example, found that for his sample of U.S. Supreme Court and state supreme court justices, party affiliation was a better predictor of judicial votes than ethnic background: Democratic justices were more liberal in fifteen policy areas than were their GOP counterparts, with the differences between Democrats and Republicans statistically significant in nine of them.[5] In separate studies of the Michigan Supreme Court, Glendon Schubert and Sidney Ulmer both concluded that Democrats were generally more liberal than the Republican jurists. Schubert found, for instance, that Democrats were more favorably inclined toward workmen's compensation claims, while Ulmer also found that Democrats were more responsive to the claims of the injured and of the unemployed.[6]

In an analysis of the voting behavior of U.S. Supreme Court justices between 1941 and 1970, Donald Leavitt concluded that "Demo-

3. Frank, *Courts on Trial*, 151.

4. Many public law scholars date the beginning of the judicial behavioralist movement with the publication in 1948 of *The Roosevelt Court*, by Pritchett.

5. Nagel, "Political Party Affiliation," 843–90. Reanalysis of the data may be found in Nagel's "Multiple Correlations."

6. Schubert, *Quantitative Analysis of Judicial Behavior*, 129–42; Ulmer, "Political Party Variable." For a more recent study of the Michigan Supreme Court, see Feeley, "Another Look at the 'Party Variable.'"

crats are liberal on economic matters and Republicans conservative."[7] Sheldon Goldman examined the 2,510 cases heard by the U.S. courts of appeals between 1961 and 1964 and found that Democratic judges had significantly higher liberalism scores on economic issues; however, he found no consistent interparty differences in criminal or civil liberties cases.[8] In a more recent study (covering 1965–1971) Goldman found background characteristics to be even more salient. Party affiliation (and the age variable) emerged as major predictors of liberal-conservative decision making on the appellate courts across a wide spectrum of issues. Democrats tended to be more liberal especially on economic issues, and the amount of liberal variance increased even more dramatically when controls for region (the South) were provided.[9]

In addition, John Schmidhauser has performed some very impressive pioneering works on the significance of party affiliation (and other background factors) in judicial voting across long time spans of American history.[10] Several unpublished doctoral dissertations written during the 1960s also provided data to bolster the party variable, and a more recent study by John Prachera has given further support for the impact of political party affiliation on judicial voting in the appellate courts.[11] In sum a considerable body of literature demonstrates the significance of party affiliation in influencing judicial behavior. The various studies do not agree, however, on how strong the relationships are nor are they unanimous on the precise types of issues which seem to activate partisan voting patterns. The primary focus of all the studies is on appellate, not trial courts. Purely "political" analyses of American *trial* courts are rather scarce in the literature, and a perusal of the studies which do exist gives very little encouragement to those who would hypothesize a relationship between partisan affiliation and voting behavior of trial court judges.[12]

7. Leavitt, "Political Party and Class Influence," 18.

8. Goldman, "Voting Behavior on the United States Courts of Appeals, 1961–64."

9. Goldman, "Voting Behavior on the United States Courts of Appeals Revisited." Goldman changed his design by limiting consideration to nonunanimous cases and by using more sophisticated multivariate methodology.

10. E.g., see Schmidhauser, *Supreme Court*, and *Constitutional Law*, esp. 486–504.

11. Herndon, "Relationships"; Bowen, "Explanation of Judicial Voting Behavior"; Beatty, "Institutional and Behavioral Analysis"; Prachera, "Background Characteristics."

12. Vines, "Federal District Judges and Race Relations Cases"; Richardson and Vines, *Politics of Federal Courts;* Walker, "Note Concerning Partisan Influences"; Dolbeare, *Trial Courts in Urban Politics;* Jacob, *Urban Justice;* Dolbeare, "Federal District Courts," 373–404; and Kritzer, "Political Correlates."

In an examination of partisan differences among trial judges in an urban New York county, Kenneth Dolbeare concluded: "We begin to border on the frivolous before we find differences between judges on a party basis, at least in this gross comparison." A bit further in the study he concluded, "Perhaps the comparative effort is vitiated by methodological problems in one or both studies [comparing his study with Nagel's, as referred to in note 5, above] or between trial courts and appellate courts, but the over-all conclusion that there is no general correlation between party identification and decision-making except in one or two highly partisan areas, seems amply demonstrated."[13] When Dolbeare analyzed partisan influence on voting behavior of *federal* trial judges in twenty urban areas, his conclusions were similar to his study of state trial judges: "Other work with state trial court judges indicated that individual values and attitudes have important effects on decisions, but that political party identification and other social factors are insignificant. The data here permit replication only of . . . part of those findings; and to the extent that the small numbers of cases in various categories support any conclusions, the same is generally true at the federal trial court level also."[14]

In a study of 1,177 randomly selected civil rights decisions handed down by 193 federal district judges between 1963 and 1968, Thomas Walker was as unsuccessful as Dolbeare in relating voting patterns to party affiliation.[15] Using the phi measure of association, Walker found no relationship between the party affiliation of the opinion writer and the liberal or conservative nature of the opinion — even under controls for region.[16]

Richardson and Vines also sought to relate judicial voting to the party affiliation of federal trial judges in their 1970 study *The Politics of Federal Courts*. After examining all reported civil liberties and labor cases for the Third, Fifth, and Eighth Circuits between 1956 and 1961, the two scholars were able to make only weak and somewhat ambivalent conclusions about the relationship between party and voting trends. Democrats were more liberal than Republicans on labor issues but only by 8.6 percent; and on civil liberties issues Republicans were some 13.3 percentage points *more* favorably disposed than Democrats — a finding in contrast to most other studies. The authors conceded that the overall partisan differences

13. Dolbeare, *Trial Courts in Urban Politics,* 75, 77.
14. Dolbeare, "Federal District Courts," 387.
15. Walker, "Note Concerning Partisan Influences," 645–49.
16. It should be noted, however, that Walker's regional controls were rather crude, with divisions into only North, South, East, and West, rather than into regions defined by policy-related boundaries such as states or judicial circuits.

which they found were "not . . . great" and reflected "ambiguity."[17]
Finally, we note a more recent study by Herbert Kritzer, which analyzed the relationship between sentencing in Vietnam war draft resister cases and the partisan orientation of the judges. While Kritzer was able to relate sentencing behavior to several "environmental variables," he also noted that "judicial background variables [e.g., party orientation] seem to have little impact on sentencing."[18]

Three general and separate questions now need to be addressed. First, what theoretical basis do we have for hypothesizing a relationship between party affiliation and judicial behavior? Second, why does the party variable appear to be such a weak (although generally consistent) predictor of the voting patterns of judges? Finally, why do virtually all of the existing studies point to partisan variations in the voting behavior of *appellate* judges and not trial court jurists?

As for the initial question, David Adamany has provided a strong argument for hypothesizing an association between party identification and subsequent judicial behavior:

> If judges are party identifiers before reaching the bench, there would be a basis for believing that they — like legislators — are affected in their issue orientations by party. Nagel has shown that 271 of the 304 justices of state high courts in 1955 had clear prior party affiliations. Furthermore, judges are generally well educated and the vote studies show that the more educated tend to be stronger party identifiers, to cast policy preferences in ideological terms, to have clearer perceptions of issues and of party positions on those issues, to have issue attitudes consistent with the positions of the party with which they identify, and to be more interested and involved in politics. For judges, even more than for the general population, party may therefore be a significant reference group on issues.[19]

This theme is echoed by Malcolm Feeley, who has noted, "Party affiliation . . . seems to be regarded as a crude, but still the most effective, background indicator of judges' values because it indicates a collection of likeminded persons (especially among political activists), is an important socializing institution, and is an important reference group for people active in public affairs."[20]

Nevertheless, both Adamany and Feeley warn against an overly simplistic view of the relationship between party affiliation and subsequent voting patterns. In his critique of the several previously

17. Richardson and Vines, *Politics of Federal Courts*, 105.
18. Kritzer, "Political Correlates," 49.
19. Adamany, "The Party Variable in Judges' Voting," 59.
20. Feeley, "Another Look at the 'Party Variable,'" 93.

cited studies of partisan behavior on the Michigan Supreme Court, Feeley argues,

> A rather narrow "party factor" interpretation, as suggested by Schubert's and Ulmer's studies, while appearing quite plausible, is not *equally* persuasive in accounting for division on *all* types of issues, including those on which no clear corresponding party "positions" or even "class" positions exist. Second, there is the real possibility of the importance of the other variables, region of residence, age, and length of tenure, factors which are generally considered important in shaping social outlook, voter choice, and group organization of both the mass electorate and political leaders, such as legislative assemblies. The differences between the two groups of judges on these factors are also clear-cut, and might indirectly indicate sources of differences in outlook toward the function of law and the judicial role, legal education and practice, and friendship and association. It could be argued, in fact, that these background factors — particularly age and residence — are at least as important in affecting views on social issues and political action as is political party affiliation, and, in fact, are causal factors in the selection of party affiliation and identification.[21]

We share the concerns of Adamany, Feeley, and others about postulating an overly simplistic causal relationship between party identification and judicial voting behavior.

As to the second question, there are several reasons why party affiliation has not proven a more useful variable in the study of American judges. First, the homogeneity of the bench ensures that even judges from different parties will bring more similar than different attributes to their task.[22] Thus, party affiliation is often not a reliable surrogate for demographic, attitudinal, or environmental differences. A second general reason for weak correlations between party and judicial voting is provided succinctly by a scholar who *has* generally found relationships between the two variables in his studies. Nagel tells us that

> there are various offsetting factors which prevent the correlation from being perfect. For one thing, party choice is frequently determined by considerations other than the similarity between the values of the individual and those of the party he has chosen. Even if an individual has chosen his party on the basis of value considerations, he may deviate from others within his party on a narrow but relevant issue such as leniency toward criminal defendants. In addition, two judges may have the same value systems and thus possibly be of the same party, but one of the two judges may hold his values with a greater intensity and may

21. Ibid. 101.
22. E.g., see a discussion and literature citations for this point in Walker, "Note Concerning Partisan Influences," 645-49.

frequently dissent without being joined by his less vigorous associate of the same party. Lack of homogeneity in the cases and the presence of clerical errors may also disrupt the correlation.[23]

Finally, the very nonideological, nonprogrammatic nature of American political parties in general tends to restrain the party factor from becoming a potent indicator of liberal-conservative policy propensity.[24] Indeed, the relatively low level of party voting in an elected policymaking institution such as the U.S. House of Representatives would seem to predict an even weaker link between party affiliation and judges.[25] In spite of the relatively weak party-policy link in the Congress, however, its strength has varied over time.[26] During periods of high turnover and ideological change, party affiliation becomes more prevalent.[27] (For example, party voting on New Deal issues was more pronounced in the wake of the 1932 realignment.)[28] Because of the extensive time period covered by our data set, we shall be able to test whether party voting by *judges* is also partially a function of the era from which the data set was drawn.

Now, let us address the third question involving a link between party affiliation and judicial voting: why has there been success in demonstrating party-policy correlations for appellate judges but not for their counterparts at the trial court level? Perhaps the best response to this query was given by Dolbeare, who has invested much scholarly effort in the study of American trial courts:

> The trial court researcher is left without the tools of those who analyze the work of appellate courts because these techniques all rest on the non-unanimous behavior of several judges exposed to the same stimuli in a single case. Not even a rough form of scale analysis comparing judges' performance in cases in a single subject area is possible, assuming one were to consider the cases comparable; there are too many judges and too few cases for each to make this effort more than an exercise in arbitrariness. We *can* compare all Republicans with all Democrats in some

23. Nagel, "Relationship Between the Political and Ethnic Affiliation of Judges," 242.

24. E.g., see Lowi, "Toward Functionalism"; Burnham, "End of American Party Politics"; and Sorauf, *Party Politics in America.*

25. For a summary of the link between party affiliation and the congressional vote, see Jewell and Patterson, *Legislative Process in the United States,* ch. 16; Kingdon, *Congressmens' Voting Decisions,* esp. ch. 4; and Sinclair, "Who Wins in the House of Representatives."

26. Brady, "Research Note on the Impact of Inter-Party Competition"; Brady and Lynn, "Switched Seat Congressional Districts."

27. Brady, "Research Note on the Impact of Inter-Party Competition"; Brady and Lynn, "Switched Seat Congressional Districts."

28. Brady, "Research Note on the Impact of Inter-Party Competition"; Brady and Lynn, "Switched Seat Congressional Districts."

subject area (or all subject areas) as to their propensity to support private claims against government actions. And we can do the same for individual judges. But as soon as we try to subdivide below "support for the private claim vs. support for government" (by the nature of the private parties, for example), we run out of cases and can no longer rely on our results.[29]

We agree with the Dolbeare analysis and would add a few observations of our own. Existing studies of the relationship between trial judge party affiliation and voting patterns have been severely handicapped by data bases with too few judges deciding too few cases over unduly short time spans. More recent research based on larger data sets with careful controls for time and case content suggest that relationships between the variables have failed to appear not because they do not exist but because researchers have not yet had sufficient data sources to explore them in all their manifestations and subtleties.[30] As our subsequent analysis will show, in seeking to demonstrate the influence of party on trial judge decision making we are not flogging a dead horse; rather, we are — to correct the metaphor — attempting to ride a horse that's never been rode.

STATEMENT OF PROPOSITIONS AND DATA ANALYSIS

Our first proposition is that for the forty-four-year period under study, Democratic judges have rendered a greater percentage of liberal decisions than their Republican colleagues. We further propose that the higher liberal voting propensity of Democratic judges will manifest itself in each of the several specific case types for this same time period. After subjecting both propositions to empirical tests, we will examine voting on selected issues over time to determine whether there are any trends in the liberal-conservative voting behavior of Republican and Democratic jurists. For example, do partisan differences increase after 1969 when the trial judges could no longer look to a unified Supreme Court to set forth clear, unambiguous legal guidelines?

PARTISAN DIFFERENCES FOR ALL CASES AND CASE CATEGORIES

Table 2 indicates that our first proposition is validated by the data: 46 percent of the decisions rendered by Democratic judges

29. Dolbeare, *Trial Courts in Urban Politics*, 75.
30. C.K. Rowland and Robert A. Carp, unpubl. research.

Table 2. Liberal and Conservative Decisions by Democratic and
Republican Judges, 1933-1977

	Democrats		Republicans	
	%	n	%	n
Liberal	46	7,152	39	4,131
Conservative	54	8,541	61	6,548
Total	100	15,693	100	10,679

NOTE: α = 1.33.

were liberal, whereas only 39 percent of those by Republicans fell
into the liberal category. The cross-product ratio, or odds ratio, is
1.33, indicating that the Democrats' ratio of liberal to conservative
opinions is 1.33 times greater (more liberal) than is the Republican
ratio.[31]

While this odds ratio and this raw difference are hardly over-

31. The cross-product ratio, frequently called the odds ratio, is a measure of the
relationship between two dichotomous variables. Specifically, it is a measure of the
relative odds of respondents from each independent variable category being placed
in a single dependent variables category. In measuring the relationship between
party identification and liberal-conservative propensities, the odds ratio is the ratio
between the odds that a Democratic judge's opinion will be liberal (or conservative)
and the odds that a Republican jurist's opinion will be liberal (or conservative).
The odds ratio is computed for 2 by 2 tables by the formula:
$$\alpha = (N_{11}/N_{12}) \div (N_{12}/N_{22}).$$
Thus, for Table 2 the computation would be:
$$\alpha = (7,152/8,541) \div (4,131/6,548) = 0.84/0.63 = 1.33.$$
The odds of a Democrat's opinion being liberal (0.84) are different from the odds of a
Republican's opinion being liberal (0.63). The ration between these odds (1.33) is
therefore a measure of the relative odds of Democratic and Republican opinions being liberal.
Interpretation of the odds ratio is straightforward. If political party has no effect
on liberal propensity, the odds will be the same for both groups of judges, and the
odds ratio would be 1.0, indicating independence or no relationship. Departures
from 1.0 in either direction indicate association. Values between 0 and 1.0 suggest a
negative relationship, i.e., a relationship which contradicts the hypothesized association. Values from 1.0 to infinity indicate a positive association, i.e., a relationship
which supports the hypothesized association. Thus, an odds ratio of 2.0 would mean
that respondents from the designated category of the independent variable are twice
as likely to respond in the predicted directed on the dependent variable than are respondents from the other category. In Table 2 the odds of a Democratic jurist rendering a liberal opinion are 1.33 times greater than the odds of a GOP counterpart.
In addition to its straightforward interpretation, the odds ratio has two other

whelming, neither can be dismissed as trivial or insignificant. The data suggest that Democratic district judges, like their counterparts on the appellate courts and in the various legislative halls throughout the nation, have been for more than four decades somewhat more liberally oriented than their GOP colleagues. Our confidence in the validity of these results is based on the large size of the sample with which we are working, the fact that the disparity is in the direction predicted by the literature, and as we shall see momentarily, the fact that the difference between the judges holds up for *nineteen* of the twenty specific case categories under study. This last reason helps to answer Feeley's concern that previous judicial voting behavior studies tended "to focus on only a limited set of politically salient issues before the court, thereby giving inadequate consideration to the possible depth and breadth of division on the court."[32]

Figure 2 provides even more revealing insights into the liberal-conservative voting disparities between Democratic and Republican judges because it enables us to examine specific years and to identify visible trends. Figure 2 graphs the percentage of the liberal decisions rendered by Republican and Democratic judges for each year between 1953 and 1977. (Prior to 1953, partisan differences averaged 4 percentage points.)[33] From 1953 to 1969 the difference between Democratic and Republican judges is very small and almost random. Democrats do outscore GOP judges on the liberalism

---

properties which make it particularly useful and appropriate for measuring the relative Democratic and Republican liberal propensities. First, unlike most nominal measures, its value is not a function of sample size or of marginal distributions. Second, the log odds of the odds ratio are perfectly symmetrical. Values ranges from negative to positive infinitely, with zero indicating no relationship between the independent and dependent variables. Although log odds ratios are more difficult to interpret, they will be utilized in Chapter 6 to generate predicted or expected call values which will serve as the basis for fitting log linear models of the legal and extralegal influences on trial court decision making. Thus, the odds ratio offers a unique combination of a simple descriptive measure appropriate for this chapter and of a more sophisticated measure which serves as the basis of model building in the penultimate chapter.

For a helpful discussion of the properties and applications of the odds ratio measure, see Reynolds, *Analysis of Nominal Data,* 20–29.

32. Feeley, "Another Look at the 'Party Variable,'" 92.

33. The years prior to 1953 have been excluded from the graph because the number of Republican judges before Eisenhower appointees appear on the bench is too small for meaningful, reliable measurement and because the content of several case types and, therefore, the substance of a "liberal" opinion began to change after 1953. The pre-1953 data, however, is almost identical to the trends in voting behavior between 1953 and 1969, that is, the disparity between Republicans and Democrats on the liberalism index fluctuates almost randomly from year to year. The Democratic liberalism score for these early years is 4 percentage points greater than that for the GOP judges (46 to 52 percent) and the odds ratio is 1.19.

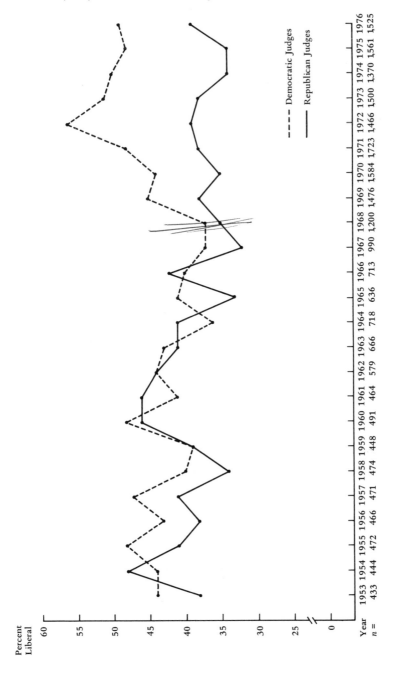

Figure 2. Liberal Decisions by Democratic and Republican Judges for All Cases, 1953-1976

index in ten of these sixteen years (and in two years the scores are identical), but the average difference between these two groups of judges is a mere 1 percent, which does indeed verge on the trivial for these years.[34] (The Democratic and Republican liberalism indexes are, respectively, 41 and 40 percent, and the odds ratio is only 1.04.) It is little wonder that previous studies of U.S. trial court behavior, nearly all of which covered the 1950s and 1960s, concluded that there was very little correlation between party affiliation and decision patterns. The conclusions of these studies were substantially correct for, indeed, the overall differences between Republican and Democratic district judges during this era is virtually nil.

Beginning in 1969, however, a most interesting phenomenon starts to appear: the tiny gap between Democrats and Republicans widens into a sizable chasm — some 17 percentage points by 1972. Not only do Democrats score higher than Republicans for each year between 1969 and 1976, but the average difference is a more impressive 11 percent, whereas the disparity had been only 1 percent for the preceding sixteen years. (The odds ratio between 1969 and 1977 jumps to 1.62.)

Figure 2 also reveals that the primary cause of the post-1968 difference between the judges was increased liberal voting tendencies among Democratic jurists rather than more conservative decisions from Republican judges. That is, between 1953 and 1969 the average liberalism score among Democratic judges was 41 percent, and after 1968 the score jumped to 48 percent. For Republicans prior to 1969, the index was 40 percent, whereas after 1968 the score declined moderately to 37 percent.[35]

We see then that for the years after 1968 the difference in voting tendencies among district judges for all cases is more impressive than it had been in prior years, and it appears that the conclusions of the previous studies of this subject were premature. There are now meaningful differences in the voting patterns between Republican and Democratic trial judges, although such disparities do appear to fluctuate over time.

Figure 2 poses an obvious question for the researcher: how does

34. Between 1953 and 1969 the coefficient of variation (which measures the relative entropy or homogeneity of aggregates which have different means) was 3.55. This indicates a good deal of fluctuation during these years. Viewing each year as a separate unit, the mean difference between Republican and Democratic judges was 1.1 percent and the standard deviation was 4.2.

35. Between 1969 and 1977 the coefficient of variation was a mere 0.28, which indicates a large degree of stability for these years. (The coefficient had been 3.55 for the preceding sixteen years.) If each year is considered as a separate unit, the mean difference between the Democratic and Republican judges is 12.5 percent and the standard deviation is 3.5.

one account for the abrupt and sustained surge of partisan voting which appeared in the late 1960s? First, with the advent of the Burger Court, the trial court jurists could no longer count on the Supreme Court for as clear and unambiguous legal guidelines as they had received from the Warren Court's more stable majority. With the decline of the fact-law congruence after 1968 the trial court judges became more free to take their decision-making cues from personal-partisan values rather than from guidelines set forth by the High Court. Consequently, the level of partisan voting increased markedly. We shall provide further evidence for this phenomenon throughout the book — especially in Chapter 6.

Another reason for increased partisanship after 1968 (manifested largely by the liberal surge among Democrats) is that the chief executive of the immediately preceding era was an individual who, unlike his predecessors, possessed both the desire *and* the political clout to put committed liberals on the district court bench, and it was in the late 1960s that the Johnson appointees began to make their impact felt among the lower federal judiciary. Thus, "Democrat" came to define a different set of political background factors. We shall deal more extensively with the impact of the appointing presidents on judicial behavior in the following chapter.

Let us now pursue our discussion of the differences over time in the voting behavior of Democratic and Republican judges by examining trends on specific types of case in which voting disparities have been the most and the least significant. Table 3 ranks these types according to the level of partisan voting they engendered. The table indicates that for this forty-four-year period differences between judges from the two parties was greatest for cases involving state and local government efforts to regulate the economic lives of their citizens, race relations issues, disputes involving interpretation of the Fourteenth Amendment (excluding racial matters), and cases involving conviction for criminal offenses. Partisan differences were almost totally absent in cases involving the interpretation of Indian laws and treaties, suits brought by the secretary of labor (or the National Labor Relations Board, NLRB) under the Fair Labor Standards Act, disputes involving rent control and excessive profits, and, finally, cases dealing with reapportionment and the right to vote. In the middle are the remaining eleven categories: items 5 through 11 (with the exception of item 8) cluster around the themes of criminal justice, class discrimination, and First Amendment freedoms, whereas items 12 through 15 deal primarily with labor-management and environmental protection issues. What tentative observations might one suggest from these rankings?

First, with the exception of item 1 (to be discussed momentarily),

Table 3. Liberal Decisions in Order of Magnitude of Partisan Voting Differences for Nineteen Types of Cases, 1933-1977

Type of Case	Overall (%)	Democrats (%)	Republicans (%)	Partisan Difference (%)	Odds Ratio
1. Local economic regulation	67	75	57	18	2.28
2. Race discrimination	51	57	42	15	1.90
3. 14th Amendment[a]	42	48	34	14	1.81
4. Criminal conviction	38	43	30	13	1.75
5. U.S. habeas corpus pleas	27	29	20	9	1.63
6. Freedom of religion	52	56	46	10	1.52
7. Freedom of expression	52	57	47	10	1.48
8. U.S. commercial regulation	68	71	64	7	1.39
9. Criminal court motions	27	30	24	6	1.35
10. State habeas corpus pleas	23	25	20	5	1.32
11. Alien petitions	40	42	35	7	1.31
12. Union vs. company	47	50	45	5	1.20
13. Employee vs. employer	38	40	35	5	1.20
14. Union members vs. union	55	57	53	4	1.14
15. Environmental protection	61	62	59	3	1.14
16. Indian rights and law	49	51	49	2	1.10
17. Fair Labor Standards Act	57	57	55	2	1.08
18. Rent control, excess profit	61	61	59	2	1.05
19. Voting rights cases	48	46	50	-4	0.86

[a] The women's rights cases are included in this category rather than listed as a separate case type, since our data on the women's rights category only includes the years after 1973.

all but one of the next ten items deal with the themes of civil rights and liberties and of criminal justice. Partisan differences among the judges have been greater on these sorts of issues than in the bottom tier of items, which deal primarily with issues of economic regulation and of labor relations. Such a revelation appears to be consistent with our overall knowledge of judicial behavior. With the decline of substantive due process after 1937 (at least at the national level), the federal courts leaned more toward self-restraint and deference to the elected branches and to the various regulatory and administrative agencies regarding the ordering of the economic lives of the American people.[36] In addition, after the 1930s, Congress legislated extensively and often with precision in the fields of economic regulation and of labor relations and this further restricted the discretion of judges in these areas. As a result of these factors, judges had less discretion to manipulate case outcomes in response to their own personal or partisan propensities.

As for the issues of criminal justice and civil rights, they seem to have evoked among the district judges the same degree of heated debate and divisiveness as they had among members of the Supreme Court after the late 1930s. The "great" and controversial decisions of the Stone, Vinson, Warren, and Burger Courts focused primarily on issues of civil liberties and of the rights of criminal defendants, and it is precisely those sorts of issues which evoked the greatest partisan schisms among the justices. Table 3 suggests that federal district judges were by no means immune to the debates and divisions which racked the nation's High Court; they, too, seem to have split along "political" lines more often on criminal justice and on civil rights matters than they did with other sorts of cases.

Fostering this propensity of the trial judges to vote along more partisan lines on Bill of Rights and Fourteenth Amendment issues is the fact that the state of the law seems to be less precise there than on issues for which there is a greater abundance of clear, unambiguous Supreme Court decisions and/or precise statutory guidelines, for example, labor and economic matters. The ambiguity (or perhaps the constant state of flux) of the law on matters such as the rights of criminal defendants, freedom of expression, equal protection of the law, and so on, reduces fact-law congruence and gives the district judges greater opportunity to respond to their personal (partisan) orientations in deciding cases than they have with other matters where their freedom of action was more circumscribed.

A recent study of federal district judges by William Kitchin supports the propositions discussed in the preceding paragraph. While interviewing twenty-one trial judges in four U.S. circuits, Kitchen asked the judges about their willingness to "innovate," that is, their inclination to make new law in areas where appellate court or congressional guidelines are ambiguous or nonexistent. He also asked the judges about which areas most lend themselves to trial court innovation. After asking why judges create new law through judicial

36. Many judicial scholars cite the 1937 Supreme Court decision of *NLRB v. Jones and Laughlin* (301 U.S. 1) as the case which marked the beginning of the end of federal court support for the doctrine of substantive due process.

innovation, Kitchin said: "One answer is that the courts innovate because other branches of government ignore certain significant problems which, to individual judges, cry out for attention. Accordingly, the individual district judge innovates in an attempt to fill a legal vacuum, as one judged commented, 'The theory is that judges should not be legal innovators, but there are some areas in which they have to innovate because legislatures won't do the job. Race relations is one of these areas. . . .' Other areas mentioned as needing judicial innovation because of legislative inaction were housing, equal accommodations, and criminal law (especially habeas corpus)."[37]

In sum, the subjects that Kitchin found to represent the greatest areas of freedom in judicial decision making are the very same subjects that we find to maximize partisan voting differences among the district judges. In situations where judges are more free to take their decision-making cues from sources other than appellate court decisions and statutes, they are more likely to rely on their personal-partisan orientations.

A second general observation about Table 3 pertains to the item which appears to evoke the greatest amount of partisan disparity among the judges — local economic regulation. Why should economic regulation at the state and local levels engender such partisan voting behavior among the judges while this tendency does not appear nearly so strong when it pertains to economic regulation by the *federal* government? We suggest that a partial answer to this may be that while substantive due process may have lost its vitality at the national level, it is still very much alive at the state and local levels vis-à-vis the local judiciaries. Robinson and Gellhorn discuss this phenomenon in their popular administrative law text:

> Although . . . the Supreme Court has now withdrawn from its erstwhile scrutiny of federal and state regulatory schemes . . . it would be a mistake to suppose that that is an end to the issue of constitutionality. Constitutional bird-watchers who have concentrated their gaze upon the United States Constitution, and upon the federal courts have frequently overlooked the path of state constitutional law, and the state courts which apply it. Sparrows they may be — and, to a crowd of eagle observers, drab and dull — state courts nevertheless can and do, exercise a significant and distinctive constitutional role in the area of economic legislation. . . . In the economic arena, the withdrawal of the United States Supreme Court from the field has left the way open for state courts to impose, under state constitutions, restrictions beyond what is mandated by federal law and Supreme Court doctrine.[38]

37. Kitchin, *Federal District Judges*, 104.
38. Robinson and Gellhorn, *Administrative Process*, 624.

In other words the doctrine of substantive due process is still alive and well at the state level in many parts of the country; it is still a topic over which economic conservatives and economic liberals are doing battle. But what does this have to do with the federal district courts? We suggest that the liaison occurs in part as a result of the 1938 Supreme Court decision of *Erie* v. *Tompkins* (304 U.S. 64). In their casebook *American Constitutional Law*, Mason and Beaney tell us that

> in matters of purely local importance the federal courts are supposed to follow decisions of state courts, but as a practical matter they are bound by the rule chiefly in cases dealing with rights in real property. . . . The Judicial Code now provides that "the laws of the several states . . . shall be regarded as rules of decision in trials at common law in the courts of the United States." Equity, admiralty, and criminal cases are excluded from the operation of this clause, and its scope was further limited by construing the word "laws" to mean only state statutes. However, since the judicial interpretation of a statute is an integral part of that statute, federal courts follow the decisions of the highest court of the state in construing a state statute.[39]

Given this reality and the fact that virtually all federal district judges practiced law in the state where they hold court and have other strong ties with the local culture, we are not too surprised that our study indicates that local economic regulation still stirs the partisan blood of federal trial judges.[40] A district judge may not feel free to give way to partisan values when it comes to determining the validity of an NLRB order for a union to end a secondary boycott. The same judge, however, may sense a bit more leeway when it comes to determining whether or not a municipal government may lawfully restrain a utility company from increasing its rates. Thus, given the viability of the substantive due process controversy at the state and local levels and given the strong district court ties to the local culture, we believe that we understand, in part at least, why the partisan orientation of the district judges is manifested in their voting on "local economic regulation" cases.

Finally, Table 3 shows what appears to be an anomaly in that the category of voting rights cases ranks last, whereas the other categories involving civil rights and liberties engendered much more intensive partisan voting. Not only is there very little difference on the liberalism index between Democratic and Republican jurists, but this is the one and only variable for which the Republican liberalism score is actually greater than that of Democratic judges. For

39. Mason and Beaney, *American Constitutional Law*, 7–8.
40. E.g., see Richardson and Vines, *Politics of Federal Courts*, ch. 4.

an explanation of this phenomenon we must examine the precise content of this category of cases. While some portion of this category includes cases in which specific individuals (often ethnic minorities) claimed a denial of their franchise, the vast majority of the cases dealt with malapportionment, that is, challenges to the "one man, one vote" principle in the way local electoral districts were drawn.

Why should apportionment challenges trigger such a nonpartisan response from Republicans in comparison with all the other case categories? To a certain degree we think the answer to this lies in the practical political effects of the various Supreme Court "one man, one vote" decisions of the 1960s. First, these decisions gave relatively specific guidelines or legal cues to trial court judges. Second, the literature indicates rather clearly that the primary beneficiaries of the reapportionment rulings have been the suburban areas in the North (as opposed to the central-city areas) and the metropolitan areas of the South; the literature is also clear that such areas tend to be the core of Republican electoral support.[41] In addition, since key electoral district boundaries are drawn by the various state legislatures, and since a large majority of the legislatures were under Democratic control during the span of our study, it is reasonable to assume that disappointed GOP candidates were well represented among those charging unconstitutional gerrymandering in their federal court suits. Finally, in those cases which do involve disputes over individual voting rights, statutory constraints are imposed on judicial discretion by the Voting Rights Act of 1965.

Considering these facts, it is not terribly surprising that there is very little difference in the solicitous attitude of Republican and Democratic judges toward "the right to vote" — or even that Republican judges tend to outscore their Democratic colleagues on this index. Thus, what appears to be an aberration may in fact be an example of "an exception which proves the rule." Undoubtedly the full explanation for this phenomenon is more complex and subtle than the one we have here provided, but we would still argue that the evidence for our explanatory hypothesis is highly suggestive.

We must conclude our discussion of Table 3 with a few words of caution. Although we believe Table 3 does suggest some patterns in the historical voting of federal judges, we are fully aware of two sobering realities: (1) none of the deviations from the mean liberalism score between Republican and Democratic judges is terribly large, and (2) the odds ratio statistic indicates that for most issues the par-

41. E.g., see Schnore, "Social and Economic Characteristics of American Suburbs"; and Wirt et al., *On the City's Rim.*

tisan difference between the judges is rather modest. Only in a few categories of cases do the differences between GOP and Democratic jurists verge on the dramatic. Thus, we are talking about behavioral *tendencies* here and not about variables that have more than moderate interrelations with one another. Also, the efficacy of case type as an estimate of case content is reduced by the extended time frame. Changes in the content of, for example, civil rights cases over time are not controlled for in our data analysis. Therefore, we extend our analysis by measuring party differences by year for selected case types.

TRENDS IN VOTING BEHAVIOR FOR SEVERAL SELECT CASE TYPES

Categories were selected for more extensive review under control for years when they met both of the following two criteria: first, the *n*'s had to be sufficiently large (>10) each year for both Republican and Democratic judges so that it would be meaningful to graph the data; and, second, the graph had to depict discernible trends in the direction of the judges' voting behavior (as opposed to more or less random fluctuations, with Democrats averaging slightly higher liberalism scores than the Republicans). Four categories of cases met these criteria, and, as one might expect, they included cases where partisan differences between the judges had been greater over time: (1) First Amendment freedoms of expression and religion, (2) criminal court motions, (3) race discrimination cases, and (4) nonracial Fourteenth Amendment issues.

Figure 3 portrays the voting patterns of Republican and Democratic judges between 1962 and 1977 on cases pertaining to the First Amendment freedoms of expression and religion.[42] The similarity in the voting patterns between this composite variable and that for the universe of cases is striking (see Figure 2). Prior to 1969 the liberalism index between Republican and Democratic judges fluctuates randomly, whereas after 1969 a wide and consistent gap emerges between the two groups of jurists. From 1962 through 1968 the Democrats are more liberal than Republican judges in three of the seven years; the Republicans lead in another three years; and the judges are equally liberal in a seventh year. The average Democratic liber-

42. The variables of "freedom of expression" and of "freedom of religion" were combined into a single First Amendment freedoms variable here because the judges' voting patterns on these separate but related issues were virtually parallel with one another and because the Republican *n*'s for some years would otherwise have been too small ($n < 10$) for use in a graph. Also, prior to 1962 the average number of cases per year in this category was fewer than five and was thus too small to be used in the graph.

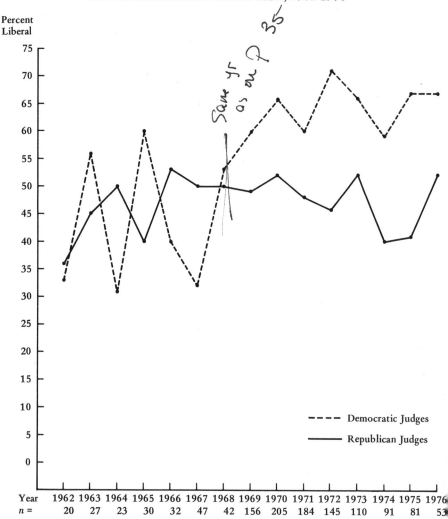

Figure 3. Liberal Decisions by Democratic and Republican Judges
for First Amendment Freedoms Cases, 1962-1976

alism score for these years is 46 percent, while for GOP judges it is
47 percent. After 1968 the Democrats lead Republicans on the liberalism index for all eight years with an average liberalism score of 64
percent. The Republican average between 1969 and 1977 is 48 percent, or a difference of 16 percent.

Figure 4 outlines the judicial voting patterns between Democratic and Republican judges on criminal court motions cases from 1956 through 1976.[43] From this figure we see that prior to 1971 the average liberal scores of the judges vary widely with no discernible differences between the Republican and Democratic judges. Between 1956 and 1970 each group of judges leads the other on the liberalism index in seven of the fifteen years and their scores are equal for one year. The average percentage of liberalism for these years is 25 percent for Democrats and 24 percent for the GOP judges. After 1970, however, a noticeable gap appears between the judges. The Democrats clearly emerge as the distinctly more liberal group of judges so that by 1976 the difference in the liberalism score between the two partisan groups is a full 16 percentage points. In other words, in 1976, Democrats were 64 percent more likely to return a liberal opinion than were their Republican counterparts. Between 1971 and 1977 the Democrats are more liberal than Republicans for all years with an average liberalism score of 37 percent; the Republican average for these years is 23 percent.

In Figure 5 the voting behavior in race discrimination cases is depicted for the years 1955 through 1976.[44] From 1955 through 1972 the Republican and Democratic indexes crisscross in virtual random fashion with the Democratic average of 56 percent being slightly greater than the GOP mean liberalism score of 51 percent. For this entire time period Democrats outscore their Republican counterparts in thirteen of the eighteen years. Between 1973 and 1977, however, a substantial gulf begins to appear between the two groups of jurists. Although both Republicans and Democrats veer in a conservative direction, this is especially true of GOP judges so that Democrats outrank Republicans on the liberalism index for all five years. The Democratic mean liberal percentage for these years is 59, while for Republican judges it is 31 percent. Thus Democrats were almost twice as likely to issue a liberal opinion. Again, we note that 1972 truly seems to represent a high-water mark of judicial liberalism. The conservative plunge on this race discrimination category after 1972 is rather dramatic.

Fourteenth Amendment cases (excluding racial issues) are portrayed in Figure 6 for the years 1963 to 1977.[45] The voting patterns for Republicans and Democrats have much in common with those

43. Prior to 1956 the average number of cases each year in this category was fewer than five and was thus too small to be used in the graph.

44. Before 1955 the number of such cases was not large enough to be meaningful; the average per year was less than five.

45. Prior to 1963 there were too few cases for analysis; the average was fewer than five per year.

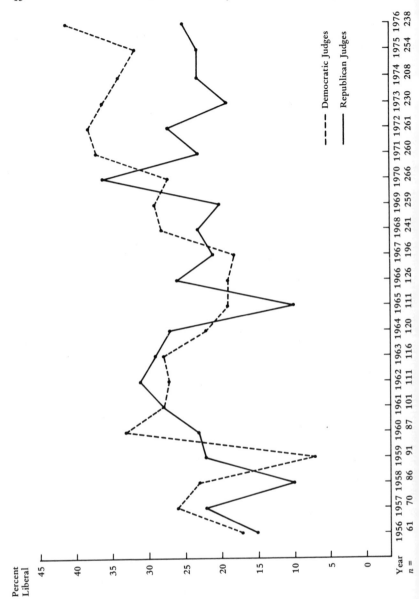

Figure 4. Liberal Decisions by Democratic and Republican Judges
for Criminal Court Motions Cases, 1956-1976

Figure 5. Liberal Decisions by Democratic and Republican Judges for Race Discrimination Cases, 1955-1976

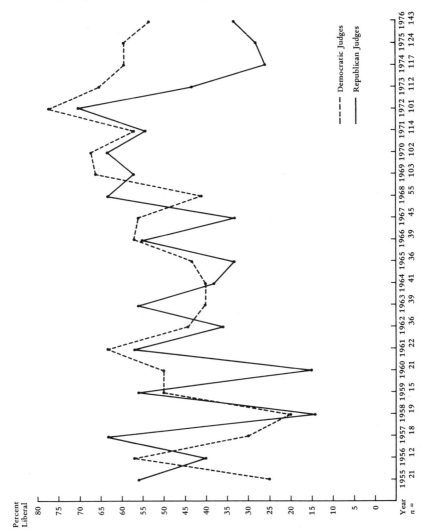

Figure 6. Liberal Decisions by Democratic and Republican Judges
for Fourteenth Amendment Cases, 1963-1976

depicted in Figures 2 through 5. Between 1963 and 1969, Democrats
are more liberal than Republicans in four of the six years, but there
is great fluctuation from year to year. The average liberalism score
for Democrats for those years is 33 percent and for Republican jurists, 24 percent. After 1969 a noticeable trend begins: Democratic

judges become distinctly more liberal for all years while Republicans veer in a slightly more conservative vein. Between 1969 and 1977 the mean liberalism score among Democrats is 51 percent and only 35 percent for the GOP judges. In addition, there is an indication that 1972 was the peak of liberal voting on Fourteenth Amendment cases for Democratic judges, although this peak seems to have been reached as early as 1970 for the Republicans.[46] The voting patterns depicted by these several figures appear to have several similar characteristics. First, prior to the 1969–72 period there appears to be very little difference in the voting patterns of Republican and Democratic judges. While Democrats are indeed a bit more liberal on the average than their GOP colleagues, the fluctuations vary almost randomly from year to year. A second common trait is that at some point between 1969 and 1972 a noticeable, discernible gap appears between Democratic and Republican judges: the Democrats become decidedly more liberal (or less conservative) than the Republican judges. This trend was clearly present for each of the several categories examined here. A third common characteristic of the figures is that 1972 appears to be the high-water mark for liberal voting — primarily for Democratic judges but to some degree for Republicans as well. This is seen vividly in Figure 2, and it is evident as well in the graphs depicting the four specific categories of cases.[47]

46. Since 1973 a significant number of Fourteenth Amendment cases have emerged pertaining to the issue of women's rights and/or sex discrimination in general. Consequently, we began to code these cases as a separate category and hence we have data on this category for a full four-year period. Because the data on this category do not cover the forty-four-year time span as do the other cases, this category was not included in the list of cases in Table 3. If we had included it, however, it would have topped the list because the voting disparity between Republicans and Democrats on this issue is greater than for any of the other categories. The average liberalism score for Democrats is 67 percent and only 45 percent for the Republican judges. The odds ratio is 2.45, which would place it even above the leading category of local economic regulation, which stands at 2.28. This finding is not too surprising in view of the evidence recently presented, which indicates that voting disparity between judges is greater with "new" issues for which there are not yet clear, firm appellate court or congressional guidelines. (See Kitchin, *Federal District Judges,* 104.) Surely the issue of women's rights in the early and mid-1970s fits in nicely with these criteria.

47. Also, one cannot help but notice that between 1975 and 1976 there is an increase in liberal voting for category of all cases and for each of the specific case categories examined here, except race relations cases. (This upsurge of the liberal trend is likewise evident in voting in the women's rights category: between 1975 and 1976 the Democratic liberal percentage increased from 54 to 69 and for Republicans the jump was from 29 to 47!) Obviously one year does not constitute a trend, but the fact that it appears so noticeably and consistently is at least worthy of mention. Perhaps President Ford's appointment of the moderate Justice Stevens in 1975 and of more liberal district judges between 1974 and 1976 is responsible for this modest swing toward more liberal voting by the lower federal judiciary.

CONCLUSION

For the time span covered by our study, meaningful differences are evident in the aggregate voting patterns of Republican and Democratic judges. From 1933 to 1977 Democrats were more liberal than Republicans by about 7 percent, and this pattern held true in nineteen of the twenty specific case categories examined here. With the exception of *local* economic regulation cases, partisan differences tended to be greater for criminal justice and for civil rights and liberties issues than for labor and economic cases.

The aggregate data also demarcate three distinct eras regarding the tendency of trial judges to use party affiliation as a significant cue in their judicial decision making: (1) 1933 through 1953, when partisan differences averaged 4 percentage points; (2) 1954 through 1968, when mean party differences were a trivial 1 percentage point; and (3) 1969 to 1977, when the schism jumped to a more impressive 11 percent. We noted that virtually all the studies that revealed little or no partisan voting among federal trial judges covered the middle period, the fifties and sixties, when indeed party voting was at a low ebb. We also suggested that the partisan surge after 1968 was the result of two factors: an unstable Supreme Court majority whose inconclusive precedents permitted trial judges more leeway to respond to their own personal-partisan values, and the impact of the exceedingly liberal Lyndon Johnson appointees.

We observed from our examination of four specific case types (First Amendment freedoms, criminal court motions, race discrimination cases, and Fourteenth Amendment issues) that prior to the 1969–72 period, partisan differences among the judges were slight, although Democrats did tend to be more liberal than Republicans. However, during those years Democrats became distinctly more liberal than their GOP colleagues, thus emulating the aggregate pattern for all cases. We also noted that for these specific cases (as with all cases) 1972 appears to mark the zenith in liberal voting by the trial judges, especially Democrats.

Although the results of this analysis are inconclusive, they support the assumptions which underlie our model and suggest that political background factors do influence trial judge policy decisions. It is particularly gratifying to note that party effects increase as controls for case type and year are added. This suggests that political effects will increase as case content estimates become more precise. The increase also suggests that fact-law congruence and, therefore, discretion to manipulate judicial outcomes vary over time as both case content and appellate court cues change.

3.

THE IMPACT OF THE APPOINTING PRESIDENT
ON JUDICIAL VOTING PATTERNS

INTRODUCTION

Despite the popular myth that judges are "nonpolitical," the evidence is overwhelming that American presidents have not shared in this naive belief. Whether it be the appointment of a Supreme Court justice or of a judge to a district court, the historical data clearly reveal that presidents have weighed the political-philosophical orientations of the would-be jurists before making their judicial appointments.[1] Usually this has meant that presidents appoint members of their own political party to fill federal judgeships, although occasionally the chief executive may cross party lines to fill a judicial vacancy. However, in the latter case, the president usually looks to those who share his basic political values, for example, President Roosevelt's 1941 appointment of the Republican—but liberal—Harlan Fiske Stone as chief justice of the United States.

Reviewing empirical data on appointment to the lower federal judiciary as far back as 1884, Richardson and Vines note,

> All but three of the thirteen Presidents before Johnson have appointed lower federal judiciary from their own party 90 percent of the time. Two Republican Presidents who fell slightly short of that figure, Taft and Hoover, did so not because of neutrality, but because there were no Southern Republican candidates for the appointments. During the administration of both, there were few Republican members of the bar in the South and probably fewer still who were sufficiently prominent to merit consideration for judicial appointment.[2]

1. Data on the need for appropriate political credentials for would-be Supreme Court justices can be found in the pioneering works of Schmidhauser, *The Supreme Court,* and "Justices of the Supreme Court." For data on the correspondence between the political party affiliation of the presidents with their appointees to the lower federal judiciary, see Goldman, "Characteristics of Eisenhower and Kennedy Appointees," and "Johnson and Nixon Appointees"; and Richardson and Vines, *Politics of Federal Courts,* 68–70. For an excellent current discussion of this phenomenon, see Walker and Hulbary, "Supreme Court Selection Process."
2. Richardson and Vines, *Politics of Federal Courts,* 68–69.

Presidents may occasionally toy with the idea of "taking political factors out of judicial selection," but such efforts tend to die aborning. For example, as a presidential candidate, Jimmy Carter proclaimed that "All federal judges . . . should be appointed strictly on the basis of merit, without any consideration of political aspects or influence."[3] Yet during his first two years in office not a single Republican found his way into the ranks of the Carter district judges, and the few GOP judges who began to appear after 1979 posed little threat to the historical tradition that over 90 percent of federal judicial appointees are of the same party as the president.[4]

Why do presidents look so consistently to members of their own political party (and occasionally to ideologically attuned members of the opposition party) in selecting candidates for judicial office? Part of the answer lies of course in the reality of routine partisan politics, that is, paying off political campaign debts, the impact of the "senatorial courtesy" requirements, and so on. In a larger sense, however, presidents consider the political values and attitudes of potential judges because they have realized intuitively what American judicial scholars have taught for almost a century: the business of judging is not merely a mechanical process of "following the law" and "being guided by past precedents"; there is considerable discretion involved in judicial decision making; the political values and orientations of the judges do affect the way they resolve judicial issues, especially when precedents are conflicting or when the court is being asked to tread in new and uncharted realms. One of the more candid and perceptive apologies for considering political factors in the appointment of federal judges was made by President Theodore Roosevelt. In a letter to Senator Henry Cabot Lodge supporting Horace H. Lurton's appointment to the Supreme Court, Roosevelt indicated why his candidate possessed the right political qualifications for the job. Said Roosevelt: "The nominal politics of the man has nothing to do with his actions on the bench. His real politics are all important. . . . He is right on the Negro question; he is right on the power of the federal government; he is right on the Insular business; he is right about corporations, and he is right about labor. On every question that would come before the bench, he has so far shown himself to be in much closer touch with the policies in which you and I believe."[5] Not only do presidents make judicial appointments based in large part on the political credentials of the potential

3. "Judging Carter's Judges: Merit Along Party Lines," *Time*, Dec. 5, 1977, p. 76.
4. For a discussion of President Carter's highly partisan and ideological appointments to the U.S. appellate courts, see Slotnick, "Carter Presidency."
5. *Selections from the Correspondence of Theodore Roosevelt and Henry Cabot Lodge, 1884–1918*, vol. II, pp. 228, 230–31.

jurist, but the evidence we will present in this chapter suggests that to an impressive degree the voting patterns of the district judges do reflect the political values of their appointing presidents.

PRESIDENTIAL CAPACITY TO INFLUENCE
THE POLITICAL CHARACTER OF
THE DISTRICT COURTS

What determines the degree to which a president is successful in obtaining a lower-court judiciary that reflects his own political philosophy?[6] We suggest that four general factors influence presidential success in this regard.

PRESIDENTIAL SUPPORT FOR IDEOLOGICALLY BASED APPOINTMENTS

One influential factor in a president's success in appointing federal district judges who mirror his own political attitudes and beliefs is the depth of his interest in and commitment to doing so. Some chief executives may be content merely with filling the federal bench with the party faithful and give scant attention to the specific ideologies of the would-be judicial candidates. Some may consider ideological factors only in the appointment of Supreme Court justices but not with members of the lower federal judiciary. The reasons for their unwillingness to place a high premium on ideology may be varied. Some presidents may eschew efforts to select trial judges on ideological grounds because they themselves are rather nonideological in their political attitudes and values, whereas other chief executives may place factors such as past political loyalty ahead of ideology in selecting district judges.

President Eisenhower is an example of a chief executive in the former category, that is, an almost apolitical man for whom ideological purity counted little. While his judicial appointees were in-

6. When we refer to the president's selecting trial judge candidates, we of course recognize that he does so with the substantial aid of the White House staff, the deputy attorney general's office, and often with members of the staff of the senator(s) from the state wherein the judicial vacancy occurs — particularly if the senator(s) and the president are of the same political party. Indeed, the president may not even know or meet the vast majority of the district judges nominated in his name. Nevertheless the president may still establish the standards and criteria — ideological or nonideological — which his subordinates are to follow in the screening of judicial candidates.

deed from primarily Republican, upper-middle-class backgrounds, there is no evidence to suggest that much attention was given to the nominee's personal political and philosophical views.[7] This is not to suggest that the Eisenhower judges were (or even could be) devoid of ideology. Rather, theirs was an ideological melange in which progressives and strong civil libertarians were mixed with jurists of more traditional, law-and-order values. The flavor of the Eisenhower nominees is well captured in this excerpt from *Judges:*

"It always amazes me," a Democratic lawyer in Washington said, "but you look back and the Eisenhower appointments are clearly the best. They've held up. Maybe it was because the Republicans had been out of office so long, they were out of practice politically. Or maybe it was that Ike's men weren't as political to begin with, they were more like amateurs. And Ike had no personal interest in the law-and-order idea like Nixon does. Ike left it to his attorneys general, to [Herbert] Brownell and [William] Rogers, and they came up with good men."

It is an opinion echoed frequently among lawyers of all political shadings, particularly when Eisenhower appointments are compared with Kennedy's. "Kennedy ruined the federal courts in the South for a generation," says William Kunstler. "Eisenhower's men were infinitely better. Ike appointed Warren and Brennan to the Supreme Court, don't forget. . . ."

Eisenhower rated "solid common sense" highly in his judicial nominees, and regarded previous judicial experience as a plus. Brownell and Rogers, both upper-echelon members of the legal Establishment, may have given less ground to senatorial sensibilities than their successors. Eisenhower-appointed [district] judges include several, such as Edward Gignoux of Maine, Frank Johnson of Alabama, and Edward Devitt of Minnesota, who are widely admired for their courage and intelligence.[8]

Harry Truman had much better credentials as a political ideologue, and yet the evidence seems to suggest that in the appointment of district judges, personal loyalty to Truman counted as much if not more than the ideological stance of the potential judges.[9] Perhaps the 1948 desertion from the Democratic party — and therefore from Truman — of the Progressives and the Dixiecrats left him unusually sensitive on the matter of personal loyalty. In any case his judicial nominations, especially after 1948, went to men who had remained personally loyal to him in the presidential campaign. So extreme was Truman's commitment to rewarding loyalty that on

7. Chase, *Federal Judges,* ch. 3.

8. Jackson, *Judges,* 262.

9. In his interviews with Truman, Harold Chase found that Truman knew surprisingly little about the activities of the judicial system, much less about the particular ideologies of the judges he appointed. See Chase, *Federal Judges,* 94.

several occasions he attempted (unsuccessfully) to violate the sacrosanct norm of senatorial courtesy.[10] Truman's interim appointment in 1949 of Carroll O. Switzer to fill the vacant judgeship in Iowa's Southern District is a case in point.

> Switzer, a bright, young Des Moines attorney, had been the attractive but unsuccessful Democratic candidate for Iowa governor in the 1948 election. Truman had first met Switzer at the time of the President's appearance in Dexter, Iowa, where he made one of his major farm belt speeches of the presidential campaign. Truman's speech was extremely well received, and many [including Truman] believe that it marked a turning point in his election prospects. The Dexter address also had an important effect on the career of Carroll Switzer, as [Iowa] Senator Gillette's administrative assistant relates in this statement:
>
> "I am sure that this day at Dexter was the first time that President Truman and his staff were sure he could win — later proved right. I am sure that he recalled that day favorably later when an appointment for a *temporary vacancy* came up in the Iowa judgeship.
>
> "I imagine the Democratic National Chairman in Washington (who had been dealing with the Iowa State Chairman for four years on the Iowa patronage while Senator Gillette was out of office) might well have been of the view that Gillette probably had no strong objection to a *temporary judgeship* for the young Gubernatorial candidate. The State Chairman, I felt, did nothing to alter this opinion.
>
> "In any event, the National Chairman or Attorney General who advised the President on court vacancies, probably acted on Switzer for the *temporary vacancy*. I don't recall that the Senator was consulted in advance."[11]

Senator Gillette did invoke senatorial courtesy against the Switzer nomination and was eventually successful in getting his own candidate installed as district judge. Still, Truman fought it for over a year. Senator Gillette's aide and confidant elaborated: "Every time the Iowa judgeship came up, Truman would hear of no one but Switzer. Truman would say, 'That guy Switzer backed me when everyone else was running away, and, by God, I'm going to see that he gets a judgeship!'"[12]

Truman's insistence on political loyalty rather than ideological factors characterized as well the overall composition of his appointments to the district court bench. For example, his personal liberal stance on civil rights and equal opportunity was by no means reflected in his choices of trial court judges: Truman appointed no

10. Richardson and Vines, *Politics of Federal Courts*, 61–63.
11. Carp, "Function, Impact, and Political Relevance of the Federal District Courts, 76–77.
12. Letter from Cy Farr, Senator Guy Gillette's long-time administrative assistant, to Robert A. Carp, Feb. 14, 1969.

blacks and no women at all, and at least three of his key southern district court appointees have been singled out as being highly conservative on civil rights matters.[13]

The disinclination of both Eisenhower and Truman to make judicial appointments primarily on ideological criteria is reflected, we suggest, in the subsequent voting patterns of the district judges they appointed. The Eisenower appointees were only slightly more conservative in their voting behavior than the Truman and Kennedy judges; similarly, it appears that the voting patterns of the Truman judges were not nearly as liberal as one might have expected. (Indeed the liberalism score of the Truman judges is identical to that of the Warren Harding judges!)

If Truman and Eisenhower exemplify presidents who eschewed ideological criteria, Richard Nixon provides a good example of a chief executive who selected his judicial nominees with a clear eye toward their ideological purity, particularly on matters of criminal justice and civil liberties. After 1960,

> "law and order" became an important political issue, with Nixon its most ardent advocate. A stout-hearted identification with the "peace forces" as against the "criminal forces" became a Nixonian criterion for judicial appointments at all levels. Judges who dissented from this simplistic interpretation, or who defended the liberal and expansive decisions of the Warren Court, were classified by the President as "softheaded."
>
> "You can't be a federal judge today," says a Washington lawyer with government experience under both parties, "unless you believe the whole hardnosed line. It's like getting ahead in the FBI — you have to be for the death penalty, you have to regard all the criminal decisions of the Warren Court as wrong. I've never seen such stereotypes. Any background of liberalism or orientation toward the Bill of Rights is a disqualifier. Or a philosophical kinship with Learned Hand, say, the idea that better one guilty man go free than an innocent man be hanged — if you feel that way, you don't make it."[14]

Sheldon Goldman, a scholar who has invested much effort in the study of the background and recruitment of federal judges, once commented, "The Nixon Administration is subjecting nominees to the most intense ideological scrutiny since FDR. They'll appoint law-and-order conservatives wherever they are strong enough to do it."[15] The empirical evidence we shall subsequently present reveals the fruits of Nixon's ideological recruitment campaign: between 1972 and 1977, for example, the Nixon judges' liberalism score is a

---

13. "Judicial Performance in the Fifth Circuit."
14. Jackson, *Judges*, 270.
15. Ibid.

full 20 percentage points lower than the Johnson judges for these same years — a difference greater than that between the appointees of any other two presidents in our data set. The contrasts among Eisenhower, Truman, and Nixon serve to illustrate the role of ideology. Studies of the Kennedy and Johnson appointment strategies, however, demonstrate that these Democrats also emphasized ideological considerations.[16] Thus, all presidents introduce some degree of ideology into the selection process. We argue, and are prepared to demonstrate, that the level of a president's commitment to select judges on primarily ideological grounds will be reflected in the subsequent voting patterns of the judges he appoints.

THE NUMBER OF DISTRICT COURT VACANCIES AVAILABLE

A second factor delimiting the chief executive's capacity to obtain a judiciary which reflects his own political philosophy is the number of trial court appointments available to the president. Obviously the more persons he can put on the bench, the greater the president's potential to influence the nature of the judicial output. The number of vacancies is of course a function of several variables: how many judges die or resign during the president's term of office, how long the president serves, and whether or not Congress passes bills that significantly increase the number of judgeships. Historically this last factor seems to have been the most important variable in influencing the number of judgeships available.[17] A good example of the dramatic impact that a new judges bill can have on the president's influence vis-à-vis the lower-court judiciary is provided by Goulden in his book *The Benchwarmers:*

> Promptly upon Kennedy's election, Congress zipped through an omnibus judgeship bill giving the new president — and, of course, the politicians who helped elect him or whose friendship he now needed — an unprecedented store of judicial boodle to distribute. The act created 71 new judgeships. That wasn't all. Because of vacancies the Democratic Senate had not permitted Ike to fill, Kennedy during his first twenty months in office appointed 147 persons to the federal bench. By way of perspec-

16. Goldman, "Characteristics of Eisenhower and Kennedy Appointees," 755–62.

17. A recent research note by Jon Bond found support for these two hypotheses: (1) that proposals to add new U.S. judges are more likely to pass if the same party controls Congress and the presidency than if different parties are in power; and (2) that proposals to add additional federal judges are more likely to pass during the first two years of the president's term than during the second two-year period. See Bond, "Politics of Court Structure."

tive, Harding, Coolidge and Hoover didn't have that many judgeships in their combined terms. In one slam-bang stretch of 47 days, from August 11 through September 27, 1961, 69 judges were nominated or appointed, an average of almost eleven per week. By mid-summer 1962 almost 40 percent of federal judges were Kennedy appointees.[18]

With the increase in the district court workload in the past fifty years, especially in the past two decades, Congress has responded by passing omnibus judges bills which have greatly enhanced the capacity of the president to influence the composition of the lower-court judiciary. Between 1884 and 1932 the average number of individuals appointed to the lower judiciary by any given president was only 48. Since the days of Franklin Roosevelt, however, the average number of appointments available to the president has averaged about three times as many. For example, the Omnibus Judge Act of 1978 created the opportunity for President Carter to appoint 152 judges to the lower federal courts.[19] In sum, one might expect a six-year president such as Nixon, who appointed 179 new district court judges (70 of whom came from a new judges act passed in 1970), to have a greater impact on the federal judiciary than a chief executive such as Ford, who served only a third as long and who was not accorded a major new judges act bonanza by the Congress. (Only 52 district judges bear the Ford label, which puts him about on a par with Calvin Coolidge.)

THE PRESIDENT'S POLITICAL CLOUT

A third variable that determines the president's capacity to fix his stamp on the trial court judiciary is the scope and proficiency of his political skills vis-à-vis all the forces and actors which might oppose his district court nominations. One such potential stumbling block in the way of a successful presidential judicial nomination is the U.S. Senate, which must confirm all lifetime judgeship appointments. If the Senate is controlled by the same political party as the president's or at least by a majority who are ideologically attuned to him, he will find it much easier to secure confirmation for his judicial nominees.[20] If opposition forces control the Senate, the going is much rougher. Several examples illustrate this point. During the

18. Goulden, *Benchwarmers*, 59.
19. See Slotnick, "Reforms in Judicial Selection," 115–18.
20. One might add that when the president and the congressional majority are of the same party, there is also a great likelihood that Congress will respond more quickly and fully to the need for a new judges bill. The reluctance of Congress to create much-needed new judgeships during the later Nixon years and during the Ford

Eisenhower years, when Democrats controlled the Senate, much greater use was made of the strategy of delaying appointments so as to force Senate action on judgeships. Harold Chase's data "suggest that the Eisenhower administration was probably less deferential to senators' wishes than the Kennedy administration, that the president's men, in order to make the appointments they wanted, more frequently applied the strategy of delay."[21] In 1959 the confirmation of thirteen Eisenhower judicial nominees was held up in the Senate by Democratic majority leader Lyndon Johnson until such time as Eisenhower agreed to Johnson's candidate for a Texas judgeship.[22] Presidents Nixon and Ford also confronted Senate majorities which were often hostile toward the names of judicial candidates sent to them by the White House. (Some of Nixon's difficulties in this regard are legendary.)[23] Sometimes these two chief executives were forced into a sort of horse-trading with senators to get their judicial nominees through the Senate. For example, both Nixon and Ford were compelled into "an agreement with the two Democratic senators from California to permit the senators to nominate one Democrat for every three Republicans selected by the President."[24]

Another roadblock between the will of the president and the composition and values of the men and women who serve as district judges is the Senate Judiciary Committee, which by Senate rules must pass on all nominations to the federal bench and make recommendations to the Senate. Historically the Judiciary Committee has had a distinctly "southern" charater to it, and, consequently, it did not look kindly upon judicial nominees thought to be too liberal on civil rights questions.[25] The powerful chairman of this committee for many years, Senator James Eastland of Mississippi, often exacted a terrible toll from presidents who attempted to put integrationist judges on the federal bench. A case in point is President Kennedy's successful attempt to secure Senator Eastland's tacit endorsement of the black and liberal Thurgood Marshall. In order to do this, Kennedy was forced to let Senator Eastland name his old college roommate, William Harold Cox, for a district judgeship in Mississippi.[26] What kind of a man is William Cox whom the liberal,

---

administration is a case in point. The Democratic congressional majority was prone to put off the passage of a new judges bill until after the 1976 election, which they hoped would be won by a Democrat.

21. Chase, *Federal Judges*, 115.
22. Jackson, *Judges*, 258.
23. E.g., see Simon, *In His Own Image*, esp. ch. 5.
24. Murphy and Pritchett, *Courts, Judges, and Politics*, 124.
25. For more information on this phenomenon, see, e.g., Chase, *Federal Judges*, 20–23; Jackson, *Judges*, 120–22; and Goulden, *Benchwarmers*, 62–64.
26. Jackson, *Judges*, 122.

civil-rights-minded Kennedy was obliged to nominate for the district court bench?

> Once on the bench Cox referred to black litigants as "niggers" and was outspokenly hostile to civil rights cases. He once wrote John Doar, then the assistant attorney general in the Justice Department's Civil Rights Division, "I spend most of my time in fooling with lousy cases brought before me by your Department in the Civil Rights field and I do not intend to turn my docket over to your department for your political advancement." During a voter registration case he stormed, "Who is telling these people they can get in line [to attempt to register] and push people around, acting like a bunch of chimpanzees?"[27]

Another political deterrent to the effective political clout of the president is the legislative norm of senatorial courtesy.[28] Many students of the American judicial process have come to regard this norm as a means by which conservative (and often segregationist) senators block the appointment of liberal, pro-civil-rights judges and force instead the nomination of judges whose views are similar to theirs.[29] While there is indeed evidence for this, one should also note that senatorial courtesy may also work in the opposite vein, that is, in assuring the appointment of liberal judges in the face of a president who would prefer law-and-order, anti-civil-rights conservatives. The Nixon administration is a case in point.

During the Nixon years, when liberal Republican senators shared the appointing power with the administration — in New York, Illinois, Massachusetts, Oregon, and New Jersey, for instance — the district judge appointees were more liberal and generally regarded to be of higher quality. As one Chicago attorney said about the Illinois judgeships for which the liberal Charles Percy held the whip of senatorial courtesy, "We draw a line here between appointments before and since Percy. His appointments are head and shoulders above what's been done around here before."[30] In screening candidates, Percy worked with a group of young, liberal attorneys in the

---

27. Goulden, *Benchwarmers*, 63–64.

28. A good current definition of this term is as follows: Since the 1930s "senatorial courtesy has come to mean that senators will give serious consideration to and be favorably disposed to support an individual senator of the president's party who opposes a nominee to an office in his state. But, as the chief clerk of the Senate Judiciary Committee has put it, 'He just can't incant a few magic words like "personally obnoxious" and get away with it. He must be prepared to fight, giving his reasons for opposing the nominee.' If his reasons are not persuasive to other senators or if he is not a respected member of the Senate, he stands a chance of losing his fight." Chase, *Federal Judges*, 7.

29. For examples of this phenomenon for the Roosevelt, Truman, and Kennedy administrations, see "Judicial Performance in the Fifth Circuit."

30. Jackson, *Judges*, 272.

ryers. "He tested us by asking judges who were ideologically cer said. "He hasn't named any lid and capable men."[31] Once or the district including East St. by racial strife, Percy checked the Advancement of Colored t his candidate had the proper ns.[32] Thus, senatorial courtesy r or worse — a president's ability d of people."

executive's political effectiveness ciary in his own image is his hav- l, local political machines, bosses lent's values regarding "the ideal Johnson were often plagued by having the big-city machines insist on selecting (or at least having a veto over) the judicial appointments to be made in their city or state. The kingpin of the Democratic political organization in Chicago, Mayor Richard J. Daley, personally approved every Chicago federal judge during the Kennedy-Johnson years.[33] Not only did many of the Daley judges possess rather poor qualifications for the judgeships, but many had little sympathy for the civil rights goals of these two presidents.[34] In Chicago, presidents not only had to cater to the wishes of the machine, but sometimes they were forced to bow to factions within the machine. For example, in 1966, leaders of the Italian division of the Chicago Democratic machine balked when it appeared that President Johnson might nominate a non-machine Italian to "their" seat on the local federal bench. One such leader told Democratic Senator Paul Douglas, "I'd rather have another nigger" (referring to U.S. District Judge James Parsons of Chicago). President Johnson then nominated a more acceptable Italian.[35]

A final element in the presidential power equation is his overall personal popularity. If the chief executive is politically popular with the electorate and commands the respect of the opinion makers in the mass media, the rank-and-file of his own party, and the leaders of the nation's various powerful interest groups, he is much more likely to prevail over any forces that seek to thwart his judicial se-

31. Ibid., 272–73.
32. Goulden, *Benchwarmers*, 157.
33. Ibid., 118–57.
34. Ibid.
35. Jackson, *Judges*, 113.

lections. This is obviously a rather general and volatile factor, but few would doubt that the president's standing with the American public is of some consequence in influencing his success in nominating judges. For example, in 1930, President Hoover's choice for a position on the Supreme Court, John J. Parker, was defeated in the Senate by a mere two-vote margin. One might well argue that had the nomination been made a year earlier, before the onset of the depression took Hoover's popularity by the throat, Parker's nomination might have been approved. Or, President Johnson's low standing with the electorate in 1968 may have been partially responsible for the refusal of the Senate to promote Abe Fortas to chief justice and to replace him with Johnson's old friend Homer Thornberry. As Henry Abraham noted about the incident, "Johnson failed largely because most members of the Senate 'had had it' with the lame-duck President's nominations."[36] Conversely, President Eisenhower's success in securing confirmation of those 13.2 percent of his nominations that were not given a "qualified" or better rating by the powerful American Bar Association must be attributed, in part at least, to Ike's generally great prestige and popularity throughout his administration.[37]

Thus, a composite variable affecting the president's capacity to influence the judicial output is the overall magnitude and effectiveness of his political clout. One can also say that such clout will be greater if the president's party controls the Senate, if the leadership of the Judiciary Committee is on the same ideological wavelength as the president, if senatorial courtesy does not become an inordinate deterrent to securing acceptable candidates, if the chief executive is not forced to yield to local political machines whose leaders retain values different from those of the president, and if the president's popular standing with the electorate is substantial.

THE JUDICIAL CLIMATE

One last factor determines the degree to which a president is successful in obtaining a trial court judiciary that reflects his own political values and attitudes: the current judicial-philosophical orientation of the other district and appellate court judges and justices with whom the president's new appointees must serve. Since U.S. federal

36. Abraham, *Judicial Process*, 77.
37. Grossman, *Lawyers and Judges*, 198. For an excellent overall discussion of the role of the American Bar Association in the judicial selection process, see Chase, *Federal Judges*, esp. ch. 4, and Grossman, *Lawyers and Judges*.

judges serve lifetime appointments during good behavior, presidents must accept the composition and orientation of the judiciary as it has been willed to him by his predecessors. What this means in practical terms is that if a new president faces a judiciary whose trial and appellate court judges already share his basic ideology, the impact of his new judicial appointees ought generally to be more immediate and substantial. Conversely, if a new chief executive is confronted with a majority of trial and appellate jurists who are committed to values radically different from his own, the impact of the subsequent judicial appointments will be much weaker and slower to materialize. New judges obviously must respect the existing judicial paradigm and are surely not free to make precedential decisions at will, lest they risk being overruled by a higher court. Such a reality circumscribes the time frame and the degree of the correlation between the ideology of the appointing president and the ideological output of the judiciary. Several examples serve to illustrate this point.

When Franklin Roosevelt became president in 1933, he was confronted with a lower-court judiciary which had been packed solidly with conservative Republican judges by his three GOP predecessors in the White House. Similarly, the Supreme Court contained a very stable working majority of justices who were greatly indisposed toward the major economic components of the New Deal. Indeed, it was not until the 1937 "switch in time" that the Supreme Court began to look with favor upon the major New Deal innovations. Thus, despite the ideological screening that went into the selection of FDR district judges, it seems fair to assume that at least between 1933 and 1938 the Roosevelt trial judges had to restrain their liberal propensities in many of the cases which were tried in their respective courts. This may explain in part why the overall liberalism score of the Roosevelt judges is not *radically* greater than the liberalism scores of the jurists appointed by Hoover, Coolidge, and Harding.

The voting record of the Eisenhower judges further serves to illustrate this phenomenon. While we will subsequently demonstrate that the Eisenhower appointees voted more conservatively than those appointed by Truman and Roosevelt, the differences are not overwhelming. Two of the major reasons are that the newly appointed Eisenhower district judges entered a realm populated almost entirely by the Democratic appointees of Roosevelt and Truman and that during the Eisenhower years the Supreme Court was controlled by a working majority of liberals whose presence must surely have dampened some of the conservative propensities of the Eisenhower appointees.

The highly conservative voting pattern of the Nixon judges may also be explained in part by this same phenomenon. When Nixon took office in 1969, he was *not* confronted with a lower federal judiciary totally devoid of conservative Republicans, since a sizable number of Eisenhower appointees were still on the bench. Similarly, with the appointment of Chief Justice Burger in 1969 and with the consolidation of the new conservative Supreme Court majority after 1972, Nixon's conservative appointees were able to work *with* the ideological grain of the federal judiciary — not against it.

JUDICIAL VOTING PATTERNS
OF THE APPOINTEES

The voting patterns of the presidential appointees show what we believe are meaningful, substantive differences between the judge aggregates defined by appointing presidents. If the differences are not greater than they are, however, we think this can be explained in terms of the four variables outlined in the preceding paragraphs. The historical evidence does not indicate that any president had all four variables working in his favor at all times. (For example, Franklin Roosevelt may have placed a high priority on the ideological purity of his nominees, but the number of new judgeships created during the depression years was not great; he often had to yield to conservative southerners, in regard to both the Judiciary Committee and senatorial courtesy; and he faced a hostile majority on the Supreme Court during his first five years in office.) This caveat notwithstanding, however, we believe the subsequent data do show that to a noticeable and substantively significant degree, the appointing president can and does have an ideological impact on the output of the trial court judiciary.

VOTING BEHAVIOR ON ALL CASES OF THE APPOINTEES OF
PRESIDENT WILSON THROUGH PRESIDENT FORD

Table 4 presents the liberalism score for all trial court appointees of Woodrow Wilson through Gerald Ford. Fifty-one percent of the decisions of the Wilson judges are liberal, which puts the Wilson jurists in a tie with those of Lyndon Johnson for having the most liberal voting record. The higher liberalism score for the Wilson judges comes as little surprise given our knowledge of his presidency. Wilson's record as a strong liberal, especially on economic matters, is well established. He also selected his judges on a highly partisan,

Table 4. Liberal Decisions for All Cases for the Appointees of President Wilson
through President Ford, 1933-1977

Appointing President	%	n
Woodrow Wilson	51	94
Warren Harding	41	538
Calvin Coolidge	43	630
Herbert Hoover	42	910
Franklin Roosevelt	47	2,827
Harry Truman	41	3,008
Dwight Eisenhower	37	4,287
John Kennedy	40	4,368
Lyndon Johnson	51	5,750
Richard Nixon	37	3,539
Gerald Ford	44	197

ideological basis, and indeed his record of appointing 98.6 percent
Democrats to the lower courts is the highest partisan percentage of
any president in the twentieth century.[38]

Following the Wilson administration came the three Republican
administrations of the 1920s, beginning with Harding's "return to
normalcy" in 1921, and followed by the two equally conservative
presidencies of Coolidge and Hoover. The conservative values of
these three chief executives (and the solid Republican control of the
Senate during their incumbencies) is reflected in the voting behavior
of the district judges appointed by these presidents. The liberalism
index drops a full 10 percentage points from Wilson to Harding, 51
to 41 percent, and remains at about that latter level for the Coolidge

38. Woodrow Wilson may have had his troubles with the conservative and progressive elements of his party, but from a realistic utilization of patronage there re-
sulted "the establishment of the President's nearly absolute personal mastery over the
Democratic party and the Democratic members of Congress." Link, "Woodrow Wilson," 156. The postmaster general had a list of senators who were the "real friends" of
the administration and "entitled to priority" in patronage; a group of less friendly
supporters could claim only "secondary consideration." Blum, *Joe Tumulty and the
Wilson Era*, 157.

and Hoover appointees, whose liberalism scores were 43 and 42 percent, respectively.

The Roosevelt judges mark a swing to the left, which should astonish no one. At 47 percent liberal, the Roosevelt jurists are about 5 percentage points more liberal than those of the immediately preceding president, Herbert Hoover. We know that FDR attempted to select his judges for their ideological purity and that he tried to use his full political skills to that end. As he told his one-time dispenser of patronage, James A. Farley: "First off, we must hold up judicial appointments in States where the delegation is not going along. We must make appointments promptly where the delegation is with us. Where there is a division we must give posts to those supporting us. Second, this must apply to other appointments as well as judicial appointments. I'll keep in close contact with the leaders."[39] The only surprise about the record of the Roosevelt jurists is that it is not more liberal than it is, given FDR's popularity with the electorate and given the sizable Democratic majorities in the Congress. As we have previously indicated, however, the very fact that the Democrats *did* control the Senate so decisively meant that senatorial courtesy would have been a stronger factor in Roosevelt's administration than in others—particularly when it came to appointments in the southern states. Also, as we have noted, between 1933 and 1938 the Roosevelt judges had to buck conservative majorities on the Supreme Court and among the lower federal judiciary, a burden not carried by the appointees of FDR's three predecessors nor by his successor.

At first blush the rather conservative voting record of the Truman judges seems a bit strange in view of Truman's personal commitment to liberal economic and social values. Only 41 percent of the Truman judges' decisions were liberal, and this is some 6 percentage points less than the FDR judges and even a point below the Hoover appointees. The voting pattern of the Truman judges is less perplexing, however, when we recall that Truman paid scant attention in general to his judicial appointments (see footnote 9 in chapter 3) and that he clearly stressed partisan and personal loyalty above ideology with the result that many conservative Democrats found their way into the ranks of the Truman appointees. Indeed, even Truman's appointments to the U.S. Supreme Court were of a rather lackluster, conservative ilk:

> Harry Truman's first [Supreme] court appointment was a Republican senator from Ohio, Harold Burton—the only Republican ever selected by a Democratic President. His three other nominees were high-ranking

39. James A. Farley, "Why I Broke with Roosevelt," *Collier's* (June 21, 1947), 13.

Democratic politicians — Chief Justice Fred Vinson had been his Secretary of the Treasury, Tom Clark had served as Attorney General, and Sherman Minton was an Indiana senator. Truman's men generally held to the modest "judicial restraint" defended so brilliantly by Frankfurter, the court's intellectual eminence. Three of Truman's appointees — Vinson, Burton, and Minton — were among eight justices rated as "failures" in the 1971 poll of professors.[40]

In light of these factors and in view of Truman's strong opposition in the Senate and general lack of popular support throughout much of his presidency, we are not surprised at the lack of a strong relationship between Truman's personal liberalism and the voting record of his trial court appointees.

The voting record of Eisenhower's judicial team is more conservative than that of Truman's but only modestly so: 37 percent of the decisions of the Eisenhower judges were liberal, whereas the percentage for the Truman men was 41. Since Ike was personally more conservative than his predecessor, the direction of the shift is not unexpected, nor is the fact that the conservative swing was not appreciably greater. We have already noted Eisenhower's disinterest in purely ideological criteria for judicial appointments and that the Eisenhower appointees had to work in the face of a steady stream of liberal decisions from the Warren Court and in the company of an overwhelmingly heavy Democratic majority in the lower federal judiciary. We suggest that these several factors mollified many of the conservative inclinations that the Eisenhower judges may have had.

The 40 percent liberalism score of the Kennedy judges marks a slight swing to the left compared with the 37 percent level of the Eisenhower jurists. While the direction of the shift would be expected, it may be surprising that the magnitude of the leftward drift is not greater. After all, Kennedy had reasonably impressive credentials as a liberal and his appointees would have been able to swim comfortably with the liberal tide of the Warren Court. Yet we must also recall Kennedy's enormous difficulty in obtaining progressive-minded judges because of the conservative, southern-dominated Senate Judiciary Committee chaired by Mississippi Senator James Eastland; Kennedy's lack of political clout in the Senate, which often made him a pawn of the senatorial courtesy norm; Kennedy's failure to overcome the stranglehold on so many appointments held by local Democratic machines, whose bosses often prized partisan loyalty over ideological purity — or even competence; and Kennedy's lack of a clear popular mandate which might have given him more leverage in the Senate.

40. Jackson, *Judges*, 340.

The voting pattern of LBJ's judges is characterized by a decided swing toward the liberal side. In fact the 51 percent liberalism score of Johnson's jurists is equaled only by the appointees of Woodrow Wilson and is 11 percentage points ahead of the Kennedy team. Why have the Johnson judges had such a liberal voting record? In terms of socioeconomic characteristics the Johnson jurists were not radically different from the judges appointed by Eisenhower and Kennedy, although the evidence does indicate that the LBJ people were somewhat younger, more diverse in religious background, and more prominent.[41] We think there are several reasons why the politically liberal Johnson was able to obtain a lower-court judiciary that more closely reflected his ideology than most of his predecessors. Johnson's great political clout and his extremely effective use of his political skills are surely primary factors. It may be true that "in contrast to his recent predecessors, President Johnson had indicated to his team that he wanted greater deference to senatorial prerogative in judicial selection."[42] Nevertheless, Johnson knew well how to barter and bargain with individual senators and was bested by no one in his ability to prod, to manipulate, and to persuade those who were initially indifferent or hostile to issues (or candidates) supported by the president. The enormous legislative successes of the Johnson administration, for example, the Civil Rights Acts and the antipoverty programs, all testify to Johnson's ability to bring initially resistant legislators around to his way of thinking. We suggest that he used this same political prowess in securing the type of district court judges who would "vote the right way on the close cases."

Harold Chase tells of Johnson's great personal interest in his district court appointments:

> The president himself took an unusual personal as well as official interest in every . . . appointment. A former staffer attributed his personal interest to . . . [several] factors. First, the president by nature was people oriented, i.e., he thought in terms of people rather than in terms of things. He had an inordinate range of acquaintanceships, and he knew personally or knew about a larger percentage of the people considered for high office than any previous president in recent history. Second, because of his humble origins, Johnson, more than most presidents, had a feeling that high posts in government, aside from their importance, were exceptionally good jobs and should go to only the most deserving and meritorious contenders. Therefore he was personally curious about those being considered for these choice prizes."[43]

41. Chase, *Federal Judges*, 179–80.
42. Ibid., 184.
43. Ibid., 183.

Johnson did have a deep personal interest in selecting well-qualified, ideologically attuned trial court judges, and he possessed a sufficient degree of political clout and skills to bring individual senators over to his way of thinking. In addition, Johnson had the opportunity to fill well over a hundred trial court vacancies, and these new liberal appointees must have felt quite at home ideologically in a judiciary capped by the Warren Court. For these reasons the dramatic liberal surge manifested by the Johnson judges might well have been anticipated.

The swing to the right of the Nixon judges is fully as compelling as the leftward shift of Johnson's judicial team. Only 37 percent of the decisions of Nixon's jurists are liberal, which is a difference of 14 points from the 51 percent score of the Johnson judges. We have already suggested the reasons why this phenomenon is not accidental: Nixon chose his 179 judges with a clear eye toward their ideological positions; he possessed the political clout to secure Senate confirmation for most judicial nominees — at least until his second term, when Watergate turned the Nixon wine to vinegar; and the rightist leanings of the Nixon judges gained more and more encouragement from a Supreme Court that was slowly moving right of center. Also, Nixon did not have to contend with an ideologically antagonistic Senate Judiciary Committee, with powerful liberal party bosses, or with more than handful of liberal GOP senators who threatened to invoke senatorial courtesy against his law-and-order judicial candidates.

The 44 percent liberalism score of the Ford judges puts them exactly halfway between the indexes of Presidents Johnson and Nixon. The more liberal voting pattern of the Ford appointees is not hard to explain. First, Ford himself was much more moderate and less ideologically oriented than Nixon, and this was reflected in the manner by which he screened his judicial candidates and in the type of individuals he chose. (Ford's choice of Justice Stevens versus Nixon's selection of Rehnquist are illustrative of this phenomenon.) Also, Ford's rather circuitous method of reaching the White House did not serve to enhance his political clout with the Senate, and so he would not have been in a position to force highly conservative Republican nominees through a liberal, Democratic Senate, even if he had had a mind to do so. We suggest that the 5 percent jump in the liberalism index among Republicans between 1975 and 1977 was due in part to the impact of the more moderate Ford appointees.

For the first time we have *hard data* on judicial voting by the appointees of eleven recent American presidents. Empirical data of this range and quantity are necessary before we can begin to make comparisons. We find it satisfying that virtually without exception the results are all in the expected direction and they conform to the body of intuitive, anecdotal, and historical information about these eleven presidents and the judges each appointed. For example, we would have expected the Harding-Coolidge-Hoover judges to be more conservative than those appointed by Wilson or Roosevelt and indeed they were; we would have predicted the appointees of Truman, Kennedy, and Johnson to be more liberal than the Eisenhower and Nixon jurists, and so they were.

We concede that many of our generalizations are rather facile. Statements such as "the presidents of the 1920s were conservative" or "Kennedy was more liberal than Eisenhower" sound a bit like extracts from a lecture to a group of undergraduate, foreign-exchange students. Still, there is historical and empirical support for the generalizations we have made; hence, to place the findings in a larger context, generalizations are necessary, facile though many may appear.

Comparing the liberalism score of one president with that of another is, of course, difficult because the meaning of the term "liberal" and the actual content of a given case category may vary from one era to another. For example, at one point (perhaps between the mid-1930s and the early 1950s) it was "liberal" to sanction judicially the expansion of state and local governmental power to engage in economic regulation in areas that touched on interstate commerce; after the early 1950s, however, "liberals" were more inclined to restrain state encroachments in the interstate commerce field with the admonition that "only the national government may legislate in this area." Also, the types of cases before the trial courts change from one time to another. For instance, prior to the 1950s very few equal protection cases came before the federal courts, whereas at the present time such cases constitute a sizable portion of the trial court docket. One must therefore be cautious in comparing the liberalism index of one president with that of another chief executive who served during a different era. To be more specific, it is probably meaningful to say that the Wilson judges, with a liberalism score of 51 percent, were more liberal than the adjacent Harding appointees whose index was 41 percent. However, to say that the Coolidge jurists, with a score of 43 percent, were more liberal than the Nixon judges, whose index has been 37 percent, is probably less valid.

One way of determining the reliability of contrasting the liberalism indexes for the various presidents is to compare them for identical periods of time when presumably their dockets were similar and the meaning of the term "liberal" was the same across various types of cases. We have done this for all cases for the period 1972–77 for the six presidencies of Truman through Ford.

When the time factor is controlled, as it is in Table 5, we find that the data are not radically different from what they were when there was no such control (see Table 4). The rank ordering of the presidents on a liberalism scale is about the same as before. Only two changes of any magnitude are discernible. During these latter years the Eisenhower appointees (at least the older judges who still remained on the bench) became markedly more conservative, whereas the liberal propensity of the Johnson judges increased noticeably. Thus, one should attempt to control for the time factor whenever possible (i.e., when the *n*'s are large enough to permit it), but it is probably not fatal to a study if this cannot be done.

Table 5. **Liberal Decisions for All Cases for the Appointees of President Truman through President Ford, 1972-1977**

Appointing President	%	n
Harry Truman	38	194
Dwight Eisenhower	29	513
John Kennedy	43	1,342
Lyndon Johnson	57	2,676
Richard Nixon	37	3,055
Gerald Ford	44	197

VOTING BEHAVIOR ON THREE CATEGORIES OF CASES BY THE APPOINTEES
OF PRESIDENT ROOSEVELT THROUGH PRESIDENT FORD

Table 6 shows the voting behavior of the judges appointed by Roosevelt through Ford on criminal justice, civil rights and liberties, and labor and economic regulation cases. Ideally, we would examine each case type separately; however, the division into seven judge cohorts forces us to collapse our case content estimates into fewer categories.

In the criminal justice cases the Truman judges are 6 percent more conservative than those appointed by FDR. This law-and-order trend is continued by the Eisenhower appointees, whose liberalism score is 19 percent compared with 22 percent for the Truman team. The Kennedy appointees are 6 percent more liberal than the Eisenhower judges, and this liberal shift is even more profound when the

Table 6. Liberal Decisions for Three Categories of Cases for the Appointees of President Roosevelt through President Ford, 1933-1977

Appointing President	Criminal Justice		Civil Rights and Liberties		Labor and Economic Regulation	
	%	n	%	n	%	n
Franklin Roosevelt	28	674	48	218	56	1,573
Harry Truman	22	1,166	44	662	61	1,062
Dwight Eisenhower	19	1,854	39	1,068	61	1,351
John Kennedy	25	2,070	42	1,114	64	1,155
Lyndon Johnson	36	2,328	61	2,041	66	1,287
Richard Nixon	26	1,195	39	1,335	47	915
Gerald Ford	33	49	41	78	54	63

NOTE: For presidents prior to FDR the n's are too small (fewer than 100 cases) in the criminal justice and in the civil rights and liberties categories to use reliably.

Johnson jurists enter the picture: the LBJ judges score 36 percent on the liberalism scale compared with 25 percent for the Kennedy jurists. A pronounced conservative trend resumes to no one's surprise with the Nixon judges, whose liberalism index falls to 26 percent. For Gerald Ford's appointees the index jumps back to 33 percent.

In the civil rights and liberties category, Truman's team was again a bit more conservative than the appointees of his predecessor, Franklin Roosevelt: 44 percent to 48 percent on the liberalism index. The Eisenhower judges, at 39 percent, are some 5 points more conservative than the Truman jurists. A slight liberal trend stems from the Kennedy team, whose liberalism score was 42. The LBJ judges represent an impressive liberal surge, as they did with criminal justice issues: 61 percent of the Johnson jurists' decisions were of a liberal nature. The Nixon team is characterized by a sharp swing to the right. Their liberalism score is only 39 percent, the same as for Eisenhower's, and 22 percentage points lower than the figure for the Johnson judges. Ford appointees are somewhat more liberal than those of Nixon; their liberalism score is 41 percent.

For labor and economic regulation cases the Truman jurists edge out the FDR team by liberalism scores of 61 to 56 percent, respectively. Eisenhower's judges score identically with those of Truman, and the Kennedy index increases a bit to 64 percent liberal decisions. The modest liberal trend continues with the LBJ judges, whose liberalism index is 66 percent. The Nixon judges carry on with their shift to the right: their liberalism score falls to 47 percent — a 19-point drop from the LBJ appointees. Ford again brings about a slight swing to the left with a liberalism index of 54 percent.

Two conclusions stand out with some clarity. First, the data are generally consistent with the anecdotal and historical literature previously discussed in this chapter and are basically harmonious with the trends outlined in Table 4, which dealt with the universe of cases. Second, we note that there is much greater variation on the liberalism index for the civil rights and liberties variable than there is for the composite variable of labor and economic regulation cases.[44] This finding is entirely consistent with our conclusion in Chapter 2 that since the late 1930s there have been in the federal judiciary much greater divisions on matters pertaining to civil liberties than there have been on labor and economic issues. After 1937, potential district judges apparently were screened more for their ideological purity on Bill of Rights and equal protection issues than they were for their beliefs about the congressional power to regulate interstate commerce or to tax and spend for the general welfare. The only exception to this generalization is the voting behavior of the Nixon judges, which does mark a sharp turn to the right even on labor and economic issues. The centrality of economic issues to Reagan's presidency suggests that this trend may be accelerated by his new appointees.

When we control for the time factor by examining the voting behavior of these various appointees for an identical period of years (1972–77), no profound changes occur (see Appendix B). The same two conclusions apply to the voting patterns when an identical time frame is chosen as when all years are considered. The only noticeable difference is that the Truman and Eisenhower judges appear to be across-the-board more conservative during their latter years than they were in their earlier years on the bench.[45]

44. For civil rights and liberties cases the mean liberalism score is 39 percent and the standard deviation is 18.1, whereas for the labor and economic regulation category the figures are 58 percent and 6.5, respectively. (For the criminal justice category the average liberalism score is 27 percent and the standard deviation is 5.9.)

45. The one exception is the voting of the Truman judges on civil rights and liber-

A closer comparison of the voting patterns of the judges appointed by Richard Nixon and Lyndon Johnson is warranted for several reasons. First, there is a greater contrast in the decisional propensities of these two groups of judges than those of any other two presidents in our data set. Not only is this interesting and significant in itself, but the fact that these judges heard their cases during substantially the same time frame adds validity to the comparison. Second, the n's for each of the nineteen separate case categories are sufficiently large for the Johnson and Nixon judges to make the comparisons meaningful. Finally, both executives go far in meeting the four criteria for maximum ideological impact on the trial court judiciary. That is, both took an inordinate interest in the values and orientations of potential judicial candidates; both had ample opportunity to fill a significant number of trial court vacancies; both possessed substantial political clout — at least during that portion of their respective administrations when most judicial appointments were made; and the nominees of each president enjoyed an ideologically harmonious Supreme Court majority throughout a significant part of their judicial tenures.[46]

The Johnson and Nixon appointees are textbook examples of judges in contrast, as our empirical data will demonstrate. Such a contrast was brought home rather clearly during a series of in-depth personal interviews with a large number of Johnson and Nixon appointees in 1971.[47] The contents of two particular interviews stand out most clearly as illustrating the difference in thinking between the Nixon-Johnson judicial appointees. The fact that the interviews were conducted successively on the same day made the contrast all the more salient. Both judges discussed their philosophy of criminal justice and, more specifically, their views about sentencing convicted felons. The rank-and-file Democrat appointed by Johnson said in part: "You know, most of the people who appear before me for sentencing come from the poorer classes and have had few of the advantages of life. They've had an uphill fight all the way and life has constantly stepped on them. . . . I come from a pretty humble

---

ties cases. On this dimension the Truman team appears to have become more liberal over time.

46. Johnson was much more likely to be *personally* acquainted with his judicial nominees than was Nixon, but, nevertheless, both presidents scrutinized the ideology of their district judge candidates to a great extent.

47. The interviews were conducted by Carp and Wheeler as part of the data base for their study, "Sink or Swim."

background myself, and I know what it's like. I think I take all this into consideration when I have to sentence someone, and it inclines me towards handing down lighter sentences, I think." One hour later a Nixon appointee addressed the same issue but with quite a different twist at the end:

> When I was first appointed, I was one of those big law-and-order types. You know — just put all those crooks and hippies in jail and all will be right with the world. But I've changed a lot. I never realized what poor, pathetic people there are who come before us for sentencing. My God, the terrible childhoods and horrendous backgrounds that some of them come from! Mistreated when they were kids and kicked around by everybody in the world for most of their lives. Society has clearly failed them. As a judge there's only one thing you can do: *send them to prison for as long as the law allows because when they're in that bad a state, there's nothing anyone can do with them. All you can do is protect society from these poor souls for as long as you can.* [Emphasis added.]

We think more is captured in these quotations than mere conflicting conclusions of two random judges.

Table 7 compares the liberalism scores of the Nixon and the Johnson appointees on nineteen separate case categories. The Nixon team is more conservative on all but one of the categories; on the voting rights cases the two groups of judges have equal scores of 51 percent. (It should be recalled that in our sample the voting rights cases consist largely of reapportionment and redistricting issues and that many of these cases are instigated by suburban GOP litigants.) The issue on which the judges were most divided was that of race relations. The Johnson judges ruled in favor of the petitioner in racial discrimination cases 66 percent of the time, whereas the Nixon judges did so in only 37 percent of the cases. The Johnson ratio of liberal to conservative opinions was three times greater than the Nixon ratio. Closely associated with this was the disparity in other types of Fourteenth Amendment cases. The Nixon judges upheld the petitioner only 35 percent of the time, while the Johnson appointees did so for 57 of the petitioners ($\alpha = 2.52$). It is significant that in no category of cases whatever were the Nixon judges more liberal than those appointed by LBJ.[48]

48. Sheldon Goldman found exactly the same phenomenon when he recently compared the voting behavior of the appeals court judges appointed by Nixon and Johnson: "Note that when the [appellate] judges were categorized by appointing administration, the median score of the Nixon appointees on the criminal procedures issue was the lowest of all groups, 0.53. In contrast, the median score of the Johnson appointees on the criminal procedures issue was the highest of all groups, 1.20. . . . On the civil liberties issue, the Nixon appointees again had the lowest median score (0.57) and the Johnson appointees the highest (1.50)." (Goldman, "Voting Behavior on the United States Courts of Appeals Revisited," 497.)

Table 7. Liberal Decisions in Order of Magnitude of Voting Differences between Nixon and Johnson Appointees

Type of Case	Nixon Appointees %	Nixon Appointees n	Johnson Appointees %	Johnson Appointees n	Raw Difference(%)	Odds Ratio $(\alpha)^a$
1. Race discrimination	37	273	66	423	29	3.24
2. 14th Amendment	35	668	57	900	22	2.52
3. Criminal court motions	23	581	37	950	14	1.91
4. Fair Labor Standards Act	44	102	70	192	26	2.92
5. Local economic regulation	53	78	83	135	30	4.16
6. Freedom of expression	43	171	66	354	23	2.61
7. Women's rights	44	99	68	94	24	3.00
8. Union members vs. union	27	63	56	72	19	2.07
9. Environmental protection	47	154	67	192	20	2.19
10. Freedom of religion	47	79	64	174	17	1.96
11. U.S. habeas corpus pleas	30	138	40	365	10	1.51
12. Criminal conviction	35	84	46	97	11	1.64
13. U.S. commercial regulation	60	210	76	384	16	2.04
14. State habeas corpus pleas	26	391	31	909	5	1.28
15. Indian rights and law	40	25	47	38	7	1.23
16. Union vs. company	44	169	52	196	8	1.37
17. Employee vs. employer	35	131	40	112	5	1.27
18. Alien petitions	49	49	54	81	5	1.24
19. Voting rights cases	51	70	51	71	0	0.97

NOTE: The category of rent control and excess profits cases was eliminated because the total n for both sets of appointees was only 6.

[a] The odds ratio = $(n_1/n_2) \div (n_3/n_4)$, where n_1 = number of Johnson liberal opinions; n_2 = number of Johnson conservative opinions; n_3 = number of Nixon liberal opinions; n_4 = number of Nixon conservative opinions.

The rank order of cases in this table is somewhat similar to that in Table 3, which compared all Republicans with all Democratic judges. First of all, four of the five case types that appear at the top of Table 7 also head the list in Table 3. This suggests that the primary issues which have divided Republicans and Democrats for the past several decades — the Fourteenth Amendment, criminal procedure, and economic regulation at the *local* level — are the same sorts of issues which separated the Nixon and Johnson judicial teams. Second, there is virtually no difference between the judges on voting rights cases: in both tables this issue is last in the rank-ordering of cases. The reason that the judges do not differ more on this issue may be that both Republicans and Democratic appointees are under some cross-pressure on the reapportionment-redistricting cases. As we noted in Chapter 2 the primary beneficiaries of the "one man, one vote" rulings have been the suburbs—the heart of Republican voting strength. This fact may cause the Republicans to respond in a more liberal manner for such cases and the Democratic judges to take a more conservative stance. In fairness to the judges, however, it must be pointed out that given the rather strict guidelines for reapportionment and redistricting, the amount of leeway accorded the district judges is not terribly great. The less discretion possessed by the judges, the less one would expect them to disagree in the way cases are resolved.

We must reemphasize the highly conservative nature of the Nixon judges. Candidate Nixon proclaimed that if elected president, he would fill the courts with "strict constructionists" who would take a narrower view of the Fourteenth Amendment and with judges who favored "eliminating technicalities that favor the criminal." This is one promise to the American people that Richard Nixon seems to have kept.

THE VOTING BEHAVIOR OF OPPOSITE-PARTY APPOINTEES

There are several reasons why chief executives decide, in about 10 percent of the cases, to select persons from the opposite political party to fill judicial vacancies. One is that the president may not be able to find qualified members of his own party to appoint and so he becomes obliged to look to the other party for possible candidates. We have already noted that prior to the Eisenhower administration, Republican presidents such as Hoover and Coolidge were forced to turn to Democrats for judicial appointments in the South because of the paucity of qualified GOP candidates. It is probably fair to say, however, that during the past quarter century few, if any, opposite-party appointments have been caused by the virtual absence of qualified persons of the president's own party in a given state.

Another reason for opposite-party appointments is surely the president's desire to give the appearance of nonpartisanship in his judicial appointments. Many presidential candidates have given at least lip service to "depoliticizing the judiciary," and few presidents would relish the charge of having given "every last judgeship to a member of his own political party." Indeed, during the past century only one president, Grover Cleveland, chose to select all his lower-court judges from the ranks of his own party. In times of international or domestic crises, presidents may consider it seemly to make opposite-party appointments "in the interests of national unity." Roosevelt's promotion of Harlan Stone to chief justice on the eve of World War II or Truman's selection of Harold Burton to the Supreme Court during the final days of the war are often viewed as symbolic efforts to stress nonpartisanship by the executive in the face of national stress. The 10 percent of the opposite-party appointments to the *district courts* are in part manifestations of this same desire for the appearance of nonpartisanship.

A final reason for a president to go outside his own party for trial judge appointees is simply that political realities force this upon him. For example, President Kennedy (and to a degree Lyndon Johnson during the early part of his administration) consented to let Republican minority leader Senator Everett Dirksen name several of the judges for vacancies in Illinois. This was done in exchange for Dirksen's support for some of the key Kennedy-Johnson legislative proposals.[49] In *The Benchwarmers*, Goulden provides another example of a political reality that forces a president's hand in this regard: "When the Senators [in any given state] are divided politically . . . they strike their own bargains. Patronage for the off-party senator relies upon such factors as his relations with the White House and how well he gets along with the other senator. Even under the Nixon Administration Senator Harrison J. Williams, a Democrat, gets one of four New Jersey appointees from his benign Republican colleague, Clifford Case."[50] Finally, so weak was Gerald Ford's position after assuming the presidency that he was forced by the political realities to give an unprecedented 21 percent of his district court appointments to Democrats.

When the first two of these reasons are the cause for the president's making an opposite-party appointment, it is likely that he can readily obtain an ideologically attuned individual and hence pay only a small political price for his having crossed political lines. For example, "Nixon's appointments across party lines have generally been either Southern Democrats whose ideology is indistinguishable from his, or the beneficiaries of trade-offs with [conservative] Democratic senators. Eldon Mahon of Texas (a nephew of Congressman George Mahon), Solomon Blatt, Jr., of South Carolina, and James King of Florida are all Nixon's kind of Democrat."[51] However,

49. Goulden, *Benchwarmers*, 121.
50. Ibid., 25–26.
51. Jackson, *Judges*, 273.

when a president is *forced* to make opposite-party appointments as part of a "political deal" or a series of "judicial package" appointments, the resulting opposite-party judges may feel no ideological or partisan loyalty to the executive in whose name the appointment was made. For instance, in return for Dirksen's legislative support, President Kennedy was obliged to appoint Republican Bernard Decker to the district court bench in Chicago. In 1971, Judge Decker was the author of a congressional redistricting opinion that subsequently cost Illinois three Democratic congressmen.

What does all this have to do with the voting behavior of opposite-party appointees? We hypothesize that on a liberal-conservative continuum the most liberal judges will be Democrats appointed by Democratic presidents, followed by opposite-party appointees, with Republican judges appointed by GOP presidents the most conservative. Since a certain portion of opposite-party appointments are virtually forced upon the president (in the form of "package deals" or because of political expediency), the ideological character of such appointments is likely to be less "pure" than if the nominees were of the same party as the president, and even though a president may be able to find persons in the opposite political party whose ideology is substantially the same as his own, some small portion of these persons' original partisan loyalties and values probably still remain. In the context of our model, political background cues should be less salient for judges from "mixed" backgrounds. Opposite-party appointees should be on the whole more of a "mixed ideological bag" than persons appointed from the same party as the president. Indeed, the data collected for this study tend to bear out this hypothesis.

Table 8 indicates that only 37 percent of the decisions of Republican judges appointed by GOP presidents were liberal, whereas 46

Table 8. Liberal Decisions for Same-Party and Opposite-Party Appointments for All Cases, 1933-1977

	%	n
Republicans appointed by Republicans	37	7,670
Democrats appointed by Republicans	42	416
Republicans appointed by Democrats	42	986
Democrats appointed by Democrats	46	14,967

percent of the output of Democrats selected by Democratic executives were of a liberal nature. Almost exactly in the middle of the
continuum, at 42 percent liberal, are the decisions of the two groups
of opposite-party jurists. Thus the empirical data seem to confirm
that on the whole, presidents are likely to have a slightly greater
ideological impact on the output of the judiciary when they stay
within their own partisan ranks in making their judicial selections.

We can subject this hypothesis to further scrutiny by comparing
the voting behavior of same-party and opposite-party appointments of several recent presidents (see Table 9). Because the n's are

Table 9. Liberal Decisions for Same-Party and Opposite-Party Appointments Made
by President Truman through President Ford

Appointing President	Democratic Judges		Republican Judges	
	%	n	%	n
Harry Truman	41	2,345	44	169
Dwight Eisenhower	44	92	37	4,195
John Kennedy	39	3,893	45	475
Lyndon Johnson	52	5,427	48	323
Richard Nixon	40	297	36	3,242
Gerald Ford	56	27	42	170

NOTE: For presidents prior to Truman the n's were too small (fewer than 100 cases)
to be reliable.

comparatively small for some of the opposite-party appointments,
we generalize from this table with caution. Table 9 suggests that Truman's Democratic judges were a bit less liberal than his Republican
appointees.[52] Eisenhower's Democratic jurists were more liberal
than his Republican judges, and his case thus lends support to our
hypothesis. The instance of the Kennedy judges does not serve to illustrate our hypothesis, however. As with Truman, Kennedy's GOP
judges were more liberal than his Democratic appointees.[53] Ken-

52. This may be because of Truman's many conservative Democratic appointments, particularly in the South, and because his Republicans were from the North.
53. As with Truman, this is more of a case of the Democratic judges being inordi-

nedy's inability to secure confirmation for liberal Democrats, especially in the South, has already been well documented. Thus, the relative liberalism of his Repubican appointments is not terribly surprising. Lyndon Johnson's Republicans were more conservative than his Democratic appointees, and Nixon's and Ford's Democratic judges were more liberal than their GOP nominees. The examples of these last three presidencies all serve to support our hypothesis that there will be less ideological correlation between the president and his *opposite*-party appointees than between the chief executive and his judges who wear the same party label.[54]

CONCLUSION

We have sought to demonstrate the ideological impact that presidents can and do have on the decisional output of the judges whom they appoint. Such presidential impact is circumscribed by a variety of factors, namely, the executive's desire to base appointments primarily on ideological criteria, the number of judges he is permitted to appoint, the degree to which he is able to marshal his political skills in support of his nominees, and the nature of the judicial climate into which the new appointees enter.

The empirical data on the voting behavior of the various presidential appointees meshed very closely with the existing political-historical literature: appointees of Democratic presidents were comparatively more liberal than those chosen by Republican chief executives; and politically powerful presidents who took a deep personal interest in their district court appointees (e.g., Wilson, Johnson, and Nixon) had a greater impact on the judiciary than executives who lacked the will, the opportunity, or the power to "pack the judiciary" (e.g., Truman, Eisenhower, and Ford). Since the FDR administration, there has been less variance in voting behavior on issues of labor and economic regulation than there has been on those of criminal justice and of civil rights and liberties. This corresponds with our knowledge that since the late 1930s the chief battleground

---

nately conservative rather than the Republicans being especially liberal. Kennedy's difficulty in securing the confirmation of liberal Democratic judges has already been emphasized in this chapter.

54. The table in Appendix C provides a breakdown of the voting behavior of same-party and opposite-party appointees on the issues of criminal justice, civil rights and liberties, and labor and economic regulation. Because the size of many of the *n*'s was relatively small and because none of the findings was particularly unexpected or unusual, the table was placed in the appendix rather than in the main body of the text.

of the judiciary has been the Bill of Rights and not matters of national commerce, taxation, and substantive due process.

As for the voting behavior of judges appointed from a party different from the president's, we offered two basic sets of conclusions. First, we observed that the most conservative judges are Republicans appointed by GOP presidents, that the most liberal are Democrats appointed by Democrats, and that the voting of opposite-party appointees falls almost exactly between these two extremes. Second (largely by rephrasing the previous conclusions), we noted that the greatest ideological impact on district court output is likely to be had by presidents who have the desire and political clout to appoint members of their own party to the federal district bench.

Questions about the influence of Presidents Carter and Reagan are beyond the scope of our data. However, the analysis here does suggest some anticipated patterns of influence. On the one hand, President Carter's influence should be enhanced by his unprecedented opportunity to appoint new judges. Further, his influence with the Senate probably benefited from Senator Kennedy's chairmanship of the Senate Judiciary Committee, especially from the senator's announced intention to restricted the use of blue slips.[55] In those states which choose to utilize them, the judicial nominating commissions may have expanded the range of influences on the appointment process, but preliminary evidence suggests that the Carter strategy has produced highly partisan appointments while increasing the number of minority group members and women on the lower federal bench.[56] In combination, these factors suggest that despite low presidential popularity, the Carter appointment process introduced substantial liberal influences over district court policy decisions. Although their absolute influence will be mitigated by a conservative Supreme Court, our findings suggest that discretion to manipulate outcomes in response to political propensities has actually increased since the advent of the Burger Court in 1969. Thus, the Carter cohort's relative influence should be substantial.

It is too soon to know how many judges Reagan will have the opportunity to appoint. Nonetheless, the circumstances of his campaign, his election, and the early part of his presidency predict a

55. Slotnick, "Reforms in Judicial Selection," 115–18. As a standard procedure, the Senate Judiciary Committee sends to the senator(s) of the state where a district court vacancy exists a request to approve or disapprove the nomination that is being considered by the committee. The request is printed on a standard blue form (hence its name). If the "blue slip" is not sent back to the committee in one week, the committee assumes that the the nomination will not be opposed. If the senator (or senators) does object, he explains why on this blue form.

56. Neff, "Breaking with Tradition."

substantial conservative influence over lower-court policy decisions. Certainly his campaign pledges (and the Republican platform) promised that conservative ideology would be valued. His margin of victory, the Republican majority in the Senate, and Senator Strom Thurman's chairmanship of the Judiciary Committee should enable him to keep that promise. Further, if his anticipated appointments to the Supreme Court and Justice Department change the nature of legal cues and reduce district judge discretion, Reagan's influence may be unprecedented.

Our model also predicts that voting differences on judicial policy issues between the Carter and Reagan appointees have been substantial. Not only have the Reagan judges been selected with a keen eye toward their ideological bent but the Burger Court has so far continued to render ambiguous decisions on many key issues confronting the judiciary. Such ambiguity from the unstable High Court majority means that the trial jurists are freer to take their decision-making cues from their personal ideology. Thus, we would predict that the increase in partisan voting disparities, which began in 1969, still characterizes the lower federal judiciary.

4.

GEOGRAPHIC FACTORS
AND JUDICIAL VOTING PATTERNS

INTRODUCTION AND REVIEW OF
THE LITERATURE

VOTING PATTERNS AS INFLUENCED BY THE REGION

V.O. Key, Jr., observed, "In American politics the historical sa-
lience of place — as contrasted with class, occupation, religion, and
other nongeographical categories — colors both intellectual analysis
and popular decisions. Our national politics has been regarded as a
process of reconciling the conflicting interests and ambitions of the
great geographical sections of the country."[1]
Many of these sectional cleavages have deeply affected the dynamics of American politics, that is, how congressmen, senators,
presidents, and voters have responded to the key issues of the day,
for example, slavery, the tariff, and the gold standard.[2] Even the
voting patterns of Supreme Court justices have been influenced in
part by sectional considerations. For example, John Schmidhauser
studied fifty-two U.S. Supreme Court cases involving sectional ri-
valry from 1837 to 1860.[3] He found that party background was a
major factor accounting for divisions among the justices. Because
the four justices who were most supportive of southern regional interests were all southern Democrats and since the two justices with
the strongest pro-northern voting patterns were northern Whigs,
Schmidhauser concluded that the effects of party and region were
virtually inseparable.
What manifestations are there today of sectional differences in
the United States which have significance for the political process?
First of all, public attitudes and voting patterns on a wide range of

1. Key, *Public Opinion and American Democracy*, 100. For further discussion of
this general theme, see Beard, *Economic Interpretation of the Constitution*, and Hol-
comb, *Political Parties of To-day*.
2. E.g., see Turner, *Significance of Sections*, and Jensen, *Regionalism in
America*.
3. Schmidhauser, "Judicial Behavior," 615-40.

issues vary from one region of the country to another.[4] As for national political officials, there is evidence that regionalism affects the voting patterns of congressmen and senators on many important issues, for example, civil rights, conservation, price supports for farmers, and labor legislation.[5] Furthermore, sectional considerations have their impact within each political party: on many significant issues northern Democrats are more liberal than their southern counterparts, and eastern Republicans are often more progressive than their GOP colleagues west of the Appalachians. Data collected by Stuart Nagel indicates that northern members of the federal independent regulatory commissions are more liberal than members with southern backgrounds.[6]

Spatial differences define different legal and democratic subcultures as well as differences in the content of judicial policy questions. Historically, U.S. trial judges have had strong affinities and ties with the state and region in which their courts are located; hence on many issues the decisions of the judges should reflect the parochial values and attitudes of the district. Richardson and Vines note,

> A persistent factor in the molding of lower court organization has been the preservation of state and regional boundaries. The feeling that the judiciary should reflect the local features of the federal system has often been expressed by state officials most explicitly. Mississippi Congressman John Sharp Williams declared that he was "frankly opposed to a preambulatory judiciary, to carpetbagging Nebraska with a Louisianian, certainly to carpetbagging Mississippi or Louisiana, with somebody north of Mason and Dixon's line."[7]

In sum the literature suggests that the attitudes and values of the masses and of those who govern do vary from one area to another, and it also indicates that federal district judges tend to be highly representative of their respective regional and local cultures. As a consequence, we postulate that significant differences should occur from region to region in the way our judges decide certain types of cases. For instance, if the literature is any guide, we should expect southern judges to be more conservative on race relations cases and on Fourteenth Amendment issues than their colleagues in the North; we would expect East Coast Republicans to be more liberal than

4. E.g., see Campbell et al., *American Voter;* Ladd and Hadley, *Transformations;* Key, *Politics, Parties, and Pressure Groups,* and *Public Opinion and American Democracy;* and Stouffer, *Communism, Conformity, and Civil Liberties.*

5. E.g., see Hinckley, *Stability and Change in Congress;* Ripley, *Congress;* Key, *Politics, Parties, and Pressure Groups,* esp. chs. 9 and 24; and Fenton, "Liberal-Conservative Divisions by Sections."

6. Nagel, *Legal Process from a Behavioral Perspective,* 239.

7. Richardson and Vines, *Politics of Federal Courts,* 71.

their GOP colleagues throughout the rest of the nation; and we would anticipate differences among northern and southern Democrats on issues such as civil rights and attitudes toward organized labor. Still, a word of caution is in order. Many of the studies which have depicted sectional differences throughout the United States have also stressed two other points: on many important issues, overall disparities among regions are rather modest; and as our society has become more mobile and more influenced by the mass media, sectionalism seems progressively to have declined.[8] Put another way, ideological divisions within regions may be increasing relative to the divisions among regions. Therefore, we do not expect spatial differences to be extreme or to extend across all issues.

VOTING BEHAVIOR AS INFLUENCED BY THE CIRCUIT

Not only is there reason to believe that judicial policy propensities vary from region to region but studies also suggest that each circuit differs from others in its interpretation of the law and in its decisional tendencies.[9] Perhaps more than region, "circuit" combines elements of the legal and democratic subcultures. In his study of voting behavior on the United States courts of appeals, Sheldon Goldman found evidence of "organized liberal-conservative voting patterns" by the judges and discovered that party affiliation was associated with voting behavior on economic liberalism issues. Nevertheless, Goldman was obliged to conclude that despite certain characteristics common to all circuits, "the eleven United States courts of appeals . . . differ in their rates of dissension and intracircuit conflict as well as the sources of conflict" and that "the institutional diversity of the appeals courts . . . imposed limitations on data collection and analysis."[10]

Interviews with district judges provided a host of specific examples of how judicial administration differed among circuits. For example, the following judicial policies were said to have been affected in whole or in part by unique circuit appeals court decisions:

8. E.g., see Key, *Public Opinion and American Democracy*, ch. 5, and *Politics, Parties, and Pressure Groups*, ch. 9.

9. See the citations contained in Goldman, "Voting Behavior on the United States Courts of Appeals, 1961–64," p. 375n6; and "Conflict on the U.S. Courts of Appeals," 636n3. Also see Morris, "Second Most Important Court"; Howard, "Litigation Flow"; Atkins, "Opinion Assignments"; Atkins and Zavoina, "Judicial Leadership"; Lamb, "Warren Burger and the Insanity Defense"; and Goldman, "Voting Behavior on the United States Courts of Appeals Revisited."

10. Goldman, "Voting Behavior on the United States Courts of Appeals, 1961–1964," 382.

the disposition toward the pleas of labor unions and of civil liberties advocates, the criteria for appointment of special masters in antitrust suits, the definition of what constitutes automobile theft, the severity of sentences in criminal cases, the interpretation of patent law, and whether or not it is desirable for trial judges to prepare *written* justifications for their decisions.[11] Each judge strongly asserted that the existence of differences in judicial output from circuit to circuit is common knowledge among federal judges.

Joseph Goulden provides a colorful illustration of how a singular stance by an appellate court may cause variances in the way justice is administered at the local level from one circuit to another:

> In the trial of an accused robber, Judge Oliver Gasch, a district bench hardnose, used the so-called "Allen charge" in an attempt to blast a jury out of deadlock. Under this charge a trial judge says a dissenting juror, when the majority is voting the other way, "should consider whether his doubt is a reasonable one which makes no impression upon the minds of so many jurors, equally honest, equally intelligent with himself." In this instance, the holdout juror wanted acquittal. When the jury still couldn't agree, Gasch went even further. He refused to declare a mistrial; he said he was "sure you ladies and gentlemen know we have a substantial backlog of work, and to spend another day before another jury retrying this case just doesn't make sense to me." After another day the jury voted guilty. But the circuit court, sitting *en banc*, reversed the case 5–4, Judge Spottswood Robinson writing, "Any undue intrusion by the trial judge into [the] exclusive province of the jury is error of the first magnitude. . . . While there is need to expedite the work of the courts, this cannot be at the expense of the call of conscience." The Allen charge is used sparingly because it pressures holdout jurors to accept a majority vote, the *Third and Seventh Circuit Courts of Appeal do not permit its use.* But as Robb noted in a crisp dissent from Robinson's opinion, the D.C. circuit on three occasions had upheld its use, as had the Supreme Court twenty times in five years. "Since the Supreme Court has not disavowed the charge," Robb wrote, "it is not for us to do so." [Emphasis added.][12]

The court of appeals is in a strategically powerful position to influence the nature and scope of the decisions of its trial judges. As James Eisenstein has noted, "Within the same circuit, of course, the behavior of district judges is even more similar. Since they all look to the same appellate body, the judges within a circuit look to and

---

11. Interview with U.S. federal district judge Henry N. Graven in Greene, Iowa, on Nov. 1, 1968; interview with U.S. federal district judge Edward J. McManus in Cedar Rapids, Iowa, on Nov. 14, 1968; interview with U.S. federal district judge Roy L. Stephenson in Davenport, Iowa, on Nov. 18, 1968; and interview with U.S. Eighth Circuit chief judge Martin D. Van Oosterhout in Sioux City, Iowa, on Dec. 6, 1968. Also see Flanders, *Case Management and Court Management.*

12. Goulden, *Benchwarmers,* 268–69.

cite the same body of decisions and rulings."[13] This was supported in a recent study by William Kitchin in which he interviewed a large number of U.S. trial court judges about their judicial behavior and perceptions. In discussing the importance of precedent to these jurists, Kitchin concluded that "most district judges . . . considered precedent as binding only if it were from their own circuit or from the U.S. Supreme Court.[14]

Circuits also follow important sectional lines that mark off historical, social, and political differences, which give them a distinctly regional character. Some of the circuits are entirely regional, such as the Fifth (only southern states), and the Seventh (only midwestern states). Others are predominantly regional but include one or more outside states, such as the First, which contains New England states and Puerto Rico, and the Eighth, which takes in six midwestern states, a border state (Missouri), and a southern state (Arkansas). (A United States map divided according to circuits may be found in Appendix D.) To the extent that circuits incorporate extralegal influences from the democratic subculture as well as legal influences, differences among circuits may be expected to increase. Thus some of the circuit-to-circuit variance may be caused by extralegal political and environmental influences on the district judges rather than by appellate court rulings.[15]

Whatever the cause of circuit-by-circuit differences, they appear not only to exist but also to persist over time. In his study of the Eighth Circuit, Carp advanced the hypothesis that "variances in the judicial behavior of U.S. trial judges from circuit to circuit can be largely accounted for because for these federal district judges the circuit is a semi-closed system, a system within which there is a considerable interaction among its members and almost no interaction between the members of one system (circuit) and another."[16] To support this hypothesis he provided data for these three propositions: that federal district judges have ample sources of communication to

13. Eisenstein, *Politics and the Legal Process*, 146.
14. Kitchin, *Federal District Judges*, 77.
15. Appellate judges also have strong ties to their respective regions. Richardson and Vines note that for their 1963 sample, 77 percent were born in one of the states in their circuit, and 86 percent were educated at a law school found within the circuit boundaries. Richardson and Vines, *Politics of Federal Courts*, 72. Nevertheless, Vines also noted in a separate study that "the circuit judge is much less tied to a particular locality than is the district judge who has strong ties with his district. The constituency of the circuit judge, the interests represented before his court, the variety of litigants appearing and the nature of policies litigated will normally be much wider in the circuit court than for the district judges in district courts." Vines, "The Role of Circuit Courts of Appeals," 311.
16. Carp, "Scope and Function of Intra-Circuit Judicial Communication," 422.

interact with one another; that these judges use the communications channels almost exclusively for intracircuit rather than intercircuit interaction; and that intracircuit communication functions adequately to socialize, to discipline, and to provide mutual support for the members of the circuit, thereby partially maintaining the circuit as a viable system.

VOTING PATTERNS AS INFLUENCED BY THE STATE

At first blush it may appear strange to argue that federal judicial policy outcomes vary significantly state by state, since the state is not an official level of the federal judicial hierarchy, which advances from district to circuit to nationwide system. Still, direct and indirect evidence does suggest that each state is unique in the way its federal judges administer justice and thus the variation from one state to another may be systematic and measurable. We think there are four reasons why this is so.

First of all, a state, like a circuit, is often synonymous with a particular set of policy-relevant values, attitudes, and orientations. So in a general sense one would automatically expect that on some issues Mississippi federal judges would act differently from Oregon jurists, not so much because they are from different states, but because they are from a different political, economic, legal, and cultural milieu. Still, there is more to it than that. The state itself is an important unit because there are strong political, educational, and cultural links between the judge and his state's political machinery and its particular social structure. As Chief Judge Edward J. Devitt of Minnesota told a group of his colleagues at a seminar for new judges: "The truth remains . . . that we are appointed to office because, personally or vicariously, we knew the United States senators [from our respective states]."[17] Richardson and Vines observe about the judges' law school education:

> Since . . . district . . . judges frequently receive legal training in the state . . . they serve, the significance of legal education is important. If a federal judge is trained at a state university, he is exposed to and may assimilate state . . . political viewpoints, especially since state law schools are training grounds for local political elites. . . . Other than education, different local environments provide different reactions to policy issues, such as civil rights or labor relations. Indeed, throughout the history of the lower court judiciary there is evidence that various persons involved in judicial organization and selection have perceived

17. Goulden, *Benchwarmers*, 34.

that local, state, or regional factors make a difference and have behaved accordingly.[18]

These two judicial scholars then note that of those judges in district courts in the year of their analysis (1963), 58 percent had been born in the district of their court, two-thirds had been born in at least the state of their court, and 61 percent had been educated at a law school in the same state as their respective courts.[19] In a more limited but detailed study based on district judge interviews, Carp and Wheeler found that the strong ties of the trial judges to their districts and states continued to develop after appointment.[20]

Second, for twenty-six of the fifty states the state and the district are identical entities. This fact is all the more important if we take into consideration Carp and Wheeler's conclusion that for a newly appointed district judge, the "first and foremost socializing agent is that of his fellow trial judges. In fact the only point on which all thirty interviewees were unanimous was that each acknowledged assistance from other federal district judges."[21] They then outlined the relationship between the socialization of newly appointed judges and the district (state): "Having indicated that more experienced trial judges are the primary socializing agent for their junior colleagues, one turns to the geographic boundaries of this socializing process. New district judges — almost without exception — seek advice from, and are advised by, other trial judges whom they know personally and with whom they come into regular contact. For the most part, such knowledge and contact are restricted to judges within the same judicial district as the novice judge, thus making judicial socialization largely an intra-district phenomenon."[22] Thus, the state acquires meaning here because in twenty-six of the fifty states (and to some degree in the remaining twenty-four), it becomes a sort of semiclosed system that socializes its new members and that permits its own unique traits and procedures to continue from one generation of federal judges to another.

Third, there is evidence that even after their appointment to the federal bench, U.S. trial judges maintain very close links with their state judicial systems.[23] A primary reason for this may be the impact of the 1938 decision of Erie v. Tompkins (304 U.S. 64), which we discussed in Chapter 2. It will be recalled that because of this ruling,

18. Richardson and Vines, Politics of Federal Courts, 73.
19. Ibid., 72.
20. Carp and Wheeler, "Sink or Swim," 366.
21. Ibid., 374-75.
22. Ibid., 377.
23. Carp, "Influence of Local Needs."

the U.S. Judicial Code now provides that "the laws of the several states . . . shall be regarded as rules of decision in trials at common law in the courts of the United States." In his study of local effects on the manipulation of district court outcomes, Carp noted,

> the importance and implications of *Erie v. Tompkins* were fully recognized by the federal district judges with whom I spoke. All of them freely cited this precedent as one which causes variation in the administration of federal justice from state to state. . . . One judge gave the interesting example of two automobile accident injury cases with which he was familiar. The facts of both cases were almost identical except that one accident occurred in Louisiana and the other in Iowa. Because the federal judges who heard the respective cases were obliged to apply *state* law, in Louisiana there was a decision for the plaintiff; in Iowa the court held for the respondent. My interviewee felt that this phenomenon is not at all uncommon. An additional consequence of the *Erie* decision is that federal judges must be fully expert and up-to-date on state as well as federal law. One Iowa federal judge made the following observation about this situation: "Sometimes when I have to rule on a point of state law, it is not at all clear what the 'correct' ruling should be. Then I am placed in the interesting position of having to guess what the Iowa Supreme Court would rule on this case, assuming they were to hear it."[24]

And in a more recent study involving the U.S. Fifth Circuit, Carp and Wheeler gave this example of the behavior of a federal judge and his state judicial system: "The judge also mentioned that he maintains very close contacts with what he calls his 'nine state judges.' He sees them frequently at both professional and social functions, and, according to the judge, 'they help keep me up on the trends in state law, which we federal judges have to administer from time to time.'"[25]

There is one final reason why we hypothesize that on some issues federal judicial administration may vary systematically state by state. We have some evidence that judges regard the state as a meaningful judicial boundary and try to behave accordingly. For example, during the 1950s the judges of Iowa's Northern and Southern Districts attempted to develop a common set of local court rules so that the federal rules would be the same for the entire state. Judge William Riley of Iowa's Southern District explained in a letter to Iowa Senator Guy Gillette why this was desirable: "Judge Graven [of Iowa's Northern District] departed this noon after working here with me on local rules of practice in the Northern and Southern Districts which may be identical for both. Being more recently from the

---

24. Ibid., 6–7.
25. Carp and Wheeler, "Sink or Swim," 386.

practice [of law] I was perhaps more sensitive to the desirability of having lawyers who cross from one district into the other find the local rules the same in both."[26]

Federal sentencing behavior may also be circumscribed by state boundaries. A U.S. trial judge in Louisiana told us, "One thing I frequently discuss with the other judges here is sentencing matters. Judge _____ has been a big help with this. I wouldn't want to hand down a sentence which is way out of line with what the other judges are doing here [in this state] for the same crime."[27] We have evidence of this same phenomenon in the U.S. Eighth Circuit. For instance, in Iowa the federal judges

> were anxious that their sentencing practices be reasonably similar, particularly where the facts of a case were almost identical. They . . . [believed that if a person] committed a federal crime in Iowa, the criminal should expect nearly equal treatment regardless of whether he was tried in the Northern or Southern federal districts of the state. This mutual belief is nicely illustrated in these remarks made by Judge Graven to Judge Riley in 1954:
>
> "I have coming before me at Sioux City for sentencing on December 14 one . . . who apparently was splitting $20 and passing them. I am informed that there is a similar charge against him in the Southern District which is being transferred to this District under Rule 20 and that it is expected that that charge will also be disposed of at Sioux City on December 14th.
>
> "I note that you have two defendents who were associates of Mr. _____ coming up before you for sentencing. Since all the defendants committed the same crimes and presumably have much the same background, I would not want my sentence of Mr. _____ to be out of line with the sentences you impose. If you impose your sentences before December 14th at 10:00 A.M., I wish you would let me know what your sentences are.[28]

Thus, we believe that federal judicial administration will vary according to the individual state for these reasons: (1) federal judges are likely to reflect their state's own unique political, cultural, and educational traditions: (2) for half the states the district and state boundaries are identical (this is significant because each district tends to be responsible for the present and ongoing socialization of its judges, thereby encouraging and perpetuating whatever idiosyncrasies are unique to that judicial unit); (3) because federal judges are often called upon to decide points of state law, they keep in very close contact with their own state's *corpus juris* and practitioners;

26. Carp, "Influence of Local Needs," 10.
27. Carp and Wheeler, "Sink or Swim," 376.
28. Carp, "Influence of Local Needs," 17–18.

and (4) fragmentary evidence indicates that on some judicial matters federal judges attempt to synchronize their behavior so that it will be similar throughout the state in which they serve.

VARIANCE IN JUDICIAL VOTING PATTERNS BY REGION, CIRCUIT, AND STATE

The primary purpose of this chapter is to measure and compare the liberalism differences among spatial units; however, an important secondary purpose is to estimate the effects of political factors by measuring liberalism differences between party cohorts under controls for jurisdictional environment. The introduction of spatial controls could affect party differences in several ways. The disappearance of party differences would suggest that what appeared to be party differences were surrogates for regional, circuit, or state differences. On the other hand, an increase in party differences would be consistent with the decentralized nature of American political parties described in Chapter 2; that is, to the extent that each national party is actually a collection of state parties one would expect meaningful party differences within each state. Whether party differences increase or decrease, these differences will be a more accurate indicator of party effects when measured under control for jurisdictional environment.

As outlined in Chapter 1, our model assumes that case content is an important determinant of judicial outcomes and that case content can be estimated by assigning cases to case types or case categories. Given the importance of case content, our estimates of extralegal effects are accurate to the extent that this legal factor is held constant or controlled. Since region, circuit, and state define different social, legal, economic, and political environments, we would expect the efficacy of case category as an estimate of case content to increase under controls for these spatial units. To cite an easy example, "voting rights" is a more accurate estimate of case content if we know the time and whether the case was heard in Michigan or Mississippi. Thus, whether party differences increase or decrease under spatial controls, the accuracy of our estimates of party effects will increase because spatial controls increase the efficacy of our case content estimates.

The fact that case content and the accuracy of case categories as estimates of that content may vary across space raises the possibility that differences among spatial environments may be the result of spatial differences in case content. Perhaps the differences between

Michigan and Mississippi voting rights decisions reflect nothing more than interstate differences in the content of voting rights cases. To some degree this problem is inherent in research which relies on aggregate data and classification. However, we compensate for this inherent problem indirectly by using space differences as controls for party effects because we get a more accurate picture of general extralegal effects, that is, if party effects increase under controls for place, we know that more than case content differences are affecting differences in policy outcomes. The introduction of party also enables us to control for case content differences by comparing spatial differences for each party. To the extent that space effects are different for each party, we may argue that these effects reflect more than spatial differences in case content.

Because we are comparing so many aggregates of judicial decisions, we have collapsed our case categories, introduced new time controls, and added a new measure of association. We reduced the twenty case types to the three case categories described in Chapter 1 and separated the forty-four years into three discrete time periods: the pre-Warren period (1933–53), the Warren period (1954–68), and the Burger period (1969–77). We chose these three eras because of the theoretical framework outlined in Chapter 1. The two most recent periods coincide with the tenures of Earl Warren and Warren Burger as chief justice. We have confirmed that a significant increase in the exercise of lower-court discretion coincides with the transition from the Warren Court to the Burger Court. The pre-Warren years were collapsed into a single time period because the relative paucity of opinions and the high turnover of justices in general and chief justices in particular precluded the subdivision of this period into eras defined by Supreme Court leadership. Even though the three time frames cover progressively shorter periods of time, each period contains a roughly equivalent number of cases because of the exponential increase in district court caseload since 1933.

To test the effects of geography on judicial decisions we use statistics which measure variances both between and within the units of region, circuit, and state. Whenever possible we shall continue to use the odds ratio (α) introduced in Chapter 2. Since the odds ratio is appropriate only for two-by-two relationships, however, we shall also rely on a new measure of association — eta — when the odds ratio requirements are not met.

For purposes of interpretation, eta is analogous to the more familiar correlation coefficient — that is, it measures the strength of the relationship between one or more independent variables and a single dependent variable. The square of eta may be interpreted as the amount of variance in the dependent variable "explained" by differences in the independent variable. Unlike the correlation coefficient, however, eta does not assume negative values. Thus, eta ranges from 0 (no relationship) to 1 (perfect statistical association).[29]

Several factors influenced our decision to report measures of association rather than to focus on the more traditional *F* test statistic. First, the measure of association is derived from the test statistic. Second, the primary purpose of the test statistic is to test the null hypothesis that no difference in the dependent variable exists across categories of the independent variable. As with all test statistics, the significance of this test is a function of the number of cases analyzed as well as the strength of the relationship. Given the large number of cases and uneven cell sizes in this analysis, trivial differences were significant beyond the 0.001 level and test statistics were difficult to compare. Further, the cases analyzed do not represent a simple random sample of federal district court decisions or even a random sample of district court opinions; rather, they approximate the universe of opinions involving liberal-conservative questions and, to some degree, a weighted sample of those policy-relevant decisions which have been codified and added to the corpus juris. Since the primary purpose of the chapter is to measure the effects of spatial differences and to compare the effects of region, circuit, and state, the odds ratio and eta are appropriate measures and bases of comparison. Further, the use of these statistics is to a large degree an intermediate step between the descriptive analysis introduced in Chapters 2 and 3 and the more complex tests of the main and interaction effects that are reported in Chapter 6.

VARIANCE IN LIBERAL PROPENSITY FROM REGION TO REGION
BETWEEN 1933 AND 1977

We begin our analysis of sectional differences in judicial voting over time by comparing northern judges with southern jurists and by contrasting eastern judges with their western counterparts.[30] We

29. For an expanded discussion of eta and its utility in this context see Mueller et al., *Statistical Reasoning*, 325–33. Also see Costner, "Criteria for Measures of Association." Given the bivariate dependent variable, it is interesting to note that parametric and nonparametric ANOVA produced essentially identical results. When measuring differences between parties we report eta rather than the odds ratio to facilitate comparisons between space and party effects when more than two spatial units are being compared.

30. In determining which states are "southern," we decided to follow Stuart Nagel's practice of including those states which comprised the Confederacy and also those whose predominant cultural and socioeconomic character has been southern: Ala., Ark., Del., Fla., Ga., Ky., La., Md., Miss., Mo., NC., Okla., S.C., Tenn.,

will also explore partisan differences by region during three time periods: 1933–53, 1954–68, and 1969–77.

Table 10 contrasts the liberalism scores of northern with southern judges and of eastern with western jurists for three time periods. From a consideration of all cases, it is clear that regional differences are modest and that only North-South differences have been maintained over time and even these have been inconsistent. Contrary to findings of declining sectionalism in the United States, North-South differences tend to be most substantial for the 1969–77 period.

An examination of the criminal justice category shows that North-South differences have fluctuated over the years. During the first time period the North was slightly more conservative than the South, but by the last period the North had become more liberal by 7 percentage points. East-West differences were modest prior to 1954 and then declined after that time.

On the civil rights and liberties continuum, northern judges were a bit more conservative for the first two time frames than southern ones. After 1968, however, northern jurists were substantially more liberal than southerners in their support of the First and Fourteenth Amendments. East-West effects on this dimension remained modest across time.

For the composite category of labor and economic regulation, moderate sectional differences have persisted over time. For each time period and for all years judges in the northern states wrote almost 20 percent more liberal opinions than their southern colleagues ($a = 1.48$) although this regional influence declined slightly after 1968. East-West differences on these issues, relatively high from 1933 to 1953, steadily declined in the post-1968 period. Nevertheless, when all years are considered, both the northern and the eastern judges have been somewhat more liberal than southern and western judges. Though small, the relationship is stronger than for the issues of criminal justice and civil rights and liberties.

Several additional observations may be made about this table. In the 1969–77 era only, northern judges as a whole became decidedly more liberal on civil rights and liberties matters and on criminal justice questions than judges in southern states. A second general finding is that after 1932 the North-South split among the lower federal judiciary was generally greater than differences between judges living in the eastern and western sections of the nation. Such

---

Texas, Va., and W. Va. The northern states consisted of the other thirty-three. (See Nagel, *Legal Process*, 240.) The states in our "eastern" (really northeastern) category are those in the First, Second, and Third Circuits: Maine, Mass., N.H., R.I., Conn., N.Y., Vt., Del., N.J., and Pa. The western states consisted of the other forty.

Table 10. Liberal Decisions, Controlled for Region: All Cases and Criminal Justice, Civil Rights and Liberties, and Labor and Economic Regulation Cases, 1933-1977

	1933-53	1954-68	1969-77	All Years
All cases				
North (%)	46	42	47	45
South (%)	43	37	38	39
α	1.14	1.22	1.41	1.29
East (%)	46	42	43	43
West (%)	44	39	44	43
α	1.08	1.08	0.90	0.99
Criminal Justice				
North (%)	26	23	31	27
South (%)	27	21	24	24
α	0.93	1.12	1.40	1.22
East (%)	23	23	27	25
West (%)	29	23	30	27
α	0.66	0.94	0.89	0.83
Civil Rights and Liberties				
North (%)	39	39	53	47
South (%)	45	42	45	44
α	0.79	0.88	1.39	1.12
East (%)	39	39	51	55
West (%)	42	41	49	54
α	0.80	0.86	1.00	0.91
Labor and Economic Regulation				
North (%)	58	64	61	61
South (%)	49	55	55	53
α	1.48	1.40	1.30	1.40
East (%)	62	65	61	63
West (%)	51	58	58	55
α	1.59	1.32	1.08	1.34

a finding is in keeping with the historical literature cited earlier in this chapter.

We now turn to an examination of intraparty cleavages by region and the intraregional cleavages by party for the three time periods between 1933 and 1977. East-West party differences are minimal (see Appendix E). Therefore, we focus our discussion on intraparty cleavages within the North and the South.

When all cases are considered, Table 11 reveals that for the forty-four-year period of our study northern Democrats have been the most liberal group of judges. This is followed by southern Democrats, northern Republicans, and then southern Republicans. The difference between southern Republicans and northern Democrats is 16 percentage points, that is, northern Democrats are 48 percent more liberal than southern Republicans. Among Democrats, the North-South split increased modestly across the three time periods. For Republican judges the North-South cleavage fluctuated across time.

Table 11. Liberal Decisions by Party and Region (North and South) for All Cases and for Criminal Justice, Civil Rights and Liberties, and Labor and Economic Regulation Cases, 1933-1977

	1933-53			1954-68			1969-77			All Years		
	Dem.	Rep.	α	Dem.	Rep.	α	Dem.	Rep.	α	Dem.	Rep.	α
All Cases												
North	47	44	1.11	43	41	1.06	54	39	1.79	49	41	1.37
South	46	37	1.44	38	35	1.11	42	31	1.63	41	33	1.40
α	1.03	1.34	–	1.23	1.29	–	1.59	1.45	–	1.34	1.37	–
Criminal Justice												
North	27	24	1.16	26	21	1.29	37	25	1.75	31	23	1.49
South	29	27	1.10	22	20	1.13	27	19	1.60	26	20	1.36
α	0.92	0.88	–	1.19	1.05	–	1.56	1.43	–	1.32	1.20	–
Civil Rights and Liberties												
North	40	38	1.10	42	35	1.35	63	42	2.29	53	40	1.72
South	49	39	1.53	41	45	0.84	50	36	1.81	48	38	1.46
α	0.69	0.95	–	1.06	0.66	–	1.69	1.33	–	1.26	1.07	–
Labor and Economic Regulation												
North	58	56	1.06	65	63	1.09	69	54	1.90	63	56	1.26
South	53	40	1.66	57	53	1.14	59	46	1.68	56	46	1.51
α	1.23	1.93	–	1.42	1.49	–	1.54	1.36	–	1.36	1.63	–

NOTE: All figures except odds ratios are given in percent.

The intraparty regional cleavages would suggest that within each party the North-South regional split has been a very real phenomenon and that the intraparty regional schism has not on the whole abated over time. However, Table 11 indicates that substantial inter-party differences also exist within each region. In general, party differences within regions and regional differences within each party cohort have been approximately equal, with party differences somewhat greater in the North than in the South. In combination, the regional and partisan differences suggest that region and party interact to influence district court policy decisions.

In general, the pattern for each case category is similar to the pattern for all cases. The rank-ordering of criminal justice for all years is exactly the same as for all cases, with northern Democrats being the most liberal. Intraparty-regional differences over time on this continuum have again been rather modest. Between 1933 and 1953 both southern Democrats and southern Republicans were actually more liberal than their northern counterparts. After 1954, northern Democrats became a bit more liberal than their southern colleagues while among Republicans the regional factor has been negligible.

An examination of all years for the issues of civil rights and liberties shows that northern Democrats are again the most liberal, although this time northern Republicans are notably less liberal than southern Democrats; again, southern Republicans are most conservative. Moreover, for this category of cases, regional differences within party cohorts are substantial. Among Democratic jurists the regional factor has been a rather volatile one. Between 1933 and 1953, southern Democrats were 9 percentage points more liberal than their northern colleagues, but after 1968, northern Democrats became substantially more likely to be supportive of civil rights and liberties than their southern neighbors. During the first two time frames the Republican pattern was anticipated by the Democratic pattern. After 1968, however, the northern Republican judges held the same liberal lead over their southern colleagues as did the northern Democrats over the southern ones. Thus on this issue, the North-South cleavage is now consistent within the two party cohorts. This would suggest that case content, environmental influences, and political influences on this category of cases are different for each region.

The North-South sectional split appears to be stronger on labor and economic regulation than on any of the others. Northern Democrats with a liberalism index of 63 are 17 points more progressive than southern Republicans. (Northern Republicans and southern Democrats have tie scores of 56 percent.) On this issue, Democrats appear to have been rather inconsistent over the years, with the range between northerns and southerns increasing gradually across time. Such has not been the case among Republicans. For the first time frame the northern GOP judges were almost 40 percent more liberal. The differences diminished between 1954 and 1968 as both cohorts became more liberal and again after 1968 as both became more conservative. However, for both parties the 1969–77 time period witnessed a high level of disparity between the northern and southern wings of the two parties, again suggesting the influence of regional economic differences.

In sum a comparison of regional and party differences over time seems to warrant several conclusions. Regional differences occur within each party, and party differences occur within each region. On the criminal justice dimension, North-South intraparty differences were initially small, but substantial change occurred after 1968 as northern Democrats and Republicans became more liberal than their counterparts in the South. Second, the split between the North and South on the two composite variables of civil rights and liberties and labor and economic regulation has been considerable and often volatile. Further, the data reveal that intraparty voting along North-South lines on these two sets of issues began to increase in 1969 after a remission during the Warren Court period. These findings parallel the discovery in Chapter 2 that partisan voting increased markedly after 1968; thus the post-1968 increase in party differences is maintained under controls for region. On the other hand, these findings also suggest that regional differences also began to increase within each party cohort but that this regional schism is most apparent for Democrats. Thus region and party both affect district court policy decisions and party differences are not surrogates for regional differences.

Although regional differences increased after 1968, they remained rather modest. This suggests that substantial differences occur within each region. We turn our attention, therefore to differences among circuits.

VARIANCE IN LIBERAL PROPENSITY FROM CIRCUIT TO CIRCUIT
BETWEEN 1933 AND 1977

First, we shall explore the degree to which judicial voting has differed from one circuit to another on a variety of issues for three time periods. We shall then compare Republican-Democratic differences by circuit over time.

Intercircuit Differences in Judicial Voting for Three Time Periods.
Table 12 outlines differences in the percentage of liberal decisions rendered by each of the eleven circuits for three time frames be-

Table 12. Liberal Decisions by Circuit for All Cases, 1933-1977

Circuit	1933-53 %	1933-53 n	1954-68 %	1954-68 n	1969-77 %	1969-77 n	All Years %	All Years n
First	52	240	48	355	53	593	51	1,188
Second	45	856	42	1,923	44	1,968	43	4,747
Third	47	800	40	1,269	36	1,707	40	3,776
Fourth	42	282	30	1,008	35	1,310	34	2,600
Fifth	40	546	41	1,115	48	1,918	44	3,579
Sixth	43	394	42	698	48	951	45	2,043
Seventh	45	273	42	509	54	1,048	49	1,830
Eighth	48	456	38	722	38	1,261	40	2,439
Ninth	47	639	45	926	45	947	45	2,512
Tenth	38	159	43	333	32	343	38	835
D.C.	47	148	43	353	57	530	49	1,031
M	45		41		45		44	
s	3.9		4.5		8.3		5.6	
Eta	0.06		0.09		0.14		0.10	

tween 1933 and 1977. Several general observations about voting trends in the several circuits are readily apparent from this table.

First, it is clear by an examination of results for all years that some circuits have been substantially more liberal in their judicial orientation than have others. The most liberal have been the First, the Seventh, and the Eleventh (Washington, D.C.). The most conservative circuits have been the Fourth, whose index was only 34, and the Tenth, with a score of 38 percent. The relatively small eta suggests that for all cases across all years, knowledge of circuit adds slightly more than knowledge of region to one's ability to discriminate between liberal and conservative policy decisions; that is, differences among circuits are only slightly greater than differences within circuits.

A second observation pertains to the consistency of individual circuits from one time frame to another. Some circuits, such as the Ninth, have been remarkably stable over time. Between 1933 and 1953, 47 percent of the Ninth Circuit's decisions were liberal; this figure dropped to 45 percent between 1954 and 1968 and remained at precisely that same level for the following eight years. Others, however, such as the Eleventh, have fluctuated widely from era to era: the District of Columbia's scores went from 47 percent to 43 percent and then up to 57 percent for our three time periods. Some circuits seem to have moved in a more liberal direction, for example, the Fifth, which went from 40 to 41 to 48 percent; other circuits appear to have become more and more conservative, for example, the Third, which went from 47 to 40 to 36 percent on the liberalism scale.

A final observation deals with changes in the standard deviation and eta over time. While the average liberalism scores for the several circuits did not vary markedly over the forty-four-year period, the standard deviations and etas more than doubled. Thus, variances in judicial voting patterns from one circuit to another seem to have increased over time, and this trend appears to have accelerated.

Our model suggests that these increased circuit effects are related to increases in judicial discretion. At a minimum, the inconsistency and ambiguity of legal cues from the Burger Court have enhanced the judges' discretion to respond to the environmental influences, which vary from circuit to circuit. The effect of Supreme Court ambiguity has been exacerbated by the enormous increases in the workload of the courts of appeals during the past several decades.[31] The Supreme Court has been less able to screen and oversee the cases which are appealed to it from the circuit courts. For example, J. Woodford Howard, Jr., concluded that "some circuit judges now consider the Supreme Court's supervision of tribunals below to be 'patently inadequate.'"[32] As a consequence of the Supreme Court's increasing inconsistency, ambiguity, and inability to keep abreast of the behavior of the appellate courts, each of these courts may now be somewhat more independent and autonomous than it was in previous decades. This phenomenon would subsequently manifest itself in differences among the eleven groups of district judges.

31. For a brief discussion of this fact and its consequences for the federal judicial system, see Henry J. Abraham, *The Judicial Process,* 3 ed., 163.

32. Howard, "Role Perceptions," 937.

Appendixes F, G, and H provide circuit-by-circuit breakdowns for the dimensions of criminal justice, civil rights and liberties, and labor and economic regulation. Perhaps the most interesting finding of these three tables is the sharp drop in the deviation measures among the circuits in the later decades on labor and economic cases as contrasted with the other two sets of issues. Such a finding parallels the discussion and findings of Chapter 2, namely, that the major battles over the status of organized labor and of U.S. government regulation of the economy were fought primarily during the 1930s and 1940s — not during the years of the Warren and Burger courts. Just as *elected* Democrats and Republicans divided more strongly on labor and economic issues during the early years than they did after the 1950s, so, too, there was less variance in the later years from one circuit to another in the way their respective trial judges decided these matters. Despite this decline in regional and circuit differences, future studies may find rejuvenated environmental effects on this category. In combination, economic conditions, the focus on economic regulation in recent campaigns, and recent regulation cases before the Supreme Court suggest that the battle over government regulation and support for labor has been revived and that, to some degree, the battle lines will reflect circuit boundaries.[33] These divisions should be even more apparent when partisan differences are introduced.

Partisan Differences within Circuits for Three Time Periods. Table 13 outlines partisan differences on all cases within each circuit for the same three time periods used previously in this chapter. Several facets of this table are worthy of elaboration. One observation is that for all years, partisanship has obviously been more salient in some circuits than in others. These party effects are most apparent in the Fourth, First, Seventh, and Washington, D.C., circuits; and for all of these circuits the main thrust of partisanship came after 1968. (For example, after 1968, Democrats' liberal propensity in the First Circuit almost doubled that of their Republican brethren.) In some circuits, however, partisanship was minimal. In the Third, Eighth, Ninth, and Tenth circuits, Republicans and Democrats differed on the whole by no more than 3 percentage points. In two circuits, the Eighth and the Tenth, the Republican liberalism scores are actually higher than the Democratic indexes. However, this is not because the GOP judges were so liberal (their score of 40 is the same

---

33. The most visible and controversial example of this tendency is the "Benzene Case." *Industrial Union Department, AFL-CIO v. American Petroleum Institute* 448 U.S. 607 (1980).

Table 13. Liberal Decisions by Party and Circuit for All Cases, 1933-1977

Circuit	1933-53			1954-68			1969-77			All Years		
	Dem.	Rep.	α	Dem.	Rep.	α	Dem.	Rep.	α	Dem.	Rep.	α
First	51 (156)	45 (47)	1.27	54 (165)	44 (190)	1.47	72 (271)	37 (322)	4.44	61 (592)	40 (483)	2.37
Second	45 (466)	43 (381)	1.12	44 (1,009)	41 (914)	1.10	48 (1,186)	38 (782)	1.45	47 (2,661)	39 (2,172)	1.24
Third	51 (322)	44 (392)	1.34	37 (691)	43 (578)	0.79	39 (723)	35 (984)	1.92	41 (1,736)	39 (1,954)	1.08
Fourth	41 (153)	34 (129)	1.19	35 (504)	26 (504)	1.50	48 (662)	21 (648)	3.39	42 (1,319)	25 (1,281)	2.20
Fifth	44 (311)	34 (170)	1.52	40 (850)	45 (265)	0.82	50 (1,470)	41 (448)	1.42	46 (2,631)	41 (883)	1.24
Sixth	43 (319)	30 (63)	1.80	43 (560)	37 (138)	1.33	50 (620)	44 (331)	1.32	47 (1,499)	40 (532)	1.29
Seventh	51 (181)	34 (92)	1.97	41 (323)	46 (186)	0.82	60 (719)	40 (324)	2.30	54 (1,223)	40 (607)	1.72
Eighth	47 (21)	48 (245)	1.01	36 (498)	40 (224)	0.85	39 (760)	37 (501)	1.07	39 (1,468)	40 (970)	0.96
Ninth	46 (343)	47 (217)	0.96	46 (569)	43 (357)	1.12	46 (582)	44 (365)	1.06	46 (1,494)	44 (939)	1.06
Tenth	42 (67)	40 (92)	1.08	41 (213)	44 (120)	0.89	29 (168)	33 (175)	1.03	35 (448)	38 (267)	.90
D.C.	51 (114)	49 (41)	1.09	47 (156)	40 (197)	1.35	66 (267)	49 (263)	1.97	58 (498)	45 (489)	1.64
M	47	41		42	41		50	38		47	40	
s	4.3	6.6		5.2	3.6		12	7.3		7.6	5.5	
Eta	0.06	0.10 −		0.08	0.12 −		0.18	0.15 −		0.11	0.11 −	

NOTE: Figures in parentheses represent the number of cases; all other figures, except odds ratios and etas, are in percent.

as the historical Republican average); rather, it is because Democratic judges in these two circuits were inordinately right of center. It is interesting to note that party effects seem to be maximized in circuits that are more economically, politically, and culturally homogeneous and to be minimized in the more heterogeneous circuits. This pattern suggests that differences will occur among states within the more heterogeneous circuits.

Regarding the trend of partisan voting among judges in each of the eleven circuits, the data here are consistent with the overall findings of Chapter 2. Between 1933 and 1968 the differences between Republican and Democratic jurists in the eleven circuits was small; however, after 1968 the partisan gap more than doubled. Thus, in the post-1968 era, voting along party lines in the various circuits re-emerged after a doldrums period and went on to exceed the judicial partisanship which characterized the Roosevelt-Truman years.

Observations are also in order with regard to differences across circuits among Democrats and among Republicans. For Democrats the eta for the first time period is 0.06; for the second time frame it is 0.08; and for the third period it is 0.18. This would indicate that among Democratic judges the pull of the circuit has been increasing over the years—not decreasing as has often been suggested. For Republican jurists the increase in circuit effects has been more modest. Nonetheless, the combination of differences between party cohorts and increasing circuit effects within each party cohort suggests that both extralegal environmental cues and political cues are becoming more salient to federal district judges.

Given the importance of case content, one would expect the relative effects of party and circuit to be maintained under a control for case category. Tables containing a partisan breakdown over time among the eleven circuits for the dimensions of criminal justice, civil rights and liberties, and labor and economic regulation are presented in Appendixes I, J, and K. Because the contents of these tables are somewhat tedious, we present them here in summary form in Table 14.

A small increase in party effects is apparent when controls for case content are added to controls for time and circuit. Further, for each case category, the average odds ratio after 1968 is decidedly larger than the ratio for the previous period. It is also apparent that circuit differences increased within party cohorts. This increase is most substantial within the Democratic cohort, especially for criminal justice and civil rights and liberties categories. This demonstrates that the increases in party effects are not surrogates for circuit differences and suggests that differences among circuits involve more than differences in the efficacy of case category as an estimate of case content. In combination these patterns suggest that, while environmental and political cues have independent effects on judicial policy decisions, the effect of their interaction may exceed the sum of these independent effects. This possibility should become

Table 14. Mean Democratic and Republican Liberalism Across Circuits,
by Time and Case Category, 1933-1977

Years	Criminal Justice			Civil Rights and Liberties			Labor and Economic Regulation			All Cases		
	Dem.	Rep.	α	Dem.	Rep.	α	Dem.	Rep.	α	Dem.	Rep.	α
1933-53	26	21	1.57	44	43	1.09	56	47	1.60	47	41	1.47
Eta	0.17	0.13	–	0.13	0.20	–	0.12	0.20	–	0.06	0.10	–
1954-68	27	23	1.47	43	38	1.48	60	60	1.00	42	41	1.47
Eta	0.10	0.12	–	0.09	0.11	–	0.13	0.10	–	0.08	0.12	–
1969-77	35	26	1.90	56	41	2.24	66	50	2.37	50	38	2.04
Eta	0.18	0.15	–	0.17	0.15	–	0.15	0.08	–	0.18	0.15	–
All Years	30	24	1.60	51	41	1.83	61	53	1.72	47	40	1.74
Eta	0.13	0.11	–	0.12	0.12	–	0.11	0.11	–	0.11	0.11	–

NOTE: All figures except odds ratios and etas are given in percent.

even more apparent as we shift to our smallest spatial unit of analysis, judicial policy propensities among states and between partisan cohorts under control for state.

VARIANCE IN LIBERAL PROPENSITY FROM STATE TO STATE
BETWEEN 1933 AND 1977

Table 15 outlines the percentage of liberal decisions in each state for all cases between 1933 and 1977 and for each of the three discrete time frames. The states are grouped according to the U.S. circuits of which they are a part to determine whether state effects occur independently of circuit effects.[34] All cases will be examined here as a group, because for many of the states the n's for specific case categories are too small to justify more specific analysis. (Even with all cases, some states have returned a small number of opinions; for example, only 31 opinions were issued from Nevada between 1969 and 1977.) State effects on each party cohort will be compared under controls for time and case category in Table 16, and party differences by state will be presented under selected controls in Table 17.

It is apparent from Table 15 that substantial variance occurs

34. For convenience we have used "state" to indicate all divisions of circuits, which may also include territories and possessions (the Virgin Islands, the Canal Zone, Puerto Rico, Guam).

Table 15. Liberal Decisions by State or Territory for All Cases, 1933-1977

	1933-53		1954-68		1969-77		All Years	
	%	n	%	n	%	n	%	n
First Circuit								
Maine	25	20	47	32	43	40	40	92
Massachusetts	56	162	47	208	61	205	51	620
New Hampshire	55	120	56	25	75	64	67	109
Rhode Island	46	13	40	50	79	94	64	157
Puerto Rico	47	17	60	25	35	130	40	172
M	46		50		59		52	
s	12		8		19		13	
Eta	0.19		0.16		0.33		0.18	
Second Circuit								
Connecticut	50	60	46	194	43	254	45	508
New York	45	754	42	1,720	43	1,673	43	4,147
Vermont	75	4	25	8	59	34	54	46
M	57		38		48		47	
s	16		11		9		6	
Eta	0.14		0.03		0.06		0.07	
Third Circuit								
Delaware	59	51	48	95	36	170	43	316
New Jersey	51	123	43	272	46	142	46	537
Pennsylvania	46	610	38	883	35	1,356	35	2,849
Virgin Islands	33	3	46	13	48	28	43	44
M	47		44		41		42	
s	11		4		7		5	
Eta	0.10		0.09		0.07		0.07	
Fourth Circuit								
Maryland	28	90	34	265	42	236	36	591
North Carolina	63	24	37	208	60	208	49	440
South Carolina	48	63	37	123	31	101	37	287
Virginia	50	58	21	260	29	568	28	886
West Virginia	41	44	21	149	39	90	30	283
M	46		30		38		36	
s	13		8		13		8	
Eta	0.26		0.15		0.26		0.18	

Table 15 (Continued)

	1933-53		1954-68		1969-77		All Years	
	%	n	%	n	%	n	%	n
Fifth Circuit								
Alabama	49	33	42	177	46	182	44	39?
Florida	47	77	43	134	55	347	51	55?
Georgia	42	135	34	153	52	309	45	59?
Louisiana	39	109	43	306	46	355	44	77?
Mississippi	64	14	38	66	52	155	49	23?
Texas	33	172	39	268	41	551	39	99?
Canal Zone	—	—	88	8	73	11	83	1?
M	39		47		52		51	
s	20		18		10		15	
Eta	0.13		0.11		0.12		0.10	
Sixth Circuit								
Kentucky	48	124	30	100	43	96	41	32?
Michigan	34	107	42	215	53	243	45	56
Ohio	46	82	47	158	64	237	55	47?
Tennessee	49	75	44	223	36	374	38	67
M	44		41		49		45	
s	7		7		12		7	
Eta	0.18		0.11		0.22		0.13	
Seventh Circuit								
Illinois	39	172	30	463	45	432	37	1,06?
Indiana	50	36	31	88	55	64	43	18?
Wisconsin	58	62	35	145	61	541	55	74?
M	49		32		54		45	
s	9		3		8		9	
Eta	0.18		0.18		0.17		0.13	
Eighth Circuit								
Arkansas	38	47	34	141	42	100	35	28?
Iowa	62	45	45	44	65	90	60	17?
Minnesota	54	108	41	133	53	224	50	46?
Missouri	46	199	36	327	26	620	31	1,14?
Nebraska	43	23	57	21	43	111	50	15?
North Dakota	—	—	40	35	48	29	44	6?
South Dakota	100	2	33	21	44	84	43	10?
M	49		41		46		45	
s	30		8		12		10	
Eta	0.16		0.10		0.28		0.19	

Table 15 (Continued)

	1933-53		1954-68		1969-77		All Years	
	%	n	%	n	%	n	%	n
Ninth Circuit								
Arizona	80	5	37	25	44	55	48	85
California	49	348	42	538	44	631	44	1,517
Idaho	54	41	59	17	44	16	53	74
Montana	65	23	46	59	39	41	47	123
Nevada	50	16	45	22	45	31	46	69
Oregon	29	69	42	98	52	52	40	219
Washington	43	76	50	38	36	25	44	139
Hawaii	47	36	48	64	60	68	53	168
Alaska	33	18	53	53	52	21	49	92
Guam	100	1	50	12	25	4	47	17
M	55		47		44		47	
s	21		6		10		4	
Eta	0.17		0.08		0.12		0.08	
Tenth Circuit								
Colorado	59	29	51	83	49	72	51	184
Kansas	24	34	36	55	24	37	29	126
New Mexico	–	–	50	14	57	14	53	28
Utah	100	4	50	36	35	17	49	57
Oklahoma	36	73	47	111	18	56	37	240
Wyoming	27	14	–	–	44	18	37	32
M	41		39		38		43	
s	35		20		15		10	
Eta	0.34		0.14		0.27		0.16	

NOTE: Dashes = no cases.

among states within each circuit. Even under controls for circuit, knowledge of the state from which an opinion originated helps us to explain judicial policy outcomes. Table 15 also indicates that the magnitude of differences among states varies across time as well as among circuits. In general, the relationship is strongest for the most recent time period. This is especially true for the First, Eighth, Tenth, and Fourth circuits. It is interesting to note, moreover, that among-state differences show an increase within some circuits and a decrease within others. Changes in case content, shifting population and political influences, and changes in judicial personnel may account for this. However, the pattern also suggests that partisan and appointing-president effects may be increasing within each state and therefore reducing differences among states in relation to those within states.

In addition to the general pattern of state effects, interesting patterns are apparent for each circuit. In the U.S. First Circuit the liberalism score of 67 percent for the most liberal state, New Hampshire, is some 68 percent greater than the scores for Maine and the Commonwealth of Puerto Rico, whose liberal indexes are each 40 percent. The variance among states in this circuit is especially interesting in light of the large party differences within that circuit. The 1968–77 period shows more variance among the states and between the parties in this circuit than in any previous time span. By contrast, the neighboring Second Circuit seems remarkably homogeneous.

State effects within the Third Circuit also declined over the three time periods. For all years, its most liberal state (New Jersey) stands at 46 percent on the liberalism continuum as contrasted with Pennsylvania's low of 35 percent. The range between the most and the least liberal state in the Fourth Circuit is more dramatic. For the 1968–77 period, Virginia has a low score of 29 percent, whereas North Carolina stands out with a high liberalism score of 60 percent. The post-1968 eta (0.26) suggests that state is a relatively strong predictor of policy-decision outcomes in this circuit.

In the Fifth Circuit we see a progressive decline in the standard deviations among the states, but the etas remain remarkably consistent. For all years, Florida is the most liberal state at 51 percent and Texas the most conservative at 39 percent. However, each state became more liberal after 1968. (The figures for the Canal Zone are too small for meaningful analysis.) In the Sixth Circuit the relative effects of differences among states doubled, that is, eta is twice as strong in the post-1968 period (0.22) as in the 1954–68 period (0.11). The northern states of Ohio and Michigan, with respective liberalism indexes of 55 and 45 percent, lead the two border states of Kentucky and Tennessee, whose scores are 41 and 38 percent.

For each time period, the liberal lead in the three-state Seventh Circuit is held by Wisconsin. Illinois is the most conservative state, and Indiana falls approximately midway between the two. In the Eighth Circuit, state effects increase dramatically for the most recent period (eta = 0.28). Iowa is the most liberal state with a score of 60 percent; this is in contrast to Missouri's 31 percent. Clearly the southern and border states have exerted a conservative influence on this circuit as a whole.

Idaho and Hawaii are the most liberal states in the Ninth Circuit, with liberalism scores of 53 percent each. This is in contrast to Oregon's low of 40 percent. In the Tenth Circuit, Kansas is the most conservative state with a score of only 29 percent; this is contrasted with the New Mexico high of 53 percent. As with the Seventh Circuit, state effects increased after 1968 (eta = 0.27).

The relative differences among the states in each circuit seem to follow the same pattern as do the differences among the circuits and between the Republican and Democratic cohorts in each of the circuits. That is, differences among states seem to have increased in the later years just as have intercircuit disparities and partisanship in judicial behavior. In both circuits which cross North-South sectional boundaries, the Sixth and the Eighth, the border and southern states were markedly more conservative than the other states. This may suggest that local and regional values — as personified in the state — have a greater influence on judicial behavior than the circuit as a whole. The presence of differences among states within each circuit demonstrates that the state environment exerts independent influence on judicial policy decisions.

Let us now test the relative effects of state environment and judges' party affiliations. To do so we will examine state effects under control for party and party effects under control for state. The large number of states reduces our ability to compare individual states for each case category; however, in Table 16 we compare state effects on each party cohort under controls for time and case category by comparing the coefficients of association (eta) for Democrats and Republicans with the coefficients for both parties.

State effects within each party cohort have been substantial and relatively stable. Although state effects are maximized during the 1969–77 period, these effects remain relatively consistent across time and among case categories. Certainly the increases do not match the dramatic post-1968 increases in other environmental effects. Although we do not test interaction effects until the penultimate chapter, this pattern certainly suggests that such effects exert substantial influence over trial court policy decisions.

Table 16 also tells us something about the relative party effects on interstate differences. During the earlier period, state effects were greater for Republicans, but by the last period the early differences had virtually disappeared. Moreover, it is interesting to note that the eta for each party tends to be larger than the eta for both parties. Intuitively, one might expect the measure for both parties to fall in between the measure for each party, but the differences (larger under control for either party) suggest that by controlling for party, variance in judicial liberalism within states is reduced in relation to the variance among states. This, in turn, suggests that party differences are present within states and that some party effects are inde-

Table 16. Coefficient of Association (Eta) between State Differences and Judicial Liberalism, by Political Party and Case Category, 1933-1977

Case Category	1933-53			1954-68		
	Dem.	Rep.	All Judges	Dem.	Rep.	All Judges
Criminal justice	0.30	0.32	0.26	0.18	0.25	0.16
Civil rights and liberties	0.27	0.35	0.22	0.22	0.31	0.18
Labor and economic regulation	0.25	0.29	0.22	0.22	0.21	0.16

Case Category	1969-77			All Years		
	Dem.	Rep.	All Judges	Dem.	Rep.	All Judges
Criminal justice	0.30	0.31	0.26	0.21	0.22	0.17
Civil rights and liberties	0.29	0.29	0.25	0.20	0.24	0.17
Labor and economic regulation	0.23	0.19	0.18	0.17	0.17	0.14

pendent of state effects. In Table 17 we address this suggestion directly.

To the extent that apparent party effects disappear or "wash out" under controls, we may conclude that what appeared to be party effects were actually surrogates for space, time, and case content differences. On the other hand, if party effects increase under additional controls, we may conclude that these political cues impinge upon the judicial decision independently of other legal and extralegal cues. The nature of American political parties and the role of senatorial courtesy in the federal district judge appointment process combine to suggest that knowledge of a judge's state party affiliation may be more valuable than knowledge of party affiliation at the national level. Further, controls for case content should be more meaningful at the state level than they are at the national, regional, or circuit level. That is, civil rights cases resolved in Missouri during a given time frame are probably more comparable than are, for example, civil rights cases resolved in Missouri and Minnesota (also in the Eighth Circuit) during the same time frame. Finally, the preceding analysis of party effects under control for region and for circuit suggests that party effects become more important as the spatial span of control is reduced.

Unfortunately, we cannot impose perfect controls for time, space, and case content. Even with a large data set, the distribution of our cases across time, space, and case types does not permit controls for each of the twenty case types, each of the forty-four years, and each of the fifty states (plus Washington, D.C.). Such controls would generate too many empty cells and vitiate subsequent analysis. In recognition of these inescapable limitations, we tested the effects of party in each state for all cases and all times, for all cases after 1968, and for civil rights and liberties cases after 1968. Thus, each successive level of analysis imposes an additional category of control. We chose to focus on civil rights and liberties in the most recent time period for two reasons. First, earlier analysis has suggested that the importance of political cues for civil rights and liberties cases increased during the most recent time period. Second, the controversy and intensity surrounding these cases during this period generated a large number of cases throughout the fifty states. Thus, while our controls are not absolute, they are sufficient to facilitate the exploration of the effects of party under controls for state.

Table 17 illustrates several things about party effects under controls for state. First, party effects vary substantially from state to state. For all years and all cases, absolute party differences ranged from 0 percent in Nebraska to 49 percent in Utah. Further, while the

Table 17. Interparty Differences in Liberalism by State for Civil Rights and Liberties Cases and All Cases

State	Civil Rights and Liberties 1969-77					All Cases 1969-77					All Cases for All Years 1933-77				
	Dem.		Rep.		α	Dem.		Rep.		α	Dem.		Rep.		α
	%	n	%	n		%	n	%	n		%	n	%	n	
Alabama	40	40	52	82	0.61	36	67	51	115	0.53	35	151	50	241	0.54
Alaska	—	1	—	2	—	43	7	60	15	0.50	53	40	49	49	1.19
Arizona	69	13	25	4	6.75	41	44	55	11	0.58	44	71	67	15	0.77
Arkansas	31	13	57	35	0.33	28	29	48	71	0.42	35	182	43	106	0.84
California	50	149	39	92	1.53	46	408	40	226	1.28	45	966	42	498	1.08
Colorado	60	10	32	44	3.21	54	24	35	83	2.20	40	91	44	151	0.95
Connecticut	48	90	50	2	0.91	46	233	23	22	2.84	48	370	39	142	1.35
Delaware	19	21	69	29	0.11	24	102	54	68	0.26	36	169	52	147	0.66
District of Columbia	63	93	56	73	1.35	66	266	49	265	1.97	58	497	45	490	2.49
Florida	68	109	36	39	3.84	59	269	42	79	1.98	55	431	39	126	2.72
Georgia	59	76	55	62	1.20	55	193	47	116	1.35	45	440	47	158	0.94
Hawaii	100	10	58	19	3.19	62	29	62	45	1.00	56	104	51	71	1.27
Idaho	—	1	—	2	—	80	5	27	11	10.67	44	27	55	49	0.81
Illinois	58	74	41	127	2.00	55	157	38	276	1.99	50	449	40	436	1.53
Indiana	52	23	73	11	0.41	58	38	44	32	1.77	42	100	41	97	1.02
Iowa	89	9	66	32	4.19	74	27	62	69	1.73	62	66	59	124	1.17
Kansas	60	15	29	7	3.75	46	35	21	29	3.23	37	101	27	56	1.66
Kentucky	68	19	43	14	2.89	46	54	38	42	1.40	44	260	31	62	1.50
Louisiana	56	143	15	27	7.30	49	301	26	54	2.76	46	648	24	70	2.33
Maine	—	—	63	16	—	—	—	43	40	—	38	24	41	80	0.92
Maryland	51	64	45	40	1.30	42	123	40	114	1.51	43	181	33	416	1.62
Massachusetts	78	45	45	64	4.22	69	83	41	170	3.21	58	274	43	314	2.74
Michigan	83	35	39	56	7.47	76	82	41	162	4.40	51	331	37	240	2.65
Minnesota	71	52	32	31	5.18	62	146	39	78	2.57	55	236	45	232	1.65
Mississippi	55	89	—	—	—	52	154	50	2	1.08	49	235	50	2	0.98

Table 17 (Continued)

State	Civil Rights and Liberties 1969-77					All Cases 1969-77					All Cases for All Years 1933-77				
	Dem.		Rep.		α	Dem.		Rep.		α	Dem.		Rep.		α
	%	n	%	n		%	n	%	n		%	n	%	n	
Montana	45	11	50	4	0.83	42	24	32	19	1.55	50	52	44	73	1.30
Nebraska	39	46	—	—	—	—	—	43	111	—	45	53	45	119	1.00
Nevada	50	8	—	—	—	45	31	—	—	—	43	51	56	18	1.99
New Hampshire	70	33	—	—	—	75	64	—	—	—	68	100	46	11	2.74
New Jersey	30	10	42	19	0.89	53	30	43	113	1.49	48	192	44	351	1.17
New Mexico	60	10	50	6	1.50	57	21	40	10	2.00	53	30	47	15	1.29
New York	61	293	41	239	2.29	48	937	38	737	1.46	45	2,259	40	1,892	1.24
North Carolina	72	88	35	20	4.68	65	161	43	47	2.46	55	308	38	135	2.73
North Dakota	63	8	29	7	4.17	67	15	29	14	5.00	54	24	35	46	2.20
Ohio	74	61	61	43	1.84	71	156	51	81	2.33	58	345	46	134	2.04
Oklahoma	20	59	0	7	1.79	18	207	21	14	0.82	29	337	31	70	0.91
Oregon	67	6	72	18	0.77	40	20	59	32	0.46	42	88	38	130	1.22
Pennsylvania	49	167	35	254	1.76	41	553	31	773	1.52	40	1,363	36	1,425	1.22
Rhode Island	92	48	80	5	2.75	90	76	32	19	18.42	80	96	37	62	6.87
South Carolina	33	33	29	7	1.25	29	90	46	11	0.49	37	276	46	11	0.91
South Dakota	80	10	33	18	8.00	47	53	39	31	1.41	46	56	39	51	1.33
Tennessee	42	103	52	21	0.65	36	327	43	47	0.74	39	573	48	95	0.88
Texas	51	219	21	43	3.95	44	473	25	77	2.41	42	706	34	283	1.59
Utah	100	8	7	13	12.50	75	8	23	26	6.71	86	14	37	60	7.24
Vermont	80	5	46	13	4.67	75	12	50	22	3.00	69	16	45	31	4.77
Virginia	53	114	17	130	5.17	50	211	13	463	6.41	44	329	16	664	6.34
Washington	75	4	33	3	6.00	44	18	25	8	2.40	47	93	34	35	2.50
West Virginia	47	17	50	4	0.89	37	79	55	11	0.48	29	228	35	55	0.00
Wisconsin	71	223	56	9	1.96	61	522	43	21	2.10	57	667	38	74	2.48
Wyoming	—	—	50	8	—	—	—	59	17	—	—	—	41	42	—

NOTE: Dashes = no or too few cases.

table shows that Democrats are generally more liberal than Republicans, GOP judges are substantially more liberal in several states.

For purposes of this analysis, the most important message from this table concerns the increase of party effects as controls for time and case content are added. Party effects for all cases are greater within the last period than for all years. Within the last period, party effects are more important for civil rights and liberties cases than for all cases. Even if one discounts the substantive value of large odds ratios for states such as Utah, which had relatively few civil rights and liberties opinions during the last period, the overall pattern of party effects is impressive. This pattern is consistent with our earlier analysis of extralegal effects and suggests that political cues do impinge on the judicial policy decisions independently of space, time, and case content effects. Certainly we get a sharper picture of the patterns of decisions in civil rights and liberties cases by looking at the continued effects of state and party.

CONCLUSION

Our findings confirm and amplify the wealth of literature which indicates that federal judicial administration is not uniform throughout the United States, that the judges' ties with their region or locale are strong and do have an influence on judicial behavior. Our findings are also consistent with our knowledge that political parties in the United States tend to be state parties and that state party officials tend to be influential in the selection of federal district judges.

At this point we know that variance in judicial liberalism occurs among circuits and that these differences are present for both parties. This suggests that judicially defined spatial units do impose independent constraints upon judicial discretion. We also know that additional variance occurs among states within each circuit. Thus, knowing the opinion writer's state is as helpful in explaining the opinion's policy content within a given circuit as it is across all circuits. Given the relative effects of region, circuit, and state and the fact that the larger spatial units can be inferred from identification of a state, it is apparent that the state is the most important spatial influence on district court policy decisions and, therefore, the appropriate unit for subsequent tests of spatial effects on judicial liberalism.

Finally, we know that party effects are more important under controls for state than they are in the absence of spatial controls or under controls for region or circuit and that party effects increase as controls for time and case content are added to spatial controls. Therefore, subsequent analyses of environmental and political influence on judicial policy decisions should measure the interaction between state and political cues as well as the independent effects of each.

5.

THE LEVEL OF URBANIZATION
AND JUDICIAL VOTING PATTERNS

INTRODUCTION AND REVIEW
OF THE LITERATURE

BEHAVIORAL DIFFERENCES BETWEEN URBAN AND RURAL AREAS

It seems fair to generalize that to a significant degree the more urban the community, the more likely it is that the residents will possess liberal sociopolitical orientations.[1] For example, there is evidence that those living in metropolitan areas are more likely than their small-town and rural neighbors to favor public enterprise in regulating the power industries and in seeing that everyone is provided with adequate housing, to support the idea that "the government ought to help people get doctors and hospital care at low cost," to oppose curbing the power of labor unions, and to believe that "the government in Washington ought to see to it that everybody who wants to work can find a job."[2] There is also evidence that residents of rural areas are more likely to contain larger percentages of persons who rank low on questions of U.S. involvement in international politics communities.[3]

The lifestyles and morals of residents of rural areas also often differ from those of city dwellers. For instance, support for prohibition of alcoholic beverages has traditionally been twice as great among farmers and among residents of small towns than it has been among

1. Nevertheless we readily acknowledge the caveat expressed by V.O. Key, Jr., on this general subject: "The detailed evidence on gradations of opinion among places of different population size indicates that even the country is not often set off sharply from the metropolis. Rather, people of all shades of opinion inhabit both the city and the country. The opinion distributions in the two types of areas overlap; only the averages differ. [For an extensive compilation of poll results comparing farmers with other sectors of the population, see Beers, "Rural-Urban Differences."] Moreover, on many questions, differences in opinion patterns are not related with regularity to size of community." Key, *Public Opinion and American Democracy*, 111–12.

2. Ibid., 112–13.

3. Ibid., 114.

those who inhabit large cities.[4] Urban-rural attitudinal differences toward prohibition are paralleled by, and perhaps associated with, differences found by Samuel Stouffer, who developed a scale on the willingness to tolerate nonconformists. According to the Stouffer study, the percentage of the population in the "more tolerant" category was 39 in the metropolitan areas, 30 in other cities, 25 in small towns, and only 18 for the farm population.[5]

Furthermore, the authors of the *American Voter* tell us:

> Although class awareness shows little tendency to follow common sociological divisions of the population, one such correlate emerges with some clarity. Contact with modern urban life increases the likelihood of class awareness. The level of awareness is highest in the central cities of large metropolitan areas and declines steadily through smaller cities to a low among people living in sparsely settled areas. It is particularly low among people in farm occupations. Furthermore, the probability that an individual thinks of himself as a class member shows some variation according to the amount of his life that he has spent in urban areas where ideas of social class are abroad. Among people who reside in large metropolises, those who have lived in such urban concentrations all of their lives are more likely to be aware of class than metropolitan people who grew up on farms."[6]

These same authors and others have then demonstrated how social-class perceptions are related to a large variety of other political and social variables pertaining to citizens' attitudes and orientations.[7]

Not only is the size of the community related to one's basic values and attitudes, but the urban-rural continuum is also clearly associated with overt political behavior. For example, Leon Epstein demonstrated that in Wisconsin gubernatorial elections, the Democratic vote increased consistently with size of city.[8] In a more extensive study in Michigan, Nicholas Masters and Deil Wright determined that much of the variation in Democratic voting among cities of different sizes could be explained by the occupational composition of the cities. Yet workers in small cities were much less likely to vote Democratic than were laborers in large metropolitan areas. Conditions present in the large urban areas and absent in the smaller cities mobilized laborers for the Democrats. (The relative absence of unions in cities under 10,000 seemed to be the most important fac-

4. Ibid., 115.
5. Stouffer, *Communism, Conformity, and Civil Liberties,* 112.
6. Campbell et al., *American Voter,* 203–4.
7. Ibid., ch. 12. See also, for example, Lipset, *Political Man,* and Pomper, *Voters' Choice,* ch. 3.
8. Epstein, "Size of Place and the Two-Party Vote."

tor.)[9] In a study of congressional voting and occupations, Duncan MacRae, Jr., came to generally similar conclusions. In congressional districts composed mainly of farmers and small-town dwellers, MacRae found little or no association between voting and occupation. In urban districts, however, occupations tended to split their voting along predicted party lines.[10] Finally, there is evidence that one's location on the urban-rural continuum affects the likelihood of one's voting in the first place.[11] In sum, the size of the community in which one lives affects one's basic social and political attitudes and influences if and how the voter will exercise his franchise. The literature also indicates that to a significant degree the values and political behavior of urban dwellers is on the average more liberal than those who live in small towns or rural areas.

Studies reveal that not only does community size affect values and behavior of the citizenry at large but that it influences the voting patterns and behavior of elected *legislative* officials. For example, Randall Ripley examined differences in the distribution of constituency characteristics among all Democratic and Republican representatives in the Eighty-eighth Congress (1963–64). He noted that "Democrats were more likely to come from poorer, more urban districts with a relatively large non-white population and Republicans were more likely to come from richer, more suburban districts with a relatively small non-white population."[12]

Ripley then noted that most studies conclude that

constituency characteristics are wedded to ideological differences among congressmen. Democrats and Republicans generally differ in their views, particularly on domestic policy, with the Democrats being generally more liberal and the Republicans generally more conservative. Within the parties, however, differences between the districts represented by individuals are not always systematically predictive of which party members will be the more liberal or more conservative or more or less loyal to the party. A few variables are more predictive of ideological differences than others. For example, among urban southern Democrats ($N = 36$) in the Eighty-eighth Congress the percent urban population in the district was highly correlated with party unity, support for a larger Federal role, and support for President John Kennedy's programs. That is, among this subset of congressmen those from the more urban districts were the more liberal, loyal Democrats. Among rural southern Democrats ($N = 42$) the

9. Masters and Wright, "Trends and Variations in the Two-Party Vote."
10. MacRae, "Occupations and the Congressional Vote." For information on urban voting and presidential politics, see Key, *Politics, Parties, and Pressure Groups,* 245–53.
11. For example, see Campbell et al., *American Voter,* 255–59.
12. Ripley, *Congress: Process and Policy,* 290.

percentage of black population in the district was negatively correlated with party unity, support for a larger federal role, and support for the president's programs. That is, the rural southern Democrat with the greatest proportion of blacks in his district tended to be the most conservative and least loyal to his party's legislative positions."[13]

Whereas some scholars have argued that the influence of party affiliation has a greater impact on congressmen's votes than constituency characteristics, another study presented more differentiated findings. When the influence of constituency and party were compared on five policy dimensions, constituency was found to be relatively potent on civil liberties and international involvement matters, but party affiliation was found to be more important on questions of agricultural assistance, social welfare, and government management.[14] As Ripley points out, however, "the 'dispute' in the roll call literature between party influence is ultimately pointless since the type of district helps determine the party of the congressman."[15] In any case, the evidence does indicate a positive relationship between congressmen from urban districts and liberal voting on many (though surely not all) important issues.

At the level of state politics, a variety of studies have sought to determine the existence of urban-rural splits in the way legislators vote on key issues. Not all of these investigations, however, have arrived at the same conclusions.[16] This is so in part at least because of the very strong conjunction in many states between party affiliation and constituency factors. As Jewell and Patterson note:

> The correlation between urbanization-industrialization and party voting in the legislature is far from perfect, but it is strong enough to raise questions about the causal relationships that may exist. In states with high party voting, each of the parties is likely to be relatively homogeneous in its composition. The Democratic party draws its electoral strength from the metropolitan centers and particularly from labor groups, racial and ethnic minorities, Catholic voters, and persons with below-average incomes. The Republican vote is in the higher-income sections of the metropolis, the towns and cities, and some of the farm areas.[17]

Perhaps one of the best studies (and literature reviews) of this subject was conducted by Wayne Francis. In his fifty-state analysis, Francis compared his findings about urban-rural legislative splits

13. Ibid., 290–91.
14. Clausen, *How Congressmen Decide.*
15. Ripley, *Congress,* 291.
16. E.g., see MacRae, "Relation between Roll Call Votes and Constituencies." In contrast, see Derge, "Metropolitan and Outside Alignments."
17. Jewell and Patterson, *Legislative Process,* 382.

with the conclusions of an earlier four-state study by John Wahlke and his colleagues.[18]

> In our study, California legislators tended to disagree about the most significant source of controversy, but they selected the "urban versus rural" item more often than any of the others. In the four-state study, the California responses indicated "low crystallization" on the subject of the sources of conflict, but urban-rural and regional opinion conflicts were selected more often than the others. . . . In Tennessee, 74 percent of the responses in this study suggested "urban versus rural," while in the four-state study, urban-rural opinion conflict ranked very high.[19]

Francis then noted that his data disagreed with that of some studies, which

> would lead one to believe that urban-rural conflict is more typical of the northern industrial states. . . . What is more convincing evidence against the proposition that urban-rural conflict is typical of the northern industrial states is the consistency with which legislators from the more *rural* states select "urban versus rural" as the most frequent source of controversy. . . . As these states become less and less agrarian, perhaps the significance of the region will begin to vanish. No doubt the concept of region [i.e., urban versus rural] fills many psychological needs, in addition to certain functional economic needs, and the former are more likely to lag in the face of changing economic needs.[20]

Thus, although not all scholars are of one mind on the subject and despite the fact that some regard the urban-rural split as more or less synonymous with partisan differences, an impressive body of literature suggests that in many states and on many issues the nature of the legislators' constituencies does have an impact on their voting behavior.

It appears that community size also influences the decision making of the members of the important independent regulatory commissions. In his study of the voting behavior of 100 separate commissioners sampled from the years 1936, 1946, and 1956, Stuart Nagel concluded that "commissioners appointed from northern states are more likely to be found on the liberal side of split decisions than are commissioners appointed from southern states." He then noted:

> Similar decisional differences can be shown, although slightly less so if one uses region where born rather than region where appointed from for

18. Wahlke et al., *Legislative System.*
19. Francis, *Legislative Issues*, 39.
20. Ibid., 39–40.

those few commissioners whose birthplace and appointment place differ. Much of the relative conservatism of the southern commissioners can probably be attributed to the effects of their relative ruralism, which places a greater emphasis on consumer and worker self-sufficiency and on face-to-face relations between consumers and sellers and between workers and employers. . . . Commissioners who were appointed from cities larger than 100,000 were disproportionately more likely to be above their agency's liberalism score, to be Democrats, and to be Northerners than were commissioners from cities smaller than or equal to 100,000 in population.[21]

Studies have shown that the urban-rural setting is associated with the behavior of judges, as well as with that of the general public, legislators, and commissioners. The vast majority of such studies focus on the sentencing patterns of jurists, and as we shall see, the conclusions they suggest are frequently ambiguous, contradictory, or both. Using a 1962 sample of criminal cases decided in 194 counties located in all fifty states, Stuart Nagel made these observations about the relationship between community size and judicial sentencing behavior at the state level: (1) in rural areas, 50 percent of the defendants sentenced to prison in felonious assault cases received terms of more than one year, whereas in urban areas only 37 percent were given such terms; (2) in rural areas, 61 percent of those sentenced to prison in grand larceny cases were required to serve more than a one-year term, whereas in urban areas only 54 percent were so required.[22] Nagel also examined federal sentencing practices, using the year 1963 as his base. Here the findings were more ambiguous. In metropolitan areas, 70 percent of those convicted in federal assault cases were sentenced to prison terms of more than one year, but in rural areas only 63 percent faced such punishment.[23] Nagel suggests that urban areas place a greater stigma on assault, whereas rural areas place a greater stigma on grand larceny. He argues that the "assault differences may be based on notions of self-defense associated with more agricultural societies, as opposed to the defense by professional police associated with more industrialized societies."[24] In interstate larceny cases, 54 percent of those sentenced in the urban centers as opposed to 48 percent in the more rural areas were forced to serve terms of more than one year. However, for this same type of crime, defendants in rural areas were more likely to be found guilty (86 to 83 percent) and

21. Nagel, *Legal Process,* 240.
22. Ibid., 106, 107.
23. Ibid., 109.
24. Ibid., 100.

more apt to receive a prison term rather than a suspended or pro-bated sentence (52 to 46 percent).[25]

In their 1974 study of sentencing practices of the U.S. Second Circuit, scholars at the Federal Judicial Center also found evidence which suggests that *urban* judges may be more severe in their sentencing practices than jurists in more rural districts. For example, it was noted that "sentences in the Eastern District [of New York—Brooklyn] tend on the whole to be somewhat more severe than the median sentences for the entire circuit in particular cases, that sentences in the four smaller districts tend to be less severe, and that sentences in the Southern District [New York City] are about equally distributed around the median."[26] However, the Judicial Center researchers concede that their statistical tests "do not suggest that the differences among districts are particularly strong" and they add that "it also seems clear that the venue is a good deal less important than the identity of the individual judge."[27]

Beverly Cook's study of sentences in draft offender cases provides data in *support* of the hypothesis that judges in rural areas are more severe in their sentencing practices than are judges in medium-sized and smaller cities. According to her data, the average severity index was 20.2 for U.S. trial judges in cities of more than 500,000 persons, 23.5 for jurists in cities of between 50,000 and 500,000, and 29.9 for judges in cities of fewer than 50,000.[28] She notes that her conclusions contrast with those of Walter Markham, whose study of the same phenomenon did find that the size of the district population correlated positively and significantly with the percentage of offenders sentenced to prison but not with the length of the prison term nor the disparity of sentences within the district.[29]

In commenting on Cook's findings, David Danelski notes,

Judges in large communities tend to be less severe than those in small communities probably because (a) judicial attitudes underlying sentencing behavior vary with population size and (b) local opinion varies with population size and influences sentencing behavior. . . . Judges who hear few draft cases and judges who sit alone and hence take all of the draft cases in their courts give significantly more severe sentences because they tend to serve in small communities, which means (a) they tend to be conservative, and (b) local opinion in those communities tends to support severe sentences.[30]

25. Ibid., 110.
26. Partridge and Eldridge, *Second Circuit Sentencing Study*, 32.
27. Ibid.
28. Cook, "Sentencing Behavior," 612.
29. Markham, "Draft Offenders," 179–80.
30. Danelski, "Toward Explanation of Judicial Behavior," 664.

In sum, the literature provides evidence that on many issues the general U.S. population, state and national legislators, members of independent regulatory commissions, and state and federal judges tend to be somewhat more liberal if they are associated with large metropolitan areas than if they represent (or come from) smaller or rural communities. The differences are not overwhelming, but they tend for the most part to be in a consistent direction. Admittedly, studies of judicial sentencing behavior are somewhat ambiguous on the subject, and rigorous empirical studies of urban-rural judicial voting patterns on matters *other than sentencing* are virtually non-existent.

WHY JUDGES IN METROPOLITAN AREAS
ARE HYPOTHESIZED TO BE MORE LIBERAL

The previously discussed literature suggests that it is difficult for a judge to decide differently from the prevailing community opinion on an issue. The sociological impact of the community, in combination with an appointment process which tends to ensure that judges are representative of the local political culture, lead us to anticipate that judges are not likely to be greatly different from others in the community (large or small) they are serving. We reiterate that U.S. trial judges tend to preside in the judicial district in which they were born and raised. (Such was the case for 57.7 percent of Richardson and Vines's sample and for 70 percent of the Carp and Wheeler sample.)[31] If the urban culture as a whole tends to be more liberal than the rural environment, and if judges tend to sit on benches in the districts where they were born and raised, then it follows that jurists should to some degree reflect the values and attitudes of the districts they serve: judges in metropolitan districts ought to manifest in their decision making more liberal orientations than their colleagues in nonurban districts. Moreover, the greater homogeneity of smaller communities may result in even greater pressures on the judges to conform to conservative local values than there are on judges in the more pluralist urban centers.

Second, there is evidence that articulate, well-financed liberal judicial lobbying groups are more prolific and active in the urban centers than in the rural areas of the nation.[32] Whether they appear as

31. Richardson and Vines, *Politics of Federal Courts*, 72; Carp and Wheeler, "Sink or Swim," 366.
32. For direct and implicit evidence of this, see Nathan Hakman, "The Supreme Court's Political Environment: The Processing of Noncommercial Litigation," in

litigants or as *amici*, liberal groups are more likely to be based in metropolitan areas, where in turn they initiate or sponsor litigation. Labor unions, women's rights groups, the American Civil Liberties Union (ACLU), gay rights organizations, the American Jewish Congress, and the National Lawyers Guild are examples of groups more likely to have strong bases in urban America and to be involved in litigation in the courts of our larger cities. The consequences of these facts are noted by Richardson and Vines:

> In the same region there are sharp contrasts in decision making activity among district courts because litigation is sparse in some courts, such as that of southern Mississippi, compared to districts such as eastern Louisiana [New Orleans], where litigation is more frequent. Cases are simply not brought in some districts, notably those with low urban populations, because the motivation, skills, and facilities required to carry on litigation are lacking. The eastern Pennsylvania district [Philadelphia] with its large urban and industrial population presents an example in which litigation occurs more frequently than in any of the Southern districts. [In their sample for the same time period, the Southern district of Mississippi had 2 labor cases and 4 civil liberties cases; in the Eastern district of Pennsylvania there were 145 labor cases and 48 civil liberties cases.]
>
> Although one may expect that Southern districts such as southern Mississippi would be a prolific source of civil liberties litigation, the absence of much litigation indicates the inactivity which the federal judiciary can exhibit in shaping policy in an area unless initiative is taken by interested participants. For all practical purposes, during our sample period, the federal district courts — and as a result much of the higher judiciary — were excluded from these districts by the failure of litigation to develop.[33]

Just because liberally oriented judicial lobbying groups are more active and prolific in the urban districts does not mean, of course, that the cities will ipso facto become centers of judicial liberalism. Still, there can be no victories for liberal causes unless and until the appropriate cases are presented in court. Progressive-minded judges in rural areas would have little effect if presented with no cases through which they could manifest their liberal bent. Likewise, conservative judges in urban areas would be under scant intellectual pressure to be more receptive to the liberal pleas if they were not confronted frequently with teams of articulate, well-organized attorneys representing liberal causes. Thus, while the urban presence of liberally oriented lobbying groups may not automatically cause

---

Grossman and Tanenhaus, *Frontiers of Judicial Research,* 199–254. See also Carp, "Analysis of Censorship Pressures."

33. Richardson and Vines, *Politics of Federal Courts,* 95–96.

judicial liberalism, their efforts may at least create the opportunities for liberal decisions to be rendered.

We turn now to the literature on the behavior of small groups for a third reason for hypothesizing more liberal and independent behavior from jurists in large multijudge urban centers than from their more isolated colleagues in smaller communities. A well-developed body of literature demonstrates that persons are much more likely to make risky and independent decisions vis-à-vis community standards when acting as part of a collegial group than when acting as separate, isolated individuals. In 1961, J.A.F. Stoner demonstrated that groups have a tendency to be bolder and to take greater risks than individuals.[34] Since then, other studies have shown similar results over many tasks and conditions and have discovered two reasons for bolder and independent decision making by small groups: first, members of a group tend to give each other needed psychological reinforcement when faced with the prospect of making a risky, potentially dangerous decision; and, second, group decisions give the individual members greater anonymity.[35]

Although decision making by U.S. judges in urban centers is still of course performed on an individual basis, nevertheless there is reason to believe that jurists in multijudge cities do receive the necessary psychological support and anonymity to allow them to be more independent (i.e., liberal) in their decisions.[36] Obviously it is not urbanism per se which is the liberal impetus here; rather it is that populous urban centers by their very nature require more judges than do smaller communities, and hence a state of affairs is created wherein the manifestations of small-group behavior might appear.

Jurists in the larger, multijudge cities, unlike their isolated colleagues in rural areas, can obtain needed psychological support from their fellow trial judges when they render innovative and/or

34. Stoner, "Comparison of Individual and Group Decisions."

35. Wallach, Kogan, and Bem, "Group Influence on Individual Risk Taking"; Marquis, "Individual Responsibility"; Wallach, Kogan, and Bem, "Diffusion of Responsibility"; Wallach and Kogan, "Roles of Information, Discussion, and Consensus"; Bem, Wallach, and Kogan, "Group Decision Making"; and Teger and Pruitt, "Components of Group Risk Taking." For a broader discussion of small-group behavior and related phenomena, see Ofshe, *Interpersonal Behavior in Small Groups;* Wuebben et al, *Experiment as a Social Occasion;* and Biddle and Thomas, *Role Theory.*

36. It must be acknowledged, of course, that judicial independence vis-à-vis the community can be either in a liberal or a conservative direction. If the large urban center were quite liberal, then "risky behavior" might be conservative policymaking by judges and vice versa. Or, one may hypothesize — as we do here — that "risky behavior" is making policy which is *significantly more liberal* than a community's already-liberal values.

unpopular liberal decisions.[37] Carp and Wheeler indicated that one kind of problem faced by district court jurists (especially novice judges) is psychological, partly a result of the loneliness and isolation of the judicial office and the need for peer group support.[38] For example, judges are often subjected to great hostility by much of the public when law and conscience require them to render such unpopular decisions as ordering a state university to allow a professed Communist to speak on campus or invalidating the conviction of a sex offender because of an illegally obtained confession. The psychological support of other trial judges who are frequently subjected to the same type of criticism is a considerable source of strength. As Carp and Wheeler concluded,

> For help in coming to terms with such [psychological] burdens the federal district judge can turn to only one real source of aid: other U.S. trial judges, primarily those in his own district. . . . One fact with which the authors were continually confronted in the interviews was that federal district judges see themselves as part of a great national fraternity, a brotherhood of individuals who daily encounter the same demands, difficulties, and traumas. One judge who had been on the bench only a few weeks asserted that "there is really a fraternal feeling among us judges. We understand each other. We all have the same problems and we can help and sympathize with each other."[39]

The amenity of mutual psychological support is much more readily available to jurists in multijudge urban areas than to those who are geographically isolated. As one Fifth Circuit jurist in a multijudge city told us: "At the present time Judge _____ and I constantly discuss our cases. He is in the office next door, and I run over there all the time when I've got something that's bugging me. There is no doubt that things are easier for judges who sit here in New Orleans than it is for judges who are more geographically isolated. It is easier for judges here to talk over mutual problems. All I have to do is walk next door." Thus, knowing that one will have the needed psychological support from one's colleagues may be an additional factor which encourages urban judges "to go out on a limb" and render innovative and perhaps highly unpopular decisions.

Besides the mutual psychological support which emboldens

---

37. By this statement we do not mean to suggest that it is impossible to render innovative and/or *conservative* decisions. It is just that during the past several decades the vast majority of the highly unpopular district court decisions have been of a "liberal" nature, e.g., the freeing of an obviously guilty criminal on a legal technicality, an order to a state university to grant recognition to a campus gay organization, a ruling that a local obscenity ordinance is too vague.

38. Carp and Wheeler, "Sink or Swim," 372–77, 389–90.

39. Ibid., 389.

small-group decision makers, a large urban environment also provides the anonymity required for independent judicial decision making. We suggest that such anonymity provides an additional psychological incentive for judges to take the initiative in rendering unpopular, liberal decisions — especially in the areas of criminal justice and civil rights and liberties. That judges are subjected to extensive criticism and sometimes even brutal hostility after making unpopular rulings is well documented.[40] Richardson and Vines note that,

> although federal judges are insulated from formal links with popular opinions, they are aware of opinions expressed in a community context, and such expression is a variety of popular pressure. A notable example is the case in the eastern district of South Carolina in which Judge J. Waties Waring struck down an attempt by the state to block Negro voting. This action effectively isolated him from the entire Charleston community, and it was said that old friends ignored him, acquaintances refused to speak to him, and that he became the "lonesomest man in town." Other Southern judges suffered similar social indignities after decisions favorable to civil rights, among them Judge Skelly Wright of the Louisiana eastern district and Judge Frank Johnson of the middle district of Alabama. Graves of their relatives were desecrated, crosses burned on home lawns, dynamite blasts set off near relatives' homes, and professional ostracism was inflicted by local bar groups.[41]

With regard to busing and school integration matters one Louisiana judge told us that he lives "in a white, middle class suburb and my neighbors feel pretty strongly against busing, and I have to be careful not to express my thoughts on the matter in front of them. My wife gets this kind of 'static' from the neighbors all the time." And a federal judge from a small Florida community lamented, "I've lost more friends in the last four years following the Constitution of the United States than I made in the first forty."

While all federal district judges are subjected to public criticism and attack for unpopular liberal civil rights and criminal justice rulings, such hostility may be somewhat easier to bear for those judges cloaked by the anonymity of the large city. A district judge in Houston aptly portrayed this phenomenon as he compared himself with a colleague in a small East Texas community not known for its liberal values:

---

40. E.g., see Peltason, *58 Lonely Men;* Richardson and Vines, *Politics of Federal Courts,* 98–99; Carp and Wheeler, "Sink or Swim," 373; Grafton, "Lonesomest Man in Town," 20–21, 49–50; Hamilton, *Bench and the Ballot;* and Vines, "Federal District Judges and Race Relations Cases."
41. E.g., Richardson and Vines, *Politics of Federal Courts,* 98–99.

It's not so bad for us here when we have to hand down one of those bombshell rulings. The press covers it and some of the right wing groups squawk, and some people cuss you out on the local [radio] call-in shows that night, but in a day or so it blows over and some other story comes along to take its place. . . . I mean, when I leave the courthouse at night, I step outside and nobody even knows who I am. But now with Judge _____ up in _____ city it's different. Everyone in town calls him "the Red Judge." He's had death threats made on him, and at one time had to be under special guard. He can't even go into a supermarket without people pointing him out. It must be hell for him up there.

Although there are many brave judges in smaller communities and in rural areas who are not afraid to face hostile public opinion and render unpopular decisions, we suggest that the burden is greater for them than for their counterparts in the larger cities.

In sum, we hypothesize a positive relationship between urbanism and liberal judicial opinions because (1) urban centers tend to be more liberal than rural areas; (2) judges tend to preside over district courts in the same environments in which they were born and socialized and thus those who come from more pluralist, liberal metropolitan centers ought to be more liberal than jurists in more homogeneous, conservative, less urban districts; (3) articulate liberal interest groups lobby more actively in large urban centers; and (4) jurists in multijudge cities are provided with two factors which, according to small-group theory, foster bolder, more independent (liberal) decision making, namely, mutual psychological support and a greater degree of anonymity.

THE SIZE OF THE DISTRICT COURT AND VOTING PATTERNS

To represent the urban-rural character of the district court we have chosen here to use the number of judges assigned to the court when a given case was decided rather than the population figures of the cities wherein the district courts were located. Richardson and Vines, who, among other scholars, have chosen this method, discuss the interrelationship among the factors of population, the amount of litigation, and the number of judges assigned to the district court:[42]

42. E.g., Richardson and Vines, *Politics of Federal Courts*, and Markham, "Draft Offenders," 167–68.

The reasons for varying amounts of litigation [among the districts] are complicated, but certain major relationships that influence the variation are evident. Two general factors frequently cited as stimulating litigation are population and the degree of urbanism. To these two factors we have added the number of judges, as a rough measure of size of judicial facility, and have investigated their impact upon the amount of litigation. . . .

Both total population and urban population are related to the amount of litigation in the districts by moderately large correlations, although neither factor accounts for much more than about half of the variation. Undoubtedly, the number of judges overlaps with the factors of both urbanism and population, but there is a slight suggestion that size of judicial facility is related to amount of litigation.[43]

Thus while we are not suggesting a perfect correlation between the number of judges assigned to the district and its urban-rural character, the evidence indicates a strong correlation between the two phenomena, and such a correspondence seems great enough to rely on — at least as the basis of an exploratory investigation. To have used the population size of the city wherein the district court is located would have meant a number of methodological problems not inherent in the former method. Given our forty-four-year time span, the size and rank order of the cities have varied enormously, and it would be difficult indeed to select any one year during this period on which meaningfully to rank the cities. Such a problem does not exist when one uses the number of judges assigned to the court. Indeed, a rough correction factor is built in, in that as a district either gains or loses population, the number of judges assigned to that district also changes.

Finally, if the literature on small groups is correct and a workgroup effect is generated by and related to the number of judges assigned to a given court, then this variable ought to be selected over the variable of population size of the judicial district. If group dynamics is as important a factor as we hypothesize it to be, it should be tested for as directly as possible.

In discussing the size of the district court we shall use four general categories of districts arranged according to the following numbers of judges assigned to them: one, two, three to six, and seven or more. While there is nothing "magical" about these categories, the evidence gleaned from our interviews of court personnel and from the empirical data itself suggests that they are meaningful ordinal stages representing progressive sizes and types of American com-

---

43. Richardson and Vines, *Politics of Federal Courts*, 94–95.

munities. Examples of single-judge rural courts throughout all or most of the time span of our study would include the Western District of Wisconsin, the state of Maine, and the Middle District of Louisiana.[44] Courts in small-sized urban areas, generally consisting of at least 100,000 inhabitants, included two-judge cities such as Beaumont, Texas; Honolulu, Hawaii; and Providence, Rhode Island. Larger American cities with three to six jurists included such urban centers as Denver, Colorado; St. Louis, Missouri; and Houston, Texas. Finally, in the category of very large metropolitan areas with seven or more judges were New York City; Chicago, Illinois; and Los Angeles, California.

Table 18 presents data on the liberal decisions rendered by judges in districts of varying sizes for the three time periods between 1933 and 1977 and then for all years taken as a whole. Such data is available for all cases and for the three composite case categories of criminal justice, civil rights and liberties, and labor and economic regulation. As will be evident from this table and from the ones to follow, the data generally support our basic hypothesis that urban centers are more liberal than rural areas. Nevertheless the data also reveal that the relationship is relatively weak and that the phenomenon is much more complicated and subtle than we had imagined.

An examination of the all cases category in Table 18 shows that prior to 1954, urban-rural differences on the whole appear to have been negligible. The most extreme spread on the liberalism scale among our four types of district courts was no more than three points. After 1953, however, a basic pattern began to emerge which was true not just for all cases taken together but also for the categories of criminal justice and of civil rights and liberties: more liberal decisions were rendered in the courts with two judges than in those with only one; a noticeable drop in liberal voting occurred in the courts with three to six judges; and in the courts with seven or more judges there was a modest upswing in the number of liberal decisions. In all cases for all years, 41 percent of the single-judge court opinions were liberal; this jumped to 46 percent at the two-judge level but dropped back to 41 percent at the districts with three to six judges; for cities with seven or more judges, 43 of the decisions were liberal.

The composite variable of criminal justice cases reveals these same trends. Prior to 1954, differences among the various-sized district courts were small and appear not to have been in any consis-

---

44. When we suggest that single-judge districts are rural, we do not mean that the entire district is agricultural and/or devoid of towns or small cities. Rather, such districts tend to be devoid of cities with populations in excess of 100,000 residents.

Table 18. Liberal Decisions by Number of Judges Assigned to the District Court
for All Cases and for Criminal Justice, Civil Rights and Liberties, and
Labor and Economic Regulation Cases, 1933-1977

	One Judge		Two Judges		Three to Six Judges		Seven or More Judges	
	%	n	%	n	%	n	%	n
All Cases								
1933-53	44	2,295	43	1,023	46	1,374	46	953
1954-68	36	2,790	44	1,068	40	2,482	43	2,893
1969-77	43	2,993	49	1,990	40	3,362	43	4,619
All years	41	8,078	46	4,081	41	7,218	43	8,465
Criminal Justice								
1933-53	26	661	24	240	28	301	24	168
1954-68	21	1,255	25	419	21	1,106	25	1,258
1969-77	28	1,190	35	687	27	1,421	28	1,833
All years	25	3,106	30	1,346	25	2,828	27	3,259
Civil Rights and Liberties								
1933-53	42	371	45	186	39	298	37	328
1954-68	38	607	43	260	38	469	43	643
1969-77	51	1,156	52	788	47	1,176	49	1,529
All years	46	2,134	49	1,234	43	1,943	46	2,491
Labor and Economic Regulation								
1933-53	55	1,257	50	597	56	775	61	459
1954-68	54	928	65	389	64	907	65	1,000
1969-77	58	607	62	461	57	619	60	1,170
All years	55	2,792	58	1,447	59	2,301	62	2,629

tent direction. Between 1954 and 1968 and between 1969 and 1977,
however, it is clear that the most liberal districts were those with
two judges. The next most liberal districts were those with seven or
more judges; the districts with a single judge and those with three to
six jurists were about equal.

In civil rights and liberties cases, prior to 1954 the smaller districts were actually more liberal than those with a greater number of
judges; the most liberal were courts with two jurists. After 1953 the
trends fluctuated slightly, but the two-judge districts remained the
most liberal. For the entire forty-four years, the liberalism score was
49 percent for the two-judge courts, 46 percent for the single-judge

and for the seven-or-more-judge districts, and only 43 percent for the three-to-six-judge courts.

The category of labor and economic regulation appears to be the one which best fits with our basic original hypothesis. While there is no apparent relationship between number of judges and liberal voting up to 1953, after that time there is evidence that the size of the urban area *is* associated with labor and economic liberalism. For all years together, 55 percent of the single-judge opinions were liberal; this increased to 58 percent for the two-judge courts and 59 percent for districts with three to six jurists; and in the large urban centers with more than seven judges, 62 percent of the labor and economic opinions were liberal. The difference between the most and least urban districts — 7 percent — is hardly overwhelming but neither can it be dismissed as trivial.

To investigate this general phenomenon further we selected six specific case types which had previously proven useful in predicting judicial voting patterns: Fourteenth Amendment issues (excluding cases of race and sex discrimination), race discrimination, women's rights, freedom of expression, local economic regulation, and environmental protection cases.

Of the six specific case categories depicted in Table 19 only one demonstrates a consistent association between number of judges and liberal voting — race discrimination cases. With our four sizes of district courts, the liberalism scores for all years increased progressively from 47 to 51 to 52 to 58 percent. This finding accords well with the literature, which suggests more tolerant attitudes and behavior toward minority groups in metropolitan areas than in rural and small-town communities. We would also note that voting on ra-

Table 19. Liberal Decisions for Selected Issues by Number of Judges Assigned to the District Court, 1933-1977

	One Judge		Two Judges		Three to Six Judges		Seven or More Judges	
	%	n	%	n	%	n	%	n
14th Amendment	43	615	46	484	37	621	41	860
Race discrimination	47	554	51	229	52	346	58	333
Women's rights	49	41	61	54	49	74	53	87
Freedom of expression	52	302	59	174	47	254	53	401
Local economic regulation	61	241	72	107	70	131	72	197
Environmental protection	55	214	66	109	59	187	66	241

cial issues was a key factor differentiating Republican from Democratic judges (see Chapter 2) and Johnson from Nixon appointees (see Chapter 3).

Liberal voting on local economic regulation cases also reflects a clear relationship with the size of the district court; the liberalism index is substantially lower in the rural, one-judge districts. Thus judges at all three urban levels are more likely to favor state and local government efforts to regulate their respective economies than their colleagues in the more conservative, free enterprise oriented rural areas. This issue of local economic regulation also proved effective in distinguishing Democratic from GOP jurists (see Chapter 2) and Johnson from Nixon appointees (see Chapter 3).

Sensitivity to protection of the environment appears as well to be related to the size of the district court. Although there is a conservative dip at the three-to-six judge level, jurists in cities with two judges and those with seven or more are noticeably more liberal on matters of environmental protection than are jurists in the rural areas. The other three issue dimensions in Table 19 seem to display the same curious characteristics found in many of the composite variables in Table 20: in *all* cases there is a noticeable increase in liberal voting as the number of district judges increases from one to two. However, in cities with three to six judges the liberalism scores drop markedly and then increase only modestly at the level of seven or more judges.

In sum, up to this point we see that when the several issue dimensions are considered for all years, our model is correct in predicting that as the district increases from one to two judges, its liberal output increases markedly and consistently. In the medium- to large-sized metropolitan areas, however, the liberal trend may or may not continue, depending on the issue dimension involved.

Why on so many issues should liberal voting fall off so noticeably and so regularly in the larger districts?

For at least the time span of our study, presidents (especially Democratic chief executives) appear to have had less discretion in selecting judicial nominees in the larger metropolitan areas than they have had in rural and small-sized urban areas.[45] Large cities,

___

45. We do not mean to suggest that presidents had a completely free hand in selecting judges for *rural* districts or for districts with *only two* judges; "politics" and senatorial courtesy existed there just as in states with larger metropolitan districts. The literature provides some evidence, however, that the bosses of many of the big-city political machines exerted much more influence over the selection of federal trial judges than did local political leaders in states not containing large metropolitan centers. We would also concede that this general phenomenon is probably more true of appointments made by Democratic than by Republican presidents.

primarily in the North, have often been dominated by political machines whose bosses virtually hand picked the individuals who were to become federal district judges. The literature also suggests that these machine bosses tended to be persons who were liberal on economic questions but rather conservative on criminal justice and Bill of Rights matters.[46] If this is the case, it would explain why the appointees of liberal Democratic presidents more accurately reflected the president's values in rural and small-sized district courts where the president had a freer hand in personally selecting his own judicial nominees. It would also explain why the presidents' appointees in the larger cities were more liberal than their rural colleagues on labor and economic issues — but not on criminal justice and civil liberties questions, that is, the big-city federal judges reflect more the values of the economically liberal but socially conservative bosses who *really* selected them rather than the values of the chief executives in whose name the appointments were made.

This explanatory hypothesis can be explored, at least partially, by examining the trend of liberal decisions according to the size of the district court with controls for North-South regions (see Table 20). Looking at decisions rendered by judges in the North, we see the pattern articulated above: there is a marked increase in liberal decision making for all categories between the districts with one judge and those with two jurists; however, with criminal justice cases and with civil rights and liberties issues there is a sizable drop in liberal voting by judges in the medium- and large-sized cities. With labor and economic regulation cases, on the other hand, liberal voting increases in a stepwise fashion according to the size of the district court — from 56 to 59 to 60 and then to 62 percent. Again, one partial explanation for this is that in the North, presidents have usually had to cater to the choices of the socially conservative but economically liberal big-city political bosses and machines.

In the South, on the other hand, our predictive model works almost perfectly. With one minor exception, for all cases and for each of the three separate categories, the greater the number of judges assigned to the district court, the larger are the liberalism scores.[47] Apparently in areas of the country where economically liberal but

46. Indeed, the literature suggests that the ideology of the traditional Democratic electorate in the big northern cities tends to be quite conservative on criminal justice and civil liberties issues while remaining liberal on most economic and labor questions. E.g., see Ladd, *Ideology in America,* and *Where Have All the Voters Gone?,* ch. 2.

47. There is a slight *drop* in the liberalism index in the South on civil rights and liberties issues between district courts with one judge and those with two jurists.

Table 20. Liberal Decisions by Number of Judges Assigned to the District Court According to North-South Regions for All Cases and for Criminal Justice, Civil Rights and Liberties, and Labor and Economic Regulation Cases, 1933-1977

	One Judge		Two Judges		Three to Six Judges		Seven or More Judges	
	%	n	%	n	%	n	%	n
North								
All cases	43	4,688	48	2,988	41	5,926	43	7,999
Criminal justice	27	1,663	31	996	25	2,388	26	2,542
Civil rights and liberties	46	1,041	54	801	44	1,621	44	1,912
Labor and economic regulation	56	1,762	59	702	60	2,268	62	1,963
South								
All cases	38	3,388	40	1,090	41	1,291	49	466
Criminal justice	21	1,416	26	317	29	530	33	151
Civil rights and liberties	45	1,048	40	414	49	407	57	203
Labor and economic regulation	52	911	53	319	54	309	56	97

NOTE: For this study, southern states are Ala., Ark., Del., Fla., Ga., Ky., La., Md., Miss., Mo., N.C., Okla., S.C., Tenn., Tex., Va., and W.V.; the northern states consist of the remaining thirty-three.

socially conservative big-city bosses have not intervened in the selection process, district judges *are* more liberal as the number of judges at the district court increases.

In sum, we hypothesized that as the district becomes more urban in character and as the number of judges assigned to the district court increases, so, too, will the tendency of judges to take the liberal position on the issues which come before them. Such a hypothesis was highly compelling for jurists in the South, where judicial voting has been consistently more liberal as the district court became more urban in character. In the North, however, we observed a different pattern. Whereas liberalism increased on all issues between districts with one and two jurists, we noted marked decrease in liberal voting on criminal justice and on civil rights and liberties questions in the districts with more than three judges. As a partial explanation for this anomaly in the North, we suggested that it was caused by presidents (especially Democratic chief executives) having to yield to the pressure of the big-city machines to appoint economically liberal but socially conservative judges. A full explanation for these overall findings awaits much more extensive investigation of these complex and multifarious variables.

VOTING PATTERNS OF JUDGES
IN THE LARGER CITIES

Twenty-four cities were selected for an analysis of the variance in the number of liberal decisions. To be included, their population had to be at least one million at the time of the 1970 census and there had to be at least fifty decisions in each of the three general categories of cases.[48] Table 21 ranks the cities according to whether their corporate judicial output for a forty-four-year period was most liberal, moderate, or the least liberal in the three basic issue dimensions of criminal justice, civil rights and liberties, and labor and economic regulation. The table gives a proximate indication of the comparative liberal orientation of these cities, but we approach this data with caution for several reasons. First, for many of the cities in more than one category the *n*'s are still rather small. Since opinion writing and publication varies greatly among individual judges in a city (or district), there is always the possibility that a handful of

48. The only exception was Oklahoma City, whose population is somewhat shy of one million residents.

Table 21. Cities Ranked According to Their Liberalism Index on Criminal Justice, Civil Rights and Liberties, and Labor and Economic Regulation Cases, 1933-1977

Criminal Justice[a]			Civil Rights and Liberties[b]			Labor and Economic Regulation[c]		
City	%	n	City	%	n	City	%	n
Most Liberal								
1 Baltimore	49	253	Minneapolis	64	67	Minneapolis	70	143
2 Cleveland	43	62	Milwaukee	64	195	Milwaukee	70	136
3 Atlanta	42	144	New Orleans	64	140	Boston	65	266
4 Miami	40	90	Houston	59	128	New York City	64	1,066
5 Chicago	38	180	Atlanta	55	106	Philadelphia	63	421
6 Detroit	38	116	Miami	54	52	Pittsburgh	63	251
7 San Francisco	36	209	Boston	53	191	Washington,D.C.	63	477
8 Dallas	36	58	Washington,D.C.	53	287	Newark	61	184
Moderate								
1 New Orleans	35	101	San Francisco	49	259	San Francisco	60	208
2 Denver	33	78	Chicago	47	263	Miami	60	67
3 Milwaukee	31	233	New York City	44	900	Cleveland	59	108
4 Minneapolis	31	78	Baltimore	43	168	Brooklyn	59	278
5 Washington,D.C.	31	419	Dallas	42	73	Los Angeles	58	221
6 Los Angeles	29	228	Detroit	42	137	Kansas City, Mo.	58	175
7 Boston	28	199	Philadelphia	41	343	Atlanta	57	90
8 Brooklyn	26	350	Los Angeles	40	230	New Orleans	56	119
9 Kansas City, Mo.	26	443						
Least Liberal								
1 New York City	24	1,209	Kansas City, Mo.	39	107	Chicago	55	293
2 Houston	23	162	Newark	39	69	Denver	55	91
3 Philadelphia	22	706	Cleveland	38	58	Houston	54	106
4 Newark	22	116	Brooklyn	36	198	Baltimore	53	170
5 Pittsburgh	15	296	Denver	33	69	Oklahoma City	53	105
6 Oklahoma City	11	168	Oklahoma City	31	81	Detroit	51	177
7 St. Louis	6	167	Pittsburgh	31	124	St. Louis	51	144
8			St. Louis	12	124	Dallas	45	93

[a] M for all cities = 30; s = 10.4.
[b] M for all cities = 45; s = 12.5.
[c] M for all cities = 58; s = 6.0.

prolific opinion writers in any given city may have an inordinate impact on where that city is found in the rankings. Also, the small n's do not permit explicit controls for time, and this also makes us reluctant to place too much emphasis on the precise liberalism index of any particular city. Nevertheless, given the conjunction of many of the revelations in Table 21 with other empirical findings in this and other studies and with much anecdotal literature, we can make some generalizations about the table's contents.

First, we are struck by the variability of the cities' rankings from one dimension to another.[49] Not a single city appears in the most liberal category for all three dimensions. Six cities make that list on *two* occasions, however: Minneapolis, Milwaukee, Atlanta, Miami, Boston, and Washington, D.C. Two cities, Oklahoma City and St. Louis, make the least liberal list for all three dimensions. (The extremely conservative indexes of St. Louis are of particular note, and we would add that many of our interviewees in the Eighth Circuit and elsewhere commented on the highly conservative nature of St. Louis federal judges. Apparently there is substance to such observations.) Three other cities are in the least liberal category for two of the issue dimensions: Houston, Pittsburgh, and Denver.

Second, there is no relationship between the size of these larger cities and the cities' liberalism indexes on the three dimensions. The product-moment bivariate correlation between the cities' liberalism scores and their 1970 population on the criminal justice dimension is -0.03 ($p = 0.45$); for civil rights and liberties it is -0.09 ($p = 0.35$); and for labor and economic regulation the correlation is but 0.10 ($p = 0.33$). While there is indeed a marked difference in the liberal output between district courts located in small towns and those situated in large metropolitan areas, this disparity appears to vanish after the urban area exceeds about one million in population.

Third, our analysis of the data in Table 21 reveals that the standard deviations of the cities' liberalism scores were greater for the dimensions of criminal justice and of civil rights and liberties ($s = 10.4$ and 12.5, respectively) than they were for the dimension of labor and economic regulation ($s = 6.0$). This is entirely consistent with the findings in Chapters 2 and 4 that after 1937 much greater disparities appeared among judges and between spatial entities on Fourteenth Amendment and Bill of Rights matters than on issues involving regulation of the economy by the federal government.

Table 21 also adds strength to the conclusions of Vines and of Dolbeare that southern cities are responsible for an inordinate number of liberal civil rights decisions.[50] While our civil rights and liberties category is somewhat broader than the ones used by these two

49. This conclusion is supported by statistical analysis of the interrelation between the cities' rankings on these three issue dimensions. The correlation between the variable of criminal justice and labor and economic regulation is -0.08; between criminal justice and civil rights and liberties it is 0.51; and between civil rights and liberties and labor and economic regulation it is -0.45.

50. Vines, "Federal District Judges and Race Relations Cases," and "Role of the

scholars, Table 21 reveals that southern cities are well represented among the most liberal metropolitan areas. Four of the six most liberal cities are clearly from the Deep South: New Orleans, Houston, Atlanta, and Miami. None of the cities in the least liberal civil rights and liberties category is a traditional southern community.

In *The Benchwarmers,* Goulden notes that "the Labor Department has a tough time with wage-and-hour and industrial safety cases in the U.S. district court in Dallas."[51] This tidbit of information would suggest that Dallas should rate low on the labor and economic regulation dimension, and indeed this is the case. The liberal index of 45 percent for Dallas is the lowest for the twenty-four cities and is 25 points more conservative than the Minneapolis and Milwaukee highs of 70 percent.

The legal grapevine also regards the district court in San Francisco as more liberal on civil rights and liberties questions than its Los Angeles counterpart.[52] The empirical data in Table 21 lend some modest support to this perception. San Francisco's liberalism index in this dimension is 49 percent, while Los Angeles's is 40 percent.

Not all anecdotal information finds uniform support in the Table 21 data, however. Goulden marshals a good deal of impressionistic evidence to suggest that Chicago is a highly conservative city on criminal justice and Bill of Rights cases.[53] In fact, Chicago ranks among the most liberal cities with the first category and toward the top of the moderate list in the second category. Goulden also suggests, however, that Chicago should rank as quite conservative in the field of labor and economic regulation. He quotes a lawyer who works with a public interest law group in the environmental field as saying: "Going before some Chicago judges is like playing Russian roulette with all the chambers loaded. You'll get your brains blown out one way or another, so you might as well make a record and hope to hell that the court of appeals bails you out."[54] According to Table 21, Chicago does rank among the least liberal American cities on labor and economic regulation issues. While we are very cautious about placing too much emphasis on the precise liberal indexes listed by each city, we suggest that such indexes might be at least a more accurate reflector of reality than mere stories and anecdotes about the judicial behavior in a given city.

Circuit Courts of Appeals,"; Dolbeare, "Federal District Courts and Urban Public Policy."

51. Joseph C. Goulden, *Benchwarmers,* 13.
52. Ibid., 13–14.
53. Ibid., ch. 3.
54. Ibid., 116.

VOTING BEHAVIOR OF ROVING
VERSUS NONROVING JUDGES

A roving judge is a jurist in a multidistrict state who is not assigned exclusively to any one district but rather has authority to
hear cases throughout the entire state. Where these judges are assigned to preside is often a function of the judicial needs and work-
loads of the district courts within the state. During the time span of
our study half of the fifty states have had more than one district and
of these, thirteen have had roving judges.

To our knowledge no studies have compared the decisional tendencies of roving jurists with those of their more geographically restricted colleagues. Several possible hypotheses seem reasonable to
explain the differences, if any, between these two sets of judges. One
might postulate that roving judges would be more independent because they are not tied to any one small locality and are therefore
more liberal — especially on matters of civil rights and liberties and
criminal justice issues. Such judges would presumably be less both-
ered by and responsive to parochial critics because they preside
over a broader demographic and geographic base. On the other
hand, one could well hypothesize that roving judges would be more
conservative than their more stationary brethren. Given the conservative and differential nature of legal training and traditions, it is
possible that roving judges are even more likely to defer to the
power structure, the prevailing mores, and the institutions in the
districts which they visit; hence they would be more conservative
than the nonroving jurists.

To explore these hypotheses from an empirical perspective we
compared the voting behavior or roving judges with that of their
nonroving counterparts — but only in those thirteen multidistrict
states which had roving judges. Thus there is a partial control for
geographic region, although because of the comparatively small n's
for decisions of roving judges, we did not attempt to control for
time and state.[55] Table 22 compares the two groups of judges with
regard to their decisions for all cases and for the three composite
variables.

There seems little doubt that roving judges are distinctly the
more conservative of the two groups. In the all cases category, they
are 16 percentage points less liberal than their colleagues who preside in single districts: 32 percent of the decisions of roving judges

---

55. Until the data base for roving judge decisions becomes large enough to afford
controls for time, the state, and more specific case categories, any conclusions resulting from this preliminary analysis must be regarded as highly tentative.

Table 22. Liberal Decisions of Roving Judges Compared with Nonroving Judges in the Same States for All Cases and for Criminal Justice, Civil Rights and Liberties, and Labor and Economic Regulation Cases, 1933-1977

	All Cases		Criminal Justice		Civil Rights and Liberties		Labor and Economic Regulation	
	%	n	%	n	%	n	%	n
Roving judges	32	803	13	380	46	210	51	213
Nonroving judges	48	15,268	35	5,717	54	3,136	58	6,415

NOTE: Included in this table are only those multidistrict states with roving judges: Ala., Ark., Fla., Iowa, Ky., Mo., Ohio, Pa., S.C., Tenn., Wash., and W.V.

were liberal, whereas 48 percent of those of nonroving judges were liberal. This trend continues unabated for the three more specific case types. On criminal justice matters, only 13 percent of the decisions of roving judges were liberal while almost three times as many (35 percent) of the decisions of nonroving judges were in the liberal column. Forty-six percent of the roving judges' decisions on civil rights and liberties questions were liberal, whereas this was true of 54 percent of the stationary judges' opinions. The gap is less wide for labor and economic regulation matters, but the roving judges are still more conservative by 7 percentage points (51 to 58 percent).

Thus we see that roving judges tend to be markedly more conservative than their colleagues who preside over single districts within a state. While much more theorizing and research are needed before we can fully explain this phenomenon, we offer the tentative hypothesis that the greater conservatism of roving judges is due to their strong tendency to defer to the existing parochial traditions and power structures in the areas in which they temporarily visit.

CONCLUSION

We have sought to explore several additional aspects of the degree to which district court decisions vary according to geographic-demographic factors. We presented evidence to indicate that after 1953 jurists in two-judge cities were more liberal on all types of issues than judges in rural areas where there was only one jurist per district. In the South the pattern held as well across the continuum as one advanced from district courts with three to six judges and with seven or more judges. In the North, however, the stepwise relationship between urbanization and judicial liberalism was true only for labor and economic regulation cases. For criminal justice and Bill of Rights issues the judges in the more urban centers became *more conservative.* This we suggested might be due to the influence at the judicial selection stage of the economically liberal but socially conservative big-city political bosses.

In analyzing the voting patterns of judges in twenty-four large American cities we concluded that there was no statistically or substantively significant relationship between the cities' populations and their liberalism rankings. Finally, we compared the voting patterns of roving judges with their colleagues who preside over a single district and have determined that the former group of jurists were significantly and across-the-board more conservative. We hypothesized that perhaps "visitors" to a given district are more deferential to the parochial powers-that-be and to existing conservative traditions than are jurists who regularly preside there.

6.

PRELIMINARY STEPS TOWARD A SYNTHESIS

To this point we have focused on extralegal influences on judicial decision making. We have determined that when we control for the variables of case content, geography, and time period, both political and environmental factors exert an independent influence on judges' policy decisions. Despite our focus on extralegal factors, one should not lose sight of the fact that case content still remains the primary predictor of whether a given decision is liberal or conservative. For example, the majority of criminal decisions are conservative, that is, decisions against the defendant, regardless of the time and place of the trial or hearing and regardless of the opinion writer's party or appointing president. It is *within* each case category that political influence becomes important. Indeed, the analysis to this point demonstrates that political party effects not only maintain but increase as controls are added for case content, state, and time period. The effects of state, number of judges per district court, party affiliation, and appointing president all seem to have increased dramatically after the advent of the Burger Court in 1969.

The description of legal, environmental, and political background effects on the trial judge's decision suggests that one could develop descriptive and statistical models which discriminate between liberal and conservative policy decisions without knowing the specific case content or controlling law involved. However, synthesis of the effects of time, place, party affiliation, and appointing president requires that we first answer a series of latent questions about their relative influence. We will begin this chapter, therefore, by presenting a decision-tree model derived from the analytic framework introduced in Chapter 1.

THE MODEL OF JUDICIAL POLICY DECISIONS

District judges tend to issue formal written opinions when they have exercised discretion in the manipulation of judicial outcomes.

The opinion serves to explain the judgment and may serve as the basis or rationale for analogous future decisions. If one assumes judicial discretion, the judicial policy decision may be depicted as a decision tree.

As depicted in Figure 7, the different liberal propensities associated with economic, criminal, and civil rights and liberties cases lead us to develop separate branches for each case category in recognition of the different constraints on judges' discretion to manipulate outcomes associated with each category. The separation of each case category branch into subbranches defined by time periods and place recognizes the influence of environment on judicial manipulation. It also enhances the efficacy of time, place, and case categories as estimates of case content. Finally, the model suggests that as discretion increases, the influence of political cues on decisions will increase. Thus, accuracy in predicting outcomes will be increased by knowing the judge's party affiliation and appointing president.

As indicated in Figure 7 the application of this general model for a specific policy decision guides the researcher to ask several manifest questions. First, what is the case category? Second, when and where was the opinion issued? Third, what was the opinion writer's party affiliation? Finally, who was the opinion writer's appointing president? Even though presidents tend to appoint judges from their party, Chapter 3 suggests that appointing presidents may exert independent effects on subsequent policy decisions.

Each manifest question raised by this model can be answered by reference to the exploratory findings reported to this point; however, the decision-tree model also suggests a set of latent questions about the relative predictive powers of its components which must be resolved before the model can be fit to this aggregate data. Most important, our general framework does not distinguish the relative influence of party and appointing president. Given the tendency of presidents to appoint judges from their own party, the possibility is raised that partisan and appointing-president effects are indistinguishable. If so, the model should be simplified by the exclusion of redundant influences.

In recognition of the primacy of case content in our framework and the effect of time controls on the accuracy of case category as an estimate of case content, we shall address the question for a single case category, namely, civil rights and liberties during the post-1968 era of Contemporary Conservatism. To facilitate discussion, liberal propensities in civil rights and liberties cases will be referred to as civil liberalism and defined for a given aggregate unit of analysis as the percentage of civil rights and liberties opinions that are lib-

Figure 7. Descriptive Decision-Tree Model of Judicial Policy Decisions

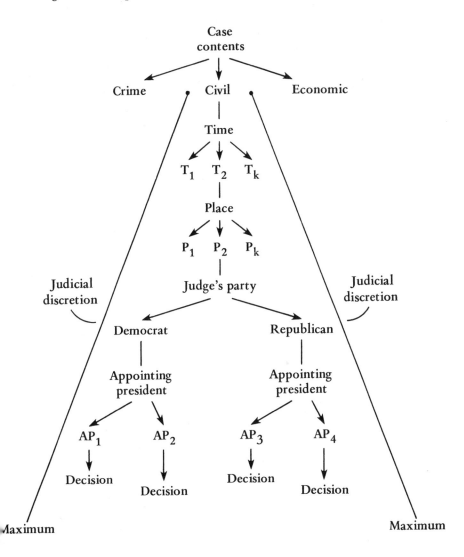

eral.[1] Civil liberalism is an appropriate category for analysis because analysis to this point demonstrates that civil liberalism questions tend to maximize democratic subculture effects and because the number of liberal opinions (2,472) and of conservative opinions (2,434) are virtually equal for the nine-year time period. Thus the discriminatory power of the model may be described and understood intuitively as its ability to discriminate between equally probable policy outcomes. Although this focus enables us to develop only one branch of the decision tree in the short run, the results will also suggest strategies for the future development of the criminal justice and economic branches.

RELATIVE EFFECTS OF APPOINTING PRESIDENT AND PARTY AFFILIATION

Despite the utility of our model for explaining the post-1968 increase in party effects, party affiliation may not be the most important political or extralegal cue for district judges. Given the tendency of presidents to appoint judges from their own party, what appears to be a dramatic increase in party effects after 1968 could be at least partially an increase in appointing-president effects. District judges on the bench during the Contemporary Conservatism era may be responding to political cues associated with their appointing president's selection strategy rather than to political cues associated with party affiliation.

---

1. The definition used here of civil liberties closely parallels that developed by Glendon Schubert and also by us in some of our earlier work. See Schubert, *Judicial Policy Making;* Rowland and Carp, "Longitudinal Study of Party Effects."

Students of the Supreme Court have divided its history into discrete eras defined by the Court's liberal or conservative policy propensities. Three of these periods have relevance for this study. The period from 1890 to 1937 has been characterized as the era of Modern Conservatism. During this era the Court mustered a rather bewildering array of doctrines to restrict government regulation of private economic activity. In 1937 the Court's ideological opposition to government regulation shifted to support for regulation under pressure from President Roosevelt and public support for the New Deal agenda. This shift marked the beginning of the Modern Liberalism era (1937–68). The era of Modern Liberalism saw the Court's primary attention shift from economic issues to questions of civil right and liberties. The Court developed a dual standard of restraint in economic regulation and activism in civil rights and liberties cases. The inauguration of Warren Burger in 1969 marked an ideological realignment on the Court from Modern Liberalism to an era that Glendon Schubert calls Contemporary Conservatism: "The era of Modern Liberalism had come to an abrupt end, and in its place the prospects seemed inescapable for the predominance of a strongly conservative mood in both the Supreme Court and the rest of the federal judiciary, at least throughout the seventies and probably beyond that." Schubert, *Judicial Policy Making,* 198.

The exploratory nature of Chapter 3 prevented us from imposing systematic controls for case category, time, and political party. In the absence of these controls we could not differentiate with any confidence between party cues and appointing-president cues. For example, we know that Johnson appointees demonstrated much higher liberal propensities than did Nixon appointees. We also know that for all cases over all years the Johnson judges returned more liberal opinions than did Kennedy's judicial team. We do not know at this point whether these intraparty differences will maintain under controls for year and case content. In the analysis which follows, therefore, we impose controls for case content and for year. We will review briefly the appointment strategies of Presidents Eisenhower, Kennedy, Johnson, and Nixon and also some relevant findings from Chapter 3. (We limit our analysis to these four appointee cohorts because the appointees of earlier presidents have returned only a trivial number of opinions during this later era.)

Of the four presidents, Nixon seems to have developed the most overtly ideological appointment strategy. Evidence reviewed in Chapter 3 suggests that President Nixon diligently pursued his 1968 campaign promise to appoint whenever possible ideological conservatives to the federal bench.[2] President Eisenhower, a fellow Republican, appears to have been less sensitive to ideological and policy considerations when making judicial appointments.[3] Thus the inauguration of President Nixon changed the ideological as well as the partisan source of new federal district judges. Given the conservative cues associated with the Nixon appointment strategy, it would come as no surprise if the new Nixon appointees exercise an independent conservatism or respond to ambiguous legal cues by returning more conservative opinions than do their incumbent Republican brethren.

As for Democratic presidents Kennedy and Johnson, both are widely perceived as political liberals who emphasized ideological considerations in their judicial appointment strategies.[4] Yet, in Chapter 3 we found substantial differences between the Kennedy and Johnson appointment strategies. Perhaps the most crucial difference rests in the relatively large amount of time and personal attention devoted to judicial appointments by President Johnson.

The contrast between Nixon and Johnson appointees reported in Chapter 3 suggests that differences in presidential appointment

---

2. Jackson, *Judges*, 270.

3. Goldman, "Judicial Appointments," and "Judicial Backgrounds"; Richardson and Vines, *Politics of Federal Courts*, 70–73.

4. See note 3, above. Also see Goldman "Johnson and Nixon Appointees," 940; Chase, *Federal Judges*.

strategy do translate into civil liberalism differences between their appointees. These variances between presidential appointee cohorts from opposite parties are interesting, especially in a common law system which assumes that judges reach their decisions in response to legal rather than political cues. Still, the more interesting differences occur between cohorts appointed by chief executives of the same political party. To measure this phenomenon we shall maximize control for case content by limiting our analysis to civil liberalism cases.

Figure 8 indicates that civil liberalism differences between Eisenhower and Nixon appointees increased after 1972. Although the increase is not unexpected, the pattern of the differences is surprising. The mounting differences are almost entirely a function of increases in the Eisenhower appointees' civil conservatism. Indeed, after the Nixon cohort's civil liberalism stabilized in 1972, it has remained remarkably consistent. By contrast, the Eisenhower cohort's civil liberalism began to decline after 1969 and plummeted after 1972. By 1975 its civil liberalism score was less than 30 percent of its 1969 index.

In spite of the size and configuration of these differences, one must interpret them with caution. Although at first glance it would seem that seated Eisenhower appointees are becoming more conservative, we cannot be absolutely confident that this is so. The increased conservatism may be a function of a relatively small number of prolific conservatives who have survived while more liberal Eisenhower appointees have left the bench. As suggested by the declining number of cases, most Eisenhower opinions were issued during the early years of the Contemporary Conservatism era.

Although the decreasing number of Eisenhower opinions hinders our analysis, the juxtaposition of these opinions with the increasing number of Nixon opinions after 1971 helps us to interpret the post-1968 jump in party differences with more confidence. The comparison of appointing-president cohorts indicates that by 1972, the vast majority of Republican opinions were written by Nixon appointees. By 1974, Nixon appointees issued 240 civil rights and liberties opinions, while Eisenhower appointees issued only 45 such opinions. It is therefore very difficult to distinguish partisan from appointing-president cues for GOP judges during the Contemporary Conservatism period. Indeed, Republican civil liberalism has become a virtual surrogate for Nixon appointees' civil liberalism. Thus, discussion of the contrast between the increased liberalism of seated Democrats and the stability of seated Republicans after 1969 is somewhat misleading; by 1974 the contrast may be more accurately described as the difference between Democrats and Nixon appointees.

Figure 8. Civil Liberalism Differences between Appointees of Presidents Eisenhower and Nixon by Year of Opinion

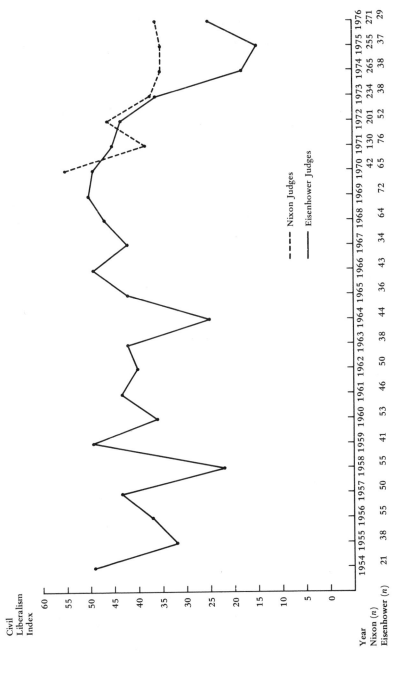

The civil liberalism differences between Kennedy and Johnson appointees depicted in Figure 9 present a somewhat different picture. As predicted by Chapter 3, the Johnson appointees issued a substantially higher percentage of liberal opinions in civil liberalism

Figure 9. Civil Liberalism Differences between Appointees of Presidents Johnson and Kennedy by Year of Opinion

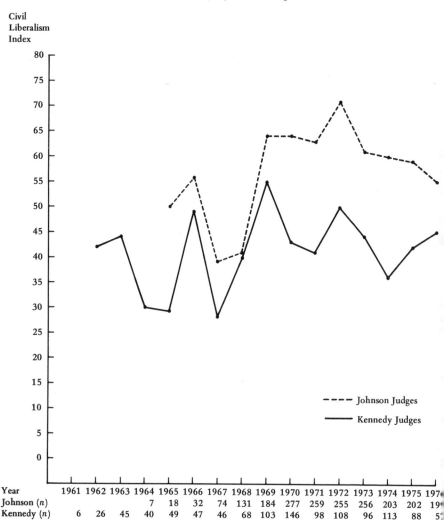

Year	1961	1962	1963	1964	1965	1966	1967	1968	1969	1970	1971	1972	1973	1974	1975	197▮
Johnson (*n*)				7	18	32	74	131	184	277	259	255	256	203	202	19▮
Kennedy (*n*)	6	26	45	40	49	47	46	68	103	146	98	108	96	113	88	5▮

cases after 1968 than did the Kennedy jurists. Moreover, the magnitude of the civil liberalism differences increases dramatically beginning in 1969 with the advent of Contemporary Conservatism and Supreme Court ambiguity. By 1974 the difference between Kennedy and Johnson appointees was more than 60 percent (Kennedy = 36 percent; Johnson = 60 percent).

To understand the increase in differences, it is instructive to compare Johnson appointees before and after 1969. The mean liberal propensity for Johnson appointees increased 16 points, from 46 to 62. Kennedy appointees' mean liberal propensity increased only half as much, from 37 to 45. Thus an important shift took place among seated Johnson appointees while a much more modest increase occurred among Kennedy judges. As with the Eisenhower appointees' decline in civil liberalism, it may be that the change was generated by the departure of conservative Johnson appointees from the bench. However, unlike the Eisenhower cohorts, the number of Johnson opinions remained substantial during the Contemporary Conservatism period, suggesting that the change is not the result of attrition among Johnson liberals.

As with the contrast between Nixon and Eisenhower judges, a comparison between the two Democratic presidential cohorts with the contemporary pattern of *partisan* differences is revealing. Previously we reported that the post-1968 increase in party effects was primarily the result of increases in Democratic liberalism while the Republican liberalism index remained largely unchanged. Now we learn that an increase in Democratic liberalism is primarily a result of the behavior of Johnson appointees after 1969. To understand the extent to which this is true, it is important to note, first, that the percentage of Democrats who are Johnson appointees increased each year after 1963, and, second, that the percentage of opinions issued by Johnson appointees also rose.

Figure 9 illustrates the relative increase in the number of opinions written by Johnson Democratic appointees and the relative decrease in the number from the Kennedy team. The figure also reveals rather clearly that the increase in the percentage of Democratic opinions that were liberal coincides with an increase in the relative number of opinions of Johnson judges.

A comparison of the four presidential cohorts indicates that most partisan differences after 1968 were actually differences among only three such cohorts. Some of the implications of this finding for understanding district judges' decisions are clear. To understand civil liberalism for the Contemporary Conservatism period we should emphasize appointing-president differences, and future research should be alert for similar effects on other times and other case cate-

gories. On the other hand, the recognition of the increasing importance of appointing-president effects does very little to explain why
these differences developed. For instance, differences between Kennedy and Johnson appointees before 1970 were relatively small.
Why, then, did the Johnson judges respond to the institutional shift
from Modern Liberalism to Contemporary Conservatism with a
dramatic increase in civil liberalism while the Kennedy appointees
responded with only a modest increase?

As with the political party variable, our conceptual framework
suggests that the increase in appointing-president effects results
from changes in fact-law congruence and in trial judge discretion.
The different presidential appointment strategies defined a different
set of policy propensities for each appointing-president cohort. The
transition to Contemporary Conservatism and the ambiguous legal
cues associated with this era provided each cohort with the discretion to exercise its unique civil liberalism propensities in the determination of judicial outcomes. Johnson appointees responded by
exercising their personal liberal propensities. A much smaller number of Kennedy appointees responded in this fashion. By contrast,
the new Nixon appointees developed a rather consistent civil conservatism compared with a declining civil conservatism among
Eisenhower jurists.

Given the bargaining between presidents and state politicians in
judicial recruitment, these conclusions suggest an interaction between
presidential recruitment strategies, environment, and appointing-
president effects on judges' civil liberalism. This should be apparent
if we examine the period of Contemporary Conservatism. We will,
therefore conclude our analysis by introducing descriptive and statistical models to measure these effects.

FITTING THE MODELS

In Chapter 1 we proposed to discriminate between alternative judicial outcomes on the basis of aggregate information about environmental variables and about personal background variables. We
also introduced a general framework to guide our analysis. We now
attempt to fit a descriptive and a statistical model derived from our
conceptual and analytic frameworks to the empirical data so far
presented. We will first demonstrate the utility of the descriptive
decision-tree model by using it to describe appointing-president differences under control for the weakest environmental effect — the
region.

DESCRIPTIVE MODEL

Our explanation of presidential effects on district judges posits that divergent appointment strategies produce cohorts with different policy propensities and that those propensities are exercised under conditions of judicial discretion. If this contention is accurate, we should be able to relate specific civil liberalism differences to variances in appointment strategy. To the extent that presidential appointment strategy varies by region, the introduction of spatial controls should increase our understanding of civil liberalism differences among appointing-president cohorts.[5] Thus, despite the virtual absence of independent regional effects reported in Chapter 4, regional variations in appointment strategy should coincide with geographic differences among presidential cohorts on the civil liberalism dimension.

Federal district judges are, of course, nominated by the president and confirmed by the Senate, and in principle the appointment initiative rests with the president. He alone can present a name to the Senate for confirmation. Still, many scholars feel that the Senate has become the dominant partner in the confirmation process.[6] The "blue slip" procedure allows home-state senators to file confidential objections to district judge nominees and it thus gives senators from the nominee's home state substantial influence over district court appointments. Indeed, home-state senators who share the presidential party affiliation may exercise a virtual veto over judicial nominations in their state.[7] Given the influence of home-state senators in the selection process, one would expect presidents to develop appointment strategies which recognize this constraint on their discretion. Thus, the effects of the appointing president on judges' policy propensities would vary among states. Moreover, to the extent that clusters of states are politically homogeneous, presidents may possibly develop regional or circuitwide appointment strategies, and the effects of the appointing president may therefore vary among these larger spatial units.

The possibility that regional controls would affect the differences among appointing-president cohorts is buttressed by studies of presidential appointment strategies reviewed in Chapter 3. This con-

5. Richardson and Vines, *Politics of Federal Courts*. The authors demonstrate throughout that the majority of lower-court judges had social, political, and legal roots in the locale or region in which they served, and they suggest that values associated with these geographic ties might be manifested in their judicial behavior.

6. Ibid. Also see Slotnick, "Reforms in Judicial Selection."

7. Ibid. Note that Senator Kennedy vowed to reduce the role of senatorial courtesy in this process. The effects of this vow remain a subject for speculation.

tingency is especially cogent for President Kennedy's appointment strategy, which featured deference to influential southern senators. Southern senators controlled key committees and were in a position to block important legislation and presidential appointments. In response to this perceived power, Kennedy deferred to southern senators in the appointment of federal district judges. Indeed, as noted earlier, Kennedy's first district court appointment was William H. Cox, a close friend and college roommate of the Senate Judiciary's conservative chairman, James Eastland of Mississippi.[8] Cox later gained notoriety and an American Bar Association censure for his alleged courtroom reference to civil rights litigants as "niggers and chimpanzees."

Although Cox is perhaps the most extreme product of the Kennedy southern strategy, he is by no means unique. Based on impressionistic and anecdotal evidence, several manifestations of this strategy seem to have developed as common sense would predict. For instance, Victor Navasky classified five of Kennedy's southern appointees as strong segregationists and noted the absence of any deep and overriding commitment to the integrity and quality of the southern judiciary.[9] In analyzing the role of Robert Kennedy in the southern appointment process, Navasky argues that no aspect of the younger Kennedy's attorney generalship is more open to criticism.[10] In contrast to the Kennedy compromise strategy, no extant study demonstrates that President Johnson felt a comparable need to appease influential senators in southern states or that any significant regional variance existed in Johnson's commitment to select liberal judges in support of his administration's social programs.

President Johnson's commitment to liberal candidates was more than matched by President Nixon's commitment to build a conservative judiciary. Indeed, Nixon's judicial appointment strategy was designed to maximize the number of political conservatives appointed to the federal bench. The success of Nixon's strategy varied among states. Evidence indicates that at the district court level, Nixon's strategy was most successful in those states with no liberal senators. The scarcity of liberal senators in the South should have maximized Nixon's strategic success in that region, and evidence suggests that his southern appointees did approximate his ideological ideal.[11] Thus one would expect his southern appointees to be more conservative than those from northern states where liberal Re-

8. Navasky, *Kennedy Justice*, 278.
9. Ibid., 272.
10. Ibid.
11. Jackson, *Judges*; but also see Chase, *Federal Judges*.

publican senators (e.g., Percy of Illinois or Javits of New York) often pushed for more liberal judicial nominees.

The potential effect of regional differences on Nixon's activist appointment strategy is relatively apparent, whereas the impact on Eisenhower's more passive strategy is less so. As noted in Chapter 3, Eisenhower seems to have been more concerned with "common sense" and judicial experience than with ideology. Further, he and his attorneys general (Brownell and Rogers) were reputedly more resistant to senatorial demands than were their Kennedy successors. The spatial differences associated with this somewhat apolitical strategy are difficult to anticipate. In combination, the focus on nonpolitical qualifications and the comparative imperviousness to Senate influence would seem to minimize the regional effects on civil liberalism differences among Eisenhower's appointees.

Together, the various appointment strategies suggest that regional differences may occur both within and among presidential appointee cohorts after 1968. One would expect substantial civil liberalism differences between Kennedy and Johnson judges in the South and also major differences between Kennedy's northern and southern appointees. Figure 10 indicates that our expectations are fulfilled rather dramatically. In the South, Johnson appointees are almost twice as likely to return a liberal opinion as are the Kennedy jurists. The disparity between the two presidential cohorts in the North is great but still not as substantial as are the differences in the South.

The centrality of civil rights questions to Kennedy's strategy of compromise with Senator Eastland and other southern senators suggests that regional differences may be even more pronounced for civil rights cases. Table 23 shows that they are. The presidential differences in the South are even greater than the disparities for the larger set of civil liberalism opinions. Indeed, in the South a Johnson judge is more than twice as likely to support a civil rights petitioner than is a Kennedy jurist. However, the more revealing difference is between the northern and southern Kennedy appointees. Kennedy's northern appointees are more than 40 percent more likely to issue a liberal opinion in civil rights cases than are his southern judges. On the other hand, only 1 percentage point separates President Johnson's southern and northern appointees. In sum, for the Kennedy and Johnson cohorts the regional differences on the civil liberalism and civil rights dimensions correspond to variations predicted by their appointment strategies.

We now turn to a comparison of the Nixon and Eisenhower cohorts under regional controls to determine whether such controls can help explain differences between the two sets of GOP appointees. Neither president was as constrained as Kennedy in southern

Figure 10. Applied Decision-Tree: Federal District Court
Civil Liberalism Policy Decisions, 1969-1976

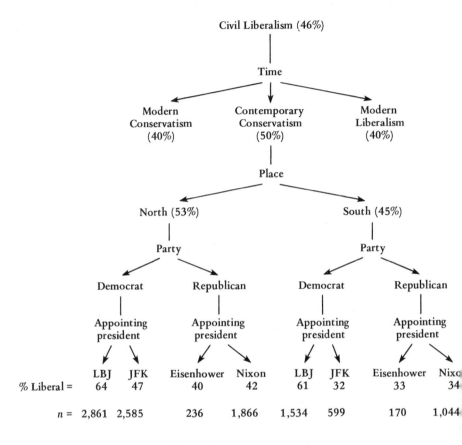

judicial appointments. Nevertheless, we have already noted Nixon's
obligation to appoint more liberal judges in the North than he
would have preferred because of the intervention of liberal GOP
senators from the big-city states. Eisenhower, too, may have been
similarly constrained, although the anecdotal literature is silent on
this matter. Table 23 and Figure 10 do reveal that the northern judges
of both Republican presidents were more liberal than their southern
judicial teams but differences *between* each set of cohorts are nil.
Hence, neither the overall civil liberalism similarities between
Nixon and Eisenhower appointees nor the differences after 1971
conceal *regional* civil liberalism differences.

Table 23. Liberal Decisions in Racial Minority Discrimination Cases of the District Court Appointees of Four Presidents, by Regional (North and South), 1969-1977

	Kennedy		Johnson		Eisenhower		Nixon	
	%	n	%	n	%	n	%	n
South	29	214	60	632	36	326	33	249
North	42	654	59	884	38	516	38	857

The utility of the decision tree defined by the descriptive model suggests that the model is a powerful tool for locating and isolating the effects of legal, environmental, and political background variables on judicial policy decisions. Although the model was developed only through differences by region among presidential appointee cohorts, these complete branches illustrate the power of the model in identifying variance in liberal propensities among judge cohorts and in describing the impact for judicial policy outcomes. If we begin with no controls for time or case content, we know only that more than 50 percent of all opinions issued from 1933 to 1977 were conservative. If we introduce the effects of time and case content by examining the Contemporary era and civil liberalism cases, we can assign a 50 percent probability to liberal and conservative outcomes in such decisions. For civil liberalism opinions, predictive accuracy is further increased by knowing whether the opinion is from a southern or northern state. As indicated by the model, knowledge of party affiliation helps organize our findings but adds little to our predictive ability. Nonetheless, the party branch remains in the model to emphasize the within-party differences between appointing-president cohorts and because party differences may prove important to developing other branches of the model. Finally, by knowing appointing president and region we can achieve a substantial reduction in error predicting the outcome of civil liberalism decisions. For instance, if we knew that a civil liberalism opinion was issued by a Kennedy appointee in the South, we would predict a conservative outcome and be wrong only 32 percent of the time. For Johnson appointees in the South we would predict a liberal outcome and reduce our predictive error to 39 percent.

Despite the utility of the descriptive decision tree, it also has obvious limitations. First, there are practical limits to the number of independent effects which can be introduced. For example, a deci-

sion tree which introduced the effects of appointing president under
controls for state would lose its utility in a thicket of 200 (50 × 4)
new limbs. More important, the inelegance of the cluttered tree
tends to focus attention on specific judge cohorts while obscuring
the overall and interaction effects which discriminate between liberal and conservative policy decisions. We will, therefore, conclude
our analysis by fitting our aggregate data to a statistical model of
judges' policy decisions which discriminates between liberal and
conservative outcomes from aggregate estimates of case content,
environment, and political influences.

STATISTICAL MODEL

To maximize the accuracy of case category as an estimate of case
content, we must introduce the effects of time and place. Thus, we
extend the descriptive analysis above by measuring background
and environmental effects on civil liberalism cases for the Contemporary Conservatism period.

As with the descriptive model, this focus on post-1968 civil liberalism cases brings a secondary benefit to the analysis. Since civil liberalism opinions for this time period are divided almost equally
between liberal (50.4%) and conservative (49.6%) decisions, our
model's discriminatory power may be judged by its improvement
over equal binomial chance.

Before fitting the model to the civil liberalism opinions, we must
choose appropriate indicators of environmental and background effects. Our focus on the Contemporary Conservatism era defines the
temporal aspect of the environment, but we must define the geographic entity as either region, circuit, or state. Based on their relative effects reported in the previous chapter, the state appears to be
the most compelling unit for testing the effects of geographic influence. Although the choice of state as the most important spatial indicator is unambiguous, the choice does present practical problems
of data analysis, that is, the introduction into the analysis of 50
additional independent variables. If one wishes to test for the interaction between state and appointing president, the number of independent variables would exceed 300. In recognition of these problems and of the independent effects of the circuit, we shall follow a
two-stage strategy of analysis and measure separately the effects of
state and appointing president for each circuit. Thus, in addition to
facilitating manageable analysis and interpretation, analysis by circuit also controls for any independent effects circuit may have on

policy outcomes and enhances the accuracy of civil liberalism as an estimate of case content.

Although our previous analysis suggests that appointing president is a more important influence than is party affiliation, we have included both indicators of political background. To the extent that the appointing-president variable dominates the political party under controls for state and number of judges per district court, the statistical analysis will remove the party effects. Also, despite the somewhat inconclusive findings reported in Chapter 5, we have included the variables of number of judges per district court in our analysis as an estimate of the urbanization level of the judicial setting.

In sum, the results of our statistical analysis will tell us whether a civil liberalism opinion between 1969 and 1977 will be liberal or conservative, under controls for circuit, when we examine the combined impact of the following variables: (1) the state in which the policy question was resolved, (2) the number of judges at the district court, (3) the president who appointed the opinion writer, and (4) the judge's political party affiliation. Or, put another way, we will learn the extent to which aggregate estimates of the decision-making environment and of the judge's political background discriminate between opinions which favor civil liberalism litigants and those which do not. To make this determination we have relied on a combination of Biomedical Computer Program (BMDP) stepwise logistic regression analysis and Statistical Package for the Social Sciences (SPSS) discriminate function analysis.[12]

Stepwise logistic regression (SLR) is a technique which measures the relationship between a binary dependent variable and two or more independent variables. Logistic regression is utilized most frequently in the biomedical setting for diagnosis or evaluation of alternative treatments. Its ability to generate interaction terms, to rank order independent variables and interaction terms, and to discriminate among large numbers of independent variables based on their maximum likelihood ratios make this technique ideal for our analysis. Since SLR is a nonlinear regression technique, the independent variables may be metric or nonmetric. The BMDP produces several statistical outputs. For our purposes the most important output is the ratio of predictive successes and predictive failures based on the information contained in the independent variables.

12. Engleman, "PLR," 517.1–527.13. Nie et al., *Statistical Package for the Social Sciences*, 434–67. For an early application of this technique in the judicial setting see S. Sidney Ulmer, "The Discriminant Function and a Theoretical Context for Its Use in Estimating the Votes of Judges," in Grossman and Tanenhaus, *Frontiers of Judical Research*, 335–69.

The BMDP does not, however, report summary measures of association between the function defined by the independent variables and the alternative judicial outcomes. For this purpose the SPSS discriminant function analysis was used. In addition to classifying probable outcomes on the basis of independent discriminating variables, SPSS discriminant function analysis reports the canonical correlation between the function defined by the set of independent discriminating variables and the alternative dependent outcomes, that is, liberal or conservative. For each case, discriminant function analysis produces a score on the discriminant function:

$$[D_i = d_{i_1}Z_1 + d_{i_2}Z_2 + \ldots \ d_{i_k}Z_k]$$

where D_i = score on the discriminant function;

d_i = weighting coefficients analogous to standardized regression coefficients

z = standardized values of the discriminating variables.

The utility of the discriminant function analysis is enhanced by the prior SLR analysis because the more powerful SLR technique identifies significant main effect and interaction terms, which reduces the number and complexity of independent variables for the discriminant analysis. This reduction is especially useful for categorical independent variables, which must be dummy or effect coded.

The results of the statistical analysis are summarized in Table 24. Party affiliation and number of judges per court were dropped from the analysis because their contribution to the discriminant function was negligible. Thus, the discriminant function is defined by two discriminating variables, state and appointing president, and—most important—by the interaction between the two.

Knowledge of state and of appointing president improve our ability to discriminate between liberal and conservative policy decisions for every circuit. This discriminatory power is most apparent for the First, Fourth, Eighth, and Tenth circuits. Indeed, in the Tenth Circuit our ability to predict policy decision outcomes improved by almost 50 percent. Even in the Ninth Circuit, where the model proved least powerful, predictive accuracy was increased by 26 percent.

The distribution of canonical correlation coefficients is consistent with the descriptive analysis in Chapters 3 and 4. For example, although state effects were relatively important in the heterogeneous Eighth Circuit, and the appointing-president variable was relatively important in the homogeneous Fourth Circuit, their interaction is important in both circuits. This is hardly surprising when one considers the interaction between presidents and home-state politicos in the judicial appointment process.

We find that a statistical model can indeed predict judicial policy

Table 24. Power of State and Appointing President to Discriminate in Each Circuit between Liberal and Conservative Civil Liberalism Decisions, 1969-1977

Circuit	Canonical Correlation	Discrimination Success(%)	Discriminant Function Reduction in Error (%)
First	0.41	70	40
Second	0.32	65	30
Third	0.36	68	36
Fourth	0.42	68	36
Fifth	0.30	64	28
Sixth	0.36	66	32
Seventh	0.32	64	28
Eighth	0.44	70	40
Ninth	0.26	63	26
Tenth	0.45	73	46
D.C.[a]	0.28	61	22

[a] Analysis limited to appointing-president effects.

decisions based on aggregate estimates of the environment and of judges' political backgrounds under controls for case content and time. One can discriminate between liberal and conservative policy decisions on the basis of aggregate estimates of political and environmental effects on those decisions. Moreover, this prediction improves as controls for legal factors are increased. By controlling for content, circuit, and time, we control for fact-law congruence and differences in the legal environment or legal subculture. Thus the influence of the democratic subculture increases as one adds controls for the legal subculture.

The power of environmental and political background factors to discriminate between alternative judicial outcomes is very encouraging in light of our rather rudimentary understanding of policymaking at the trial court level. In many ways, the contribution of this statistical model can be evaluated by comparing it with models of other policymaking institutions. Our findings are consistent with Tate's work on the Supreme Court.[13] Moreover, the combined effects of state and appointing president bear a remarkable similarity

13. Tate, "Personal Attribute Models."

to the interaction of constituency and party effects on congressmen.[14] This similarity extends to the importance of time and precedent and to the institutional constraints on legislators' discretion to respond to these environmental cues.[15] Certainly the effect of partisan realignments in the electorate on congressional decision making is analogous to the effect of Supreme Court transitions on district court decision making.[16] These similarities are particularly intriguing in light of the conventional assumption that legislatures are our most "political" policymaking institutions, while courts are ostensibly shielded from the influence of political demands.

Given these similarities, it seems reasonable to evaluate our results by comparing them with analogous studies of congressional policy decisions. The comparison makes two things clear. On the one hand, our success in explaining district court policy outcomes compares favorably with early studies of Congress. For example, the results of our aggregate data analysis are comparable to early role-call analysis of the relative effects of party and constituency in Congress by Mayhew and Shannon.[17] On the other hand, evaluation of our results in light of congressional studies also demonstrates with painful clarity the gap between the two subfields. The relative development of the congressional subfield is apparent in the relative quantity and quality of its theoretical and empirical work.[18] It is hoped that the future research suggested in the concluding chapter will narrow that gap.

14. Cooper, Brady, and Hurley, "Electoral Basis of Party Voting.

15. Clausen, *How Congressmen Decide;* Asher and Weisberg, "Voting Change in Congress."

16. Sinclair, "Policy Consequences of Realignment." It should be noted that several fine studies have delineated the effects of party realignment on Supreme Court policy directions and on the propensity of the Supreme Court to overturn legislation. In particular, see Mendelson, "Judicial Review and Party Politics"; Adamany, "Legitimacy"; Jahnige, "Critical Elections."

17. Mayhew, *Party Loyalty among Congressmen;* Shannon, *Party, Constituency, and Congressional Voting.*

18. E.g., Kingdon, "Models of Legislative Voting"; Friejohn and Fiorina, "Purposive Models of Legislative Behavior."

7.

CONCLUDING THOUGHTS ON
JUDICIAL POLICYMAKING RESEARCH

One basic premise on which our research was grounded was that the best way to predict the outcome of any given case is to determine which litigant has the weightiest evidence and the best controlling precedents. Given the values of our judicial system and the training and integrity of our jurists, we believe that this "traditional" explanation is still compelling for most judicial decisions. By the same token, we are equally persuaded that the traditional model has its limitations, and it was to the realm beyond these limitations that the thrust of our behavioral analysis was directed. For those cases for which the precedents and evidence are about equally strong, for new areas of the law where innovative decision making is required, for issues about which the precedents and evidence are ambiguous or contradictory, the traditional model is of little use. For this small but substantively important group of cases, factors such as the judges' basic philosophy, the mores and traditions of their particular circuit or state, and the attitudes and values reflected in their own political backgrounds do indeed measurably affect their judicial decision making. Thus, while paying our dues to those who contend that the quality and contents of the legal briefs provide the best explanation for judicial decisions, we also reaffirm our conviction that the key to many judicial outcomes is located in the personal mindset of the individual judge.

A second assumption which underlay this effort was that our principal data source, *Federal Supplement* opinions, does provide a sufficiently reliable source of judicial policy decisions to enable us to make meaningful generalizations about the decisional patterns of U.S. district judges. Even with its limitations, we are persuaded that the *Supplement* provides a meaningful vista of important aspects of trial judge activity even if only "as through a glass darkly." Initially, this belief was based on a variety of factors related to the *Supplement* itself, for example, its preeminence in the field and the number and breadth of cases which it reports. We now have another reason for confidence in the reliability of this data source — the general direction of virtually all of the book's primary conclusions. To a very substantial degree our findings tend to bolster and support the hypotheses of both traditional and behavioral scholars who have used a wide range of methodologies to study the behavior of federal district judges. For example, we found that Democrats have generally been more liberal than GOP judges; the Kennedy jurists indeed have been as comparatively conservative as the anecdotal literature has contended; during the 1950s and early 1960s, Republican judges in the South were more supportive of civil rights than were Democrats; and southern jurists as a whole have tended to be more conservative than their northern colleagues. That we unearthed few surprises reinforces our confidence in continued use of the *Supplement* as one measure of trial judge behavior.

It may be useful to reiterate here the more significant conclusions in each of the substantive chapters. One important contribution was to measure the degree to which political party affiliation is predictive of how judges vote on cases with clear underlying liberal-conservative dimensions. We have determined that between 1933 and 1977, Democrats were on the whole about 7 percentage points more liberal than their Republican colleagues. Indeed, Democrats historically have been more liberal on nineteen of the twenty issue dimensions studied. Equally important, however, was our finding that partisan differences have been rather uneven over time: between 1933 and 1953 the disparity was 4 percentage points; this dropped to only 1 point between 1954 and 1968; but between 1968 and 1977, Democrats were 11 percentage points more liberal than their GOP counterparts. Most studies which discounted the predictive power of partisan affiliation were conducted during the 1950s and 1960s, when party was a very weak independent variable.

The ideological impact which American presidents have had on the decisional output of their appointees has varied. Several conditions constrain a chief executive's ability to "pack the judiciary," but at least for our time span, the appointees of Democratic presidents have been distinctly more liberal than those chosen by Republican chief executives. The sharpest cleavage between the appointees of two presidents clearly has been between those selected by Lyndon Johnson and those appointed by Richard Nixon. Politically powerful presidents and/or those who placed an inordinate emphasis on the ideological purity of their judicial nominees (e.g., Wilson, Johnson, and Nixon) appear to have had a greater impact on subsequent judicial decisions than chief executives who lacked the desire or the clout to fill the judiciary with ideologically similar persons (e.g., Hoover, Truman, and Ford). Subsequent analysis also revealed that most of the political party variation among the judges could be accounted for by these differences among appointing presidents.

After the 1940s less variance could be found among judges on the labor and economic regulation dimension than on criminal justice issues and civil rights and liberties questions. For example, this was found to be the case when we examined partisan voting disparities, differences among the cohorts appointed by the various presidents and intercircuit variations in judicial behavior. We argued that this was the case because after about 1937, the chief battlegrounds of the judiciary were in the realms of criminal justice, the Bill of Rights, and equal protection rather than in taxation, substantive due process, and the commerce clause. (The only exception to this is the subject of local economic regulation, which still seems to be a source of considerable division among U.S. trial judges.)

Our examination of the voting patterns of jurists appointed from a party different from the president's revealed that the liberal propensity of Republicans appointed by Democratic presidents and of Democratic judges selected by GOP chief executives is virtually identical. We also found that Democrats appointed by Democrats have been historically the most liberal judges, whereas the most conservative jurists have been Republicans appointed by GOP presidents.

Beginning in about 1933 North-South differences generally assumed a greater magnitude than East-West differences. After 1968 the tendency for northern jurists to be more liberal than their southern colleagues increased for criminal justice and civil rights and liberties issues. For labor and economic regulation cases, however, the North-South cleavage narrowed after 1968. Intraparty differences between northern and southern jurists were greater after 1968 than they were in the previous two time frames of our study. Intraparty disparities between the East and West also increased in the more recent period, although such differences were never very large.

Variances in liberal propensity from one circuit to another are sizable — the most liberal (the First Circuit) being some 17 points more liberal than the highly conservative Fourth Circuit. Disparities among circuits followed two general modes. For the criminal justice and civil rights and liberties dimensions, the standard deviations among the circuits declined from the 1933–53 period to the 1954–68 era; for the years between 1968 and 1977, however, the standard deviations increased sharply. The other pattern is that characterized by the labor and economic regulation cases. After a reasonably high standard deviation prior to 1954, among-circuit differences declined and stabilized.

Great intracircuit partisan disparities were shown for the entire time frame and data set of our study. For example, in the First Circuit, Democrats were 21 percentage points more liberal than the Republican judges, whereas in the Tenth Circuit, GOP jurists were 3 percentage points more liberal than their Democratic colleagues. Equally important, the data reveal that intracircuit partisanship increased significantly between 1968 and 1977 in comparison with the relatively nonpartisan years between 1954 and 1968. From the early 1950s on, intercircuit differences among Democrats increased progressively, whereas among GOP judges such disparities were more volatile; after declining between 1954 and 1968 from previous years, intercircuit differences among Republicans doubled between 1968 and 1977.

Liberal variance among states increased after 1968, and this increase is apparent even under controls for circuit. Thus interstate disparities increased in the most recent period as did most sectional and intercircuit differences and overall levels of partisanship.

In the South, judicial voting became progressively more liberal as the district court became more urban in character (and as the judicial "work group" became larger). In the North, however, the findings were more difficult to interpret. Although the liberal index did increase on all issues between districts with one and two judges, the index declined on criminal justice and on civil rights and liberties issues in districts with three or more judges. We hypothesized that the phenomenon might be a function of (Democratic) presidents' having to yield to the pressure of northern big-city political bosses to appoint economically liberal *but socially conservative* judges.

In the last substantive chapter we made a preliminary effort to integrate and synthesize some of the key independent variables discussed in Chapters 2 through 5 by fitting them to descriptive and statistical models derived from the two-step framework for the analysis of judicial policy decisions. Our ultimate conclusion was that it is possible to predict district court policy decisions from aggregate estimates of the environment and judges' political background under controls for legal factors. That is, we were able meaningfully to discriminate between liberal and conservative policy decisions on the basis of aggregate estimates of political and environmental effects on those decisions. Furthermore, this can be accomplished under very strict controls for legal factors. By controlling for case content, circuit, and time, we control for fact-law congruence and differences in the legal environment or legal subculture. Thus the influence of the democratic subculture increases as one provides controls for the legal subculture.

Several areas seem promising for future research on the voting behavior of federal district judges. First, it seems desirable to update the coding of *Federal Supplement* cases to the present time. This would enable us to examine the voting patterns of the Carter and the Reagan judges, which have not been explored at all in this study. It would also enable us to compare judges nominated by Carter's special nominating commissions with their counterparts chosen in the more traditional manner.

Another promising area for future research is the relationship between the behavior of the appeals courts and that of the individual judges within each of the circuits. If the voting patterns of a circuit's appellate judges becomes more liberal or conservative, does the corporate behavior of the circuit's trial judges follow suit? The pioneering work of Sheldon Goldman would serve as a starting point for research in this area, but we would like to go beyond what he has done and compare the two levels of the judiciary under controls for time, region, political party affiliation, and so on. We would expect to find that trial court voting patterns approximate the patterns of their respective appeals courts but that a certain lag time is involved. If such is found to be so, it would be a real contribution to our understanding of judicial politics.

We have suggested that variances among trial judges increase during periods when the Supreme Court sends forth ambiguous or inconsistent guidelines. Much more research is necessary, however, before the validity of this proposition can be accepted. Research should use quasiexperimental designs to compare behavior on *specific issues* rather than on trial court decisional patterns in general. For example, although the Burger Court's decisions on many First Amendment issues left many unanswered questions (e.g., *Gannet Co. v. DePasquale*, 443 U.S. 368), its decisions discouraging trial judges from interfering in state criminal proceedings were much more exacting (e.g., *Younger v. Harris*, 401 U.S. 37). If our theory is correct, there should be as a consequence much more district judge variance on First Amendment issues than on state habeas corpus pleas.

Another related subject which is worthy of exploration is district court response to major philosophical changes on the Supreme Court. Such changes of extraordinary consequence might include the 1937 "switch in time," in which the Supreme Court majority altered its basic view about the legitimacy of state and federal efforts to regulate the economic lives of the citizenry (i.e., *West Coast Hotel Co. v. Parrish*, 300 U.S. 379, and *NLRB v. Jones & Laughlin Steel Corp.*, 301 U.S. 1), or the revolutionary determination that separate but equal educational facilities inherently violated the equal protection clause (i.e., *Brown v. Board of Education*, 349 U.S. 294). In exploring the impact of such monumental Supreme Court decisions, many questions need to be answered: how much time is required between the announcement of a significant change in Supreme Court policy and meaningful responses of district judges? Which types of judges are most (and least) likely to comply with the new High Court ruling — newly appointed jurists, judges whose political philosophy is closest to that of the Supreme Court majority, jurists who preside in regions of the country whose populace is most supportive of the Supreme Court policy change?

Another general area for which more detailed research is needed is the impact over time of a president's judicial appointments. A chief executive's ability to influence the philosophical orientation of the lower-court judiciary is limited by the number of appointments available to the president, the judicial-philosophical milieu into which the new appointees enter, and so on. There may also be a lapse between the time when the lion's share of the judicial appointments are made and the time when their impact is fully manifested. (For example, the liberal impact of the Johnson judges did not reach its zenith until several years after he left the White House.) Future research in this area might attempt to quantify and operationally define some of the generalizations we have set forth. What is the average time between the beginning of a new administration and the time when the president's impact on the judicial "output" is greatest? Which of the variables circumscribing a president's capacity to "pack the judiciary" have historically been the most and least compelling?

Finally, the promising area of the relationship between the voting behavior of a state's federal trial judges and that of the state's U.S. senators and/or congressmen would bear investigation. Given the role of senatorial courtesy in the appointment of district judges and given the fact that a state's political elite often share many of the same values and orientations, one would expect a certain degree of congruity in the decisional patterns of a state's federal judges and national legislators. If such congruity is demonstrated, it would be another illustration of the impact of regional influences in the decision making of U.S. trial judges. It would also provide evidence that senatorial courtesy is more important than we have thought: not only would this practice be significant in determining who becomes a district judge but it would serve as a policy link between a state's U.S. senator(s) and the policy decisions of the federal judges in that state.[1]

---

1. In states where senatorial courtesy is not practiced (because neither U.S. senator is from the president's party), the policy link between senators and judges should be much weaker. Still, since there is evidence that the chief executive may sometimes yield to a senator's wishes in the appointment of federal judges even when the senator is not of the president's party (see Chapter 3 for examples of this phenomenon), there may still be some correlation between senators' and judges' voting patterns in states where senatorial courtesy is not *formally* practiced.

If these substantive suggestions for additional research are undertaken and if more sophisticated models and methodological techniques are developed to analyze the data, we will have a more precise and theoretically integrated understanding of district judge policy decisions.

Appendixes

APPENDIX A:
DESCRIPTION OF ANALYZED CASE CATEGORIES

CRIMINAL JUSTICE:
PETITIONS AND CONVICTIONS

1. Habeas corpus, United States: includes all petitions for habeas corpus by criminal defendants in the custody of the U.S. government.
2. Habeas corpus, state: includes all petitions for habeas corpus and any other pleas from state prisoners to the federal district courts.
3. Motions immediately before, during, or after trial made by U.S. criminal defendants to federal district judges. Examples include a motion for a change of venue, motions to suppress evidence, motions for a new trial, or a motion for a reduction of sentence.
4. Conviction or nonconviction for a criminal offense.

GOVERNMENT REGULATION OF THE ECONOMY

1. Federal commercial regulation: includes all suits brought by an agency of the national government (e.g., the Agriculture Department, an independent regulatory agency, the antitrust division of the attorney general's office) which deal with regulation of the economy.
2. Environmental protection, pure food and drug, and consumer protection cases: includes all suits brought by both private or governmental litigants involving any of the aforementioned issues.
3. Local economic regulation: includes all cases testing the authority of a state or local government to regulate the economic lives of their citizens. Examples include the right of a state to tax a company within its jurisdiction or the authority of a city to regulate the profits of a utility. Not included in this or any other category is the right of eminent domain.

4. Rent control, excessive profit, and price control: includes all cases dealing with the power of the federal government to regulate specifically any of the aforementioned special economic matters.
5. Fair Labor Standards Act: includes most FLSA cases and other labor cases in which either the secretary of labor or the National Labor Relations Board is the plaintiff.

SUPPORT FOR LABOR

1. Union versus company: includes all cases where a labor union and a corporation are involved in a labor dispute.
2. Union members versus union: includes all cases where specific members of a union (or nonunion employees of a company) are suing the union at the company. Not included in this or any other category are suits between various unions.
3. Employees versus employer: includes all labor disputes between a company and its nonunion employees.

CLASS DISCRIMINATION

1. Alien petitions: includes all petitions to federal district courts from aliens. Examples include petitions to become U.S. citizens or petitions to enjoin revocation of citizenship proceedings commenced by the secretary of state.
2. Indian rights and law: includes all suits between Indian tribes and a local or state government or the national government and suits between an Indian tribe and a private party. This category does not include suits between various Indian tribes.
3. Voting rights cases: includes all cases where the primary issue is the right to vote. Examples include challenges to one's right to vote because of race, education, or place of residence. Also included in this category are reapportionment cases.
4. Racial minority discrimination: includes all cases where the defendants are non-Anglo and where the racial factor is obviously the primary issue at stake. This also includes cases involving labor relations in which a black or a Mexican-American is suing a union or a company.
5. Fourteenth Amendment and U.S. civil rights cases: includes all cases involving the Fourteenth Amendment equal protection

clause, privileges and immunities, and the various pieces of congressional legislation which have been passed to implement the Fourteenth Amendment. However, not included in this category are cases involving the right to vote or cases dealing with race relations, which are coded in separate categories.

6. Women's rights: includes all cases where the issue is primarily one of sex discrimination.

FIRST AMENDMENT FREEDOMS

1. Freedom of expression: includes all cases dealing with the right to petition the government, the freedom of the press, and the freedom of speech.
2. Freedom of religion: includes all cases dealing with the establishment or free exercise clauses of the First Amendment. Also included in this category are cases involving conscientious objectors.

Appendix B

Liberal Decisions for Three Categories of Cases for the Appointees of President Truman through President Ford, 1972-1977

Appointing President	Criminal Justice		Civil Rights and Liberties		Labor and Economic Regulation	
	%	n	%	n	%	n
Harry Truman	17	76	52	65	53	47
Dwight Eisenhower	14	207	29	188	49	104
John Kennedy	29	539	43	440	62	335
Lyndon Johnson	40	364	63	1,059	67	659
Richard Nixon	27	1,001	38	1,156	46	799
Gerald Ford	33	49	41	78	54	63

NOTE: For presidents prior to Truman the n's were too small (fewer than 50 cases in each category) to use meaningfully.

Appendix C

Liberal Decisions for Three Categories of Cases by Same-Party and Opposite-Party Appointees of President Truman through President Ford

| | Criminal Justice | | | | Civil Rights and Civil Liberties | | | | Labor and Economic Regulation | | | |
| | Dem. | | Rep. | | Dem. | | Rep. | | Dem. | | Rep. | |
Appointing President	%	n	%	n	%	n	%	n	%	n	%	n
Harry Truman	22	930	32	79	44	629	42	33	62	780	63	57
Dwight Eisenhower	25	24	19	1,830	46	37	39	1,031	55	31	61	1,320
John Kennedy	25	1,881	29	189	41	991	50	123	65	994	60	161
Lyndon Johnson	36	2,207	30	121	61	1,961	51	80	67	1,168	64	119
Richard Nixon	35	95	25	1,100	44	116	38	1,219	38	76	48	839
Gerald Ford	57	7	29	42	55	11	39	67	56	9	54	54

NOTE: For presidents prior to Truman the n's were too small (fewer than 50 cases in each category) to use meaningfully.

Appendix D
The Eleven Federal Judicial Districts*

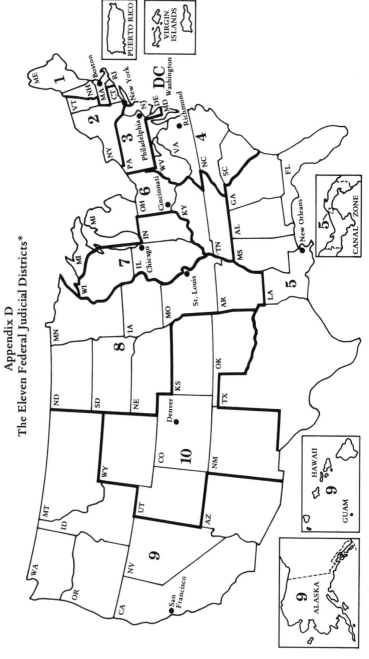

*Circuit boundaries as of 1977

Appendix E

Liberal Decisions by Party and Region (East and West) for All Cases and for Criminal Justice, Civil Rights and Liberties, and Labor and Economic Regulation Cases

	1933-53			1954-68			1969-77			All Years		
	Dem.	Rep.	α	Dem.	Rep.	α	Dem.	Rep.	α	Dem.	Rep.	α
All Cases												
East	47	43	1.21	45	41	1.19	54	40	1.84	50	41	1.70
West	46	42	1.29	39	39	1.00	47	35	1.77	44	38	1.66
α	1.02	1.01	–	1.24	1.17	–	1.30	1.18	–	1.23	1.16	–
Criminal Justice												
East	22	23	0.98	26	21	1.24	36	26	1.84	27	22	1.28
West	29	26	1.16	24	21	1.15	31	22	1.72	30	22	1.71
α	1.27	1.16	–	1.16	1.00	–	1.18	1.17	–	0.92	1.00	–
Civil Rights and Liberties												
East	38	34	1.20	44	37	1.32	64	45	2.23	50	38	1.75
West	45	40	1.30	41	39	1.16	55	39	2.16	51	39	1.75
α	0.00	0.00	–	0.00	0.00	–	1.40	1.22	–	1.00	0.97	–
Labor and Economic Regulation												
East	62	57	1.27	70	64	1.27	70	57	1.91	67	59	1.65
West	54	49	1.26	59	60	0.96	63	49	1.92	57	52	1.24
α	1.60	1.60	–	1.79	1.18	–	1.61	1.10	–	1.67	1.60	–

NOTE: All figures except odds ratios are given in percent.

Appendix F

Liberal Decisions by Circuit for Criminal Justice Cases, 1933-1977

Circuit	1933-53		1954-68		1969-77		All Years	
	%	n	%	n	%	n	%	n
First	13	32	25	131	33	189	28	349
Second	21	156	23	781	34	793	26	1,828
Third	23	280	26	482	21	788	22	1,623
Fourth	28	72	15	541	15	608	19	1,221
Fifth	27	141	26	406	36	586	32	1,111
Sixth	22	79	23	293	35	367	28	738
Seventh	32	53	27	190	38	352	34	595
Eighth	22	94	20	326	27	574	24	984
Ninth	37	126	27	347	35	344	32	799
Tenth	29	38	30	159	15	193	22	390
D.C.	21	38	21	177	39	125	34	339
M	25		25		30		27	
s	6.5		4.5		8.9		5.2	
Eta	0.13		0.09		0.15		0.11	

NOTE: The figures in this table are in harmony with the increasing body of literature on sentencing behavior of federal district judges, which indicates that there are great differences among U.S. circuits in the sentencing of convicted felons. See, for example, Sutton, *Federal Sentencing Patterns;* Zumwalt, "Anarchy of Sentencing in the Federal Courts"; and Harris and Lura, "The Geography of Justice."

Appendix G

Liberal Decisions by Circuit for Civil Rights and Liberties Cases, 1933-1977

Circuit	1933-53 %	1933-53 n	1954-68 %	1954-68 n	1969-77 %	1969-77 n	All Years %	All Years n
First	46	59	43	53	64	244	58	356
Second	31	252	39	440	52	621	44	1,313
Third	50	111	35	185	40	482	40	778
Fourth	42	57	38	221	43	479	41	757
Fifth	39	70	43	357	52	898	49	1,325
Sixth	44	36	34	165	55	329	48	530
Seventh	44	41	38	109	60	447	55	597
Eighth	33	45	30	161	41	419	37	625
Ninth	43	221	47	262	51	319	48	802
Tenth	48	29	38	50	34	166	37	245
D.C.	51	43	47	70	60	144	55	257
M	43		39		50		47	
s	6.4		5.3		9.5		7.3	
Eta	0.12		0.09		0.15		0.11	

Appendix H

Liberal Decisions by Circuit for Labor and
Economic Regulation Cases, 1933-1977

Circuit	1933-53		1954-68		1969-77		All Years	
	%	n	%	n	%	n	%	n
First	63	149	66	171	59	150	63	470
Second	61	448	66	702	61	428	63	1,578
Third	63	409	63	502	60	406	62	1,317
Fourth	49	153	55	246	53	184	53	583
Fifth	46	335	55	352	56	403	53	1,090
Sixth	50	279	59	290	58	231	55	800
Seventh	49	179	59	210	65	228	58	617
Eighth	57	317	56	285	59	249	57	851
Ninth	53	292	61	317	53	260	56	869
Tenth	39	92	61	124	57	93	53	309
D.C.	58	67	61	106	65	243	63	416
M	53		60		59		58	
s	7.6		3.8		4.0		4.2	
Eta	0.14		0.08		0.08		0.08	

Appendix I

Liberal Decisions by Party and Circuit for Criminal Justice Cases, 1933-1977

Circuit	1933-53			1954-68			1969-77			All Years		
	Dem.	Rep.	α	Dem.	Rep.	α	Dem.	Rep.	α	Dem.	Rep.	α
First	15	0	15.00	31	21	1.66	51	24	3.30	36	22	3.00
	(25)	(4)		(58)	(73)		(67)	(122)		(150)	(199)	
Second	19	21	0.89	25	20	1.29	33	26	1.41	28	23	1.33
	(72)	(82)		(463)	(318)		(568)	(325)		(1,103)	(725)	
Third	2	24	0.91	21	23	0.92	23	19	1.28	22	21	1.04
	(96)	(157)		(372)	(210)		(365)	(423)		(833)	(790)	
Fourth	21	24	0.82	17	14	1.25	32	14	3.02	24	14	1.77
	(42)	(30)		(243)	(298)		(235)	(373)		(520)	(701)	
Fifth	32	20	1.10	27	26	1.04	37	32	1.25	33	29	1.12
	(88)	(31)		(317)	(89)		(492)	(94)		(897)	(214)	
Sixth	23	14	1.83	27	31	0.79	36	30	1.32	31	29	1.08
	(64)	(14)		(195)	(98)		(277)	(90)		(536)	(202)	
Seventh	43	24	2.39	28	23	1.27	43	23	2.50	39	23	2.09
	(25)	(28)		(120)	(70)		(253)	(99)		(398)	(197)	
Eighth	27	20	1.45	21	15	1.43	26	29	0.87	24	24	1.00
	(36)	(58)		(127)	(199)		(224)	(350)		(387)	(607)	
Ninth	40	34	1.27	32	22	1.62	35	34	1.06	35	28	1.41
	(61)	(47)		(195)	(152)		(240)	(104)		(496)	(303)	
Tenth	33	45	0.65	24	33	0.65	10	29	0.38	18	33	.44
	(28)	(10)		(97)	(62)		(145)	(48)		(270)	(120)	
D.C.	25	0	25.00	36	24	1.86	54	28	2.96	42	26	2.33
	(16)	(6)		(69)	(108)		(54)	(71)		(149)	(185)	
M	26	21		27	23		35	27		30	24	
s	9.9	12.6		5.9	6.0		12.0	5.9		7.3	5.1	
Eta	0.17	0.13 −		0.10	0.12 −		0.18	0.15 −		0.13	0.11 −	

NOTE: Figures in parentheses represent the number of cases in the sample; all other figures, except odds ratios and etas, are in percent.

Appendix J

Liberal Decisions by Party and Circuit for Civil Rights and Liberties Cases, 1933-1977

Circuit	1933-53 Dem.	Rep.	α	1954-68 Dem.	Rep.	α	1969-77 Dem.	Rep.	α	All Years Dem.	Rep.	α
First	41 (29)	50 (18)	0.67	56 (24)	38 (29)	2.04	78 (133)	46 (111)	4.16	69 (186)	46 (158)	2.71
Second	35 (145)	28 (103)	1.40	43 (209)	37 (231)	1.29	58 (382)	41 (239)	2.01	49 (736)	37 (673)	1.75
Third	56 (44)	46 (55)	1.49	38 (104)	31 (81)	1.36	42 (192)	38 (290)	1.17	43 (340)	38 (426)	1.29
Fourth	53 (34)	29 (23)	2.71	41 (117)	35 (104)	1.24	55 (293)	24 (186)	3.63	51 (444)	28 (313)	3.18
Fifth	45 (35)	30 (27)	1.80	40 (247)	49 (110)	0.70	56 (654)	41 (244)	1.77	51 (936)	43 (381)	1.37
Sixth	35 (30)	43 (6)	0.71	36 (132)	34 (33)	1.08	59 (202)	49 (127)	1.55	49 (364)	46 (166)	1.20
Seventh	43 (31)	40 (10)	1.12	38 (83)	39 (26)	0.98	67 (303)	44 (144)	2.54	60 (417)	43 (180)	1.99
Eighth	44 (21)	29 (24)	1.96	44 (68)	41 (93)	1.12	46 (202)	35 (217)	1.57	46 (291)	36 (284)	1.52
Ninth	42 (116)	44 (71)	0.91	50 (184)	43 (78)	1.31	54 (187)	46 (132)	1.38	49 (487)	45 (281)	1.14
Tenth	50 (10)	47 (19)	0.92	40 (38)	33 (12)	1.36	40 (87)	28 (79)	2.17	40 (135)	32 (110)	1.38
D.C.	50 (18)	64 (11)	0.56	46 (42)	44 (28)	1.10	63 (83)	56 (61)	1.14	57 (143)	54 (100)	1.20
M	44	43		43	38		56	41		51	41	
s	5.8	13.6		5.3	5.9		11.1	9.3		8.1	7.4	
Eta	0.13	0.20 −		0.08	0.11 −		0.17	0.15 −		0.12	0.12 −	

NOTE: Figures in parentheses represent the number of cases in the sample; all other figures, except odds ratios and etas, are in percent.

Appendix K

Liberal Decisions by Party and Circuit for
Labor and Economic Regulation Cases, 1933-1977

Circuit	1933-53			1954-68			1969-77			All Years		
	Dem.	Rep.	α	Dem.	Rep.	α	Dem.	Rep.	α	Dem.	Rep.	α
First	65 (102)	48 (25)	1.95	69 (83)	65 (88)	1.18	81 (67)	42 (83)	5.69	70 (252)	53 (196)	2.22
Second	61 (249)	59 (196)	1.06	71 (337)	62 (365)	1.49	66 (226)	55 (202)	1.55	66 (812)	60 (763)	1.35
Third	68 (182)	60 (180)	1.33	65 (215)	61 (287)	1.19	68 (159)	54 (247)	1.79	66 (556)	58 (714)	1.83
Fourth	51 (77)	45 (76)	1.25	59 (144)	52 (102)	1.32	57 (112)	47 (72)	1.49	56 (333)	48 (250)	1.82
Fifth	49 (188)	36 (112)	1.74	54 (286)	62 (66)	0.69	58 (306)	50 (97)	1.41	55 (780)	47 (275)	1.36
Sixth	50 (225)	33 (43)	2.10	66 (233)	44 (57)	2.43	67 (124)	49 (107)	2.14	59 (582)	44 (207)	1.77
Seventh	55 (125)	38 (54)	1.94	54 (120)	64 (90)	0.65	74 (144)	50 (84)	2.89	62 (389)	52 (228)	1.90
Eighth	56 (141)	58 (175)	0.94	54 (186)	60 (99)	0.80	64 (143)	54 (106)	1.50	58 (470)	57 (380)	1.06
Ninth	53 (166)	56 (99)	0.88	56 (190)	66 (127)	0.66	53 (141)	52 (119)	1.11	54 (497)	58 (345)	1.17
Tenth	50 (29)	36 (63)	1.74	62 (78)	61 (46)	1.08	69 (48)	44 (45)	2.57	61 (155)	46 (154)	2.00
D.C.	63 (41)	50 (12)	1.83	60 (45)	62 (61)	0.92	73 (120)	58 (123)	1.99	68 (206)	59 (196)	1.49
M	56	47		60	60		66	50		61	53	
s	7.1	10.8		5.9	6.5		8.2	4.8		5.5	5.8	
Eta	0.12	0.20 −		0.13	0.10 −		0.15	0.08 −		0.11	0.11 −	

NOTE: Figures in parentheses represent the number of cases in the sample; all other figures, except odds ratios and etas, are in percent.

Bibliography

Abraham, Henry J. *The Judicial Process*. 3rd ed. New York: Oxford Univ. Press, 1975.

Adamany, David W. "Legitimacy, Realigning Elections and the Supreme Court." *Wisconsin Law Review* 3 (1973):790–846.

———. "The Party Variable in Judges' Voting: Conceptual Notes and a Case Study." *American Political Science Review* 63 (1969): 57–74.

Anderson, James E. *Public Policy-Making*. New York: Praeger, 1975.

Asher, Herbert B., and Herbert F. Weisberg. "Voting Change in Congress: Some Dynamic Perspectives on an Evolutionary Process." *American Journal of Political Science* 22 (1978):391–425.

Atkins, Burton M. "Opinion Assignments on the United States Court of Appeals: The Question of Issue Specialization." *Western Political Quarterly* 27 (1974):409–28.

Atkins, Burton M., and Justin Green. "Problems in the Measurement of Conflict on the United States Courts of Appeals." Paper presented at the Annual Meeting of the American Political Science Association, Chicago, Aug. 29–Sept. 2, 1974.

Atkins, Burton M., and William Zavoina. "Judicial Leadership on the Court of Appeals: A Probability Analysis of Panel Assignments in Race Relations Cases on the Fifth Circuit." *American Journal of Political Science* 18 (1974):701–11.

Baum, Lawrence. "Responses of Federal District Judges to Court of Appeals Policies: An Exploration." *Western Political Quarterly* 33 (1980):217–24.

Beard, Charles A. *An Economic Interpretation of the Constitution of the United States*. New York: Macmillan, 1913.

Beatty, Jerry. "An Institutional and Behavioral Analysis of the Iowa Supreme Court 1965–1969." Ph.D. diss., Univ. of Iowa, 1970.

Beers, Howard W. "Rural-Urban Differences: Some Evidence from Opinion Polls." *Rural Sociology* 18 (1953):1–11.

Bem, D.J., M.A. Wallach, and N. Kogan. "Group Decision Making under Risk of Aversive Consequences." *Journal of Personality and Social Psychology* 1 (1965):453–60.

Biddle, Bruce J., and Edwin J. Thomas, eds. *Role Theory: Concepts and Research.* New York: Wiley, 1966.

Black, Merle. "Regional and Partisan Bases of Congressional Support for the Changing Agenda of Civil Rights Legislation." *Journal of Politics* 41 (1979):665–79.

Blum, John M. *Joe Tumulty and the Wilson Era.* Boston: Houghton Mifflin, 1951.

Blumberg, Abraham S. *Criminal Justice.* Chicago: Quadrangle Books, 1967.

Bond, Jon R. "The Politics of Court Structure." *Law and Policy Quarterly* 2 (1980):181–88.

Bowen, Don. "The Explanation of Judicial Voting Behavior from Sociological Characteristics of Judges." Ph.D. diss., Yale Univ., 1965.

Brady, David W. "A Research Note on the Impact of the Inter-Party Competition on Congressional Voting in a Competitive Era." *American Political Science Review* 67 (1973):153–57.

Brady, David W., and Naomi Lynn. "Switched Seat Congressional Districts: Their Effect on Party Voting and Public Policy." *American Journal of Political Science* 17 (1973):528–43.

Burnham, Walter Dean. "The End of American Party Politics." *Transaction* 7 (1969):12–23.

Campbell, Angus, Philip E. Converse, Warren E. Miller, and Donald E. Stokes. *The American Voter.* New York: Wiley, 1960.

Cardozo, Benjamin. *The Growth of the Law.* New Haven: Yale Univ. Press, 1924.

_____. *The Nature of the Judicial Process.* New Haven: Yale Univ. Press, 1921.

Carp, Robert A. "An Analysis of Censorship Pressures on Iowa High School Social Studies Teachers." Master's thesis, Univ. of Iowa, 1967.

_____. "The Function, Impact, and Political Relevance of the Federal District Courts: A Case Study." Ph.D. diss., Univ. of Iowa, 1969.

_____. "The Influence of Local Needs and Conditions on the Administration of Federal Justice." Paper presented at the Annual Meeting of the Southwestern Political Science Association, Dallas, March 25–27, 1971.

_____. "The Scope and Function of Intra-Circuit Judicial Communication: A Case Study of the Eighth Circuit." *Law and Society Review* 6 (1972):405–27.

Carp, Robert A., and Claude K. Rowland. "Opinion Writing by Federal District Judges: Its Impact for the Study of Judicial Behavior and Administration." Paper presented at the Annual Conference of the American Society of Public Administration, Phoenix, Ariz., April 11–14, 1978.

———. "The Relationship Between Opinion Writing by Federal Trial Courts and Termination Rates of the District Courts." *Justice System Journal* 5 (1979); 187–96.

Carp, Robert A., and Russell Wheeler. "Sink or Swim: The Socialization of a Federal District Judge." *Journal of Public Law* 21 (1972):359–93.

Casper, Jonathan D. *Lawyers Before the Warren Court: Civil Rights and Civil Liberties.* Urbana: Univ. of Illinois Press, 1972.

Casstevens, Thomas W., and James R. Ozinga. "The Soviet Central Committee Since Stalin: A Longitudinal View." *American Journal of Political Science* 18 (1974):559–68.

Chase, Harold W. *Federal Judges: The Appointing Process.* Minneapolis: Univ. of Minnesota Press, 1972.

Church, Thomas. *Justice Delayed: The Pace of Litigation in Urban Trial Courts.* Williamsburg, Va.: National Center for State Courts, 1978.

Clausen, Aage R. *How Congressmen Decide.* New York: St. Martin's, 1973.

Cook, Beverly Blair. "Decision-Making by Federal Trial Judges: Reference Groups and Local Culture." Paper presented at the Annual Meeting of the American Political Science Association, New Orleans, Sept. 4–8, 1973.

———. "Public Opinion and Federal Judicial Policy." *American Journal of Political Science* 21 (1977): 567–600.

———. "Sentencing of Federal Judges: Draft Cases: 1972." *University of Cincinnati Law Review* 42 (1972):597–634.

Cooper, Joseph, David Brady, and Patricia Hurley. "The Electoral Basis of Party Voting: Patterns and Trends in the U.S. House of Representatives, 1887–1969." In *Sage Electoral Studies Yearbook.* New York: Sage Books, 1976.

Costner, Herbert. "Criteria for Measures of Association." *American Sociological Review* 30 (1965):341–51.

Danelski, David J. "Toward Explanation of Judicial Behavior." *University of Cincinnati Law Review* 42 (1972):659–67.

Derge, David R. "Metropolitan and Outside Alignments in Illinois and Missouri Legislative Delegations." *American Political Science Review* 52 (1958):1051–65.

Deutsch, Karl. *The Nerves of Government.* New York: Free Press, 1966.

Dolbeare, Kenneth M. *Trial Courts in Urban Politics.* New York: Wiley, 1967.

———. "The Federal District Courts and Urban Public Policy: An

Exploratory Study (1960–1967)." In J.B. Grossman and J. Tanenhaus, eds., *Frontiers of Judicial Research*. New York: Wiley, 1969.

Downes, Bryan T., ed. *Cities and Suburbs: Selected Readings in Local Politics and Public Policy*. Belmont, Calif.: Wadsworth, 1971.

Early, Stephen. *Constitutional Courts of the United States*. Totowa, N.J.: Littlefield, Adams, 1977.

Easton, David. *A Framework for Political Analysis*. Englewood Cliffs, N.J.: Prentice-Hall, 1965.

Eisenstein, James. *Politics and the Legal Process*. New York: Harper & Row, 1973.

Eisenstein, James, and Herbert Jacob. *Felony Justice: An Organizational Analysis of Criminal Courts*. Boston: Little, Brown, 1977.

Engleman, Laszlo. "PLR: Stepwise Logistic Regression." In *BMDP: Biomedical Computer Programs, P-Scores*. Los Angeles: Univ. of California Press, 1979.

Epstein, Leon. "Size and Place and the Two-Party Vote." *Western Political Quarterly* 9 (1956):138–50.

Federal Supplement. Vols. 1–431. Washington D.C.: U.S. Government Printing Office, 1933–76.

Feeley, Malcolm. "Another Look at the 'Party Variable' in Judicial Decision Making: An Analysis of the Michigan Supreme Court," *Polity* 4 (1971):91–104.

Fenton, J.H. "Liberal-Conservative Divisions by Sections of the United States," *Annals* 344 (1962):122–27.

Flanders, Steven (Project Director). *Case Management and Court Management in United States District Courts*. Washington, D.C.: U.S. Government Printing Office, 1977.

Francis, Wayne L. *Legislative Issues in the Fifty States: A Comparative Analysis*. Chicago: Rand McNally, 1967.

Frank, Jerome. *Courts on Trial: Myth and Reality in American Justice*. Princeton, N.J.: Princeton Univ. Press, 1950.

Friejohn, John, and Morris Fiorina. "Purposive Models of Legislative Behavior." *American Economic Review* 65 (1975):407–14.

Giles, Michael W., and Thomas G. Walker. "Judicial Policy-Making and Southern School Segregation." *Journal of Politics* 37 (1975): 917–37.

Goldman, Sheldon. "Characteristics of Eisenhower and Kennedy Appointees to the Lower Federal Courts." *Western Political Quarterly* 18 (1965):755–62.

_____. "Conflict on the U.S. Courts of Appeals 1965–1971: A Quantitative Analysis." *University of Cincinnati Law Review* 42 (1973):635–58.

_____. "Johnson and Nixon Appointees to the Lower Federal Courts." *Journal of Politics* 34 (1972):934–43.

_____. "Judicial Appointments to the United States Courts of Appeals." *Wisconsin Law Review* 1967 (1967):186–214.

_____. "Judicial Backgrounds, Recruitment, and the Party Variable: The Case of the Johnson and Nixon Appointees to the United States District and Appeals Courts." *Arizona State Law Journal* 2 (1974):211–22.

_____. "Voting Behavior on the United States Courts of Appeals, 1961–64." *American Political Science Review* 60 (1966):370–85.

_____. "Voting Behavior on the United States Courts of Appeals Revisited." *American Political Science Review* 69 (1975):491–506.

Goldman, Sheldon, and Thomas P. Jahnige. *The Federal Courts as a Political System.* 2d ed. New York: Harper & Row, 1976.

Goldstein, Leslie. "The Politics of the Burger Court toward Women." *Political Studies Journal* 7 (1978):213–18.

Goulden, Joseph C. *The Benchwarmers.* New York: Weybright and Talley, 1974.

Grafton, Samuel. "Lonesomest Man in Town." *Colliers* (April 29, 1950):20–22, 49–50.

Greenias, George C., and Duane Windsor. "Is Judicial Restraint Possible in an Administrative Society?" *Judicature* 69 (1981): 400–13.

Grossman, Joel B. *Lawyers and Judges: The ABA and the Politics of Judicial Selection.* New York: Wiley, 1965.

Grossman, Joel B., and Joseph Tanenhaus, eds. *Frontiers of Judicial Research.* New York: Wiley, 1969.

Gunther, G. "In Search of Evolving Doctrine on a Changing Court: A Model for a Newer Equal Protection." *Harvard Law Review* 86 (1972):1–48.

Hamilton, Charles V. *The Bench and the Ballot: Southern Federal Judges and Black Voters.* New York: Oxford Univ. Press, 1973.

Harris, Keith D., and Russell P. Lura. "The Geography of Justice: Sentencing Variations in U.S. Judicial Districts." *Judicature* 57 (1974):392–402.

Hendron, James. "Relationships Between Partisanship and the Decisions of the State Supreme Courts." Ph.D. diss., Univ. of Michigan, 1963.

Heydebrand, Wolf. "The Context of Public Bureaucracies: An Organizational Analysis of Federal District Courts." *Law and Society Review* 11 (1977):759–823.

Hinckley, Barbara. *Stability and Change in Congress.* New York: Harper & Row, 1978.

Holcomb, Arthur N. *The Political Parties of To-day.* New York: Harper, 1924.

Howard, J. Woodford, Jr. "Litigation Flow in Three United States Courts of Appeals." *Law and Society Review* 8 (1973):33–53.

———. "Role Perceptions and Behavior in Three U.S. Courts of Appeals." *Journal of Politics* 39 (1977):916–39.

Jackson, Donald Dale. *Judges.* New York: Atheneum, 1974.

Jacob, Herbert. *Urban Justice.* Englewood Cliffs, N.J.: Prentice-Hall, 1973.

Jahnige, Thomas P. "Critical Elections and Social Change." *Polity* 4 (1971):465–500.

Jahnige, Thomas P., and Sheldon Goldman, eds. *The Federal Judicial System: Readings in Process and Behavior.* New York: Holt, Rinehart, 1968.

Jensen, Merrill, ed. *Regionalism in America.* Madison: Univ. of Wisconsin Press, 1952.

Jewell, Malcolm E., and Samuel C. Patterson. *The Legislative Process in the United States.* 3d ed. New York: Random House, 1977.

Johnson, Charles A. "Lower Court Reactions to Supreme Court Decisions: A Quantitative Explanation." *American Journal of Political Science* 23 (1979):792–804.

"Judicial Performance in the Fifth Circuit." *Yale Law Journal* 73 (1963):90–133.

Key, V.O., Jr. *Politics, Parties, and Pressure Groups.* 5th ed. New York: Crowell, 1964.

———. *Public Opinion and American Democracy.* New York: Knopf, 1967.

Kingdon, John. *Congressmen's Voting Decisions.* New York: Harper & Row, 1973.

———. "Models of Legislative Voting." *Journal of Politics* 39 (1977): 563–95.

Kitchin, William. *Federal District Judges: An Analysis of Judicial Perceptions.* Baltimore: Collage Press, 1978.

Kort, Fred. "Regression Analysis and Discriminant Analysis: An Application of R.A. Risher's Theorem to Data in Political Science." *American Political Science Review* 67 (1973):555–59.

Kritzer, Herbert M. "Federal Judges and Their Political Environment." *American Journal of Political Science* 23 (1979):194–207.

———."An Introduction to Multivariate Contingency Table Analysis." *American Journal of Political Science* 22 (1978):187–213.

———. "Political Correlates of the Behavior of Federal District Judges: A 'Best Case' Analysis." *Journal of Politics* 40 (1978):25–58.

Ladd, Everett Carll, Jr. *Ideology in America: Change and Response in a City, a Suburb, and a Small Town.* Ithaca, N.Y.: Cornell Univ. Press, 1969.

_____. *Where Have All the Voters Gone?: The Fracturing of America's Political Parties.* New York: Norton, 1978.

Ladd, Everett Carll, Jr., and Charles D. Hadley. *Transformations of the American Party System.* 2d ed. New York: Norton, 1978.

Lamb, Charles M. "Warren Burger and the Insanity Defense: Judicial Philosophy and Voting Behavior on a U.S. Court of Appeals." *American University Law Review* 24 (1974):91–128.

Leavitt, Donald. "Political Party and Class Influence on the Attitudes of Justices of the Supreme Court in the Twentieth Century." Paper presented at the Annual Meeting of the Midwest Political Science Association, Chicago, April 27–29, 1972.

Lieberman, Jethro. *The Litigious Society.* New York: Basic Books, 1981.

Link, Arthur S. "Woodrow Wilson and the Democratic Party." *Review of Politics* 18 (1956):146–56.

Lipset, Seymour Martin. *Political Man: The Social Basis of Politics.* Garden City, N.Y.: Doubleday, 1960.

Lodge, Henry Cabot. *Selections from the Correspondence of Theodore Roosevelt and Henry Cabot Lodge, 1884–1918.* Vol. II. New York: Scribner's, 1925.

Lowi, Theodore. "Toward Functionalism in Political Science: The Case of Innovation in Party Systems." *American Political Science Review* 57 (1963):570–83.

Lowi, Theodore, and Alan Stone, eds. *Nationalizing Government.* Beverly Hills, Calif., Sage, 1978.

MacRae, Duncan, Jr. "Occupations and the Congressional Vote, 1940–1950." *American Sociological Review* 20 (1955):332–40.

_____. "The Relation Between Roll Call Votes and Constituencies in the Massachusetts House of Representatives." *American Political Science Review* 46 (1952):1046–55.

Maine, Sir Henry. *Ancient Law.* New York: Everyman's Library, 1974.

Markham, Walter G. "Draft Offenders in the Federal Courts: A Search for the Social Correlates of Justice." Ph.D. diss., Univ. of Pennsylvania, 1971.

Marquis, D.C. "Individual Responsibility and Group Decisions Involving Risk." *Industrial Management Review* 3 (1962):8–23.

Mason, Alpheus Thomas, and William M. Beaney. *American Constitutional Law.* 6th ed. Englewood Cliffs, N.J.: Prentice-Hall, 1978.

Masters, Nicholas A., and Deil S. Wright. "Trends and Variations in the Two-Party Vote: The Case of Michigan." *American Political Science Review* 52 (1958):1078–90.

Mayhew, David R. *Party Loyalty Among Congressmen.* Cambridge: Harvard Univ. Press, 1966.

McFeeley, Neil. "A Change of Direction: Habeas Corpus from Warren to Burger." Paper presented at the Annual Meeting of the Southwestern Political Science Association, Dallas, March 30–April 2, 1977.

Mendelson, Wallace. "From Warren to Burger: The Rise and Decline of Substantive Equal Protection." *American Political Science Review* 66 (1972):1226–33.

———. "Judicial Review and Party Politics." *Vanderbilt Law Review* 12 (1959):447–57.

Morris, Jeffrey B. "The Second Most Important Court: The United States Court of Appeals for the District of Columbia Circuit." Ph.D. diss., Columbia University, 1972.

Mosley, William H. "Personal Attitudes and Judicial Role in Judicial Decision-Making: A Study of the United States Courts of Appeals." Ph.D. diss., Univ. of Hawaii, 1972.

Mueller, John H., Karl F. Schuessler, and Herbert L. Costner. *Statistical Reasoning in Sociology.* 2d ed. Boston: Houghton Mifflin, 1970.

Murphy, Walter F. "Lower Court Checks on Supreme Court Power." *American Political Science Review* 53 (1959):1017–31.

Murphy, Walter F., and C. Herman Pritchett. *Courts, Judges and Politics: An Introduction to the Judicial Process.* 3d ed. New York: Random House, 1979.

Murphy, Walter F., and Joseph Tanenhaus. *The Study of Public Law.* New York: Random House, 1972.

Nagel, Stuart. *The Legal Process from a Behavioral Perspective.* Homewood, Ill.: Dorsey Press, 1969.

———. "Multiple Correlations of Judicial Backgrounds and Decisions." *Florida State University Law Review* 2 (1974):258–80.

———. "Political Party Affiliation and Judges' Decision." *American Political Science Review* 55 (1961):843–90.

———. "The Relationship between the Political and Ethnic Affiliation of Judges, and their Decision-Making." In G. Schubert, ed., *Judicial Behavior.* Chicago: Rand McNally, 1964.

Navasky, Victor. *Kennedy Justice.* New York: Atheneum, 1971.

Neff, Alan. "Breaking with Tradition: A Study of the U.S. District Judge Nominating Commissions." *Judicature* 64 (1981):256–78.

Nie, Norman H., C. Hadlai Hull, Jean G. Jenkins, Karin Steinbrenner, and Dale H. Bent. *Statistical Package for the Social Sciences.* 2d ed. New York: McGraw-Hill, 1975.

Ofshe, Richard J., ed. *Interpersonal Behavior in Small Groups.* Englewood Cliffs, N.J.: Prentice-Hall, 1973.

O'Neill, Timothy. "The Language of Equality in a Constitutional Order." *American Political Science Review* 75 (1981):628–39.

Parsons, Talcott. *Structure and Process in Modern Societies*. New York: Free Press, 1960.

Partridge, Anthony, and William B. Eldridge. *The Second Circuit Sentencing Study: A Report to the Judges of the Second Circuit*. Washington, D.C.: Federal Judicial Center, 1974.

Peltason, Jack W. *Federal Courts in the Political Process*. New York: Random House, 1955.

––––––. *58 Lonely Men: Southern Federal Judges and School Desegregation*. New York: Harcourt, Brace & World, 1961.

Pomper, Gerald. *Voters' Choice: Varieties of American Electoral Behavior*. New York: Dodd, Mead, 1975.

Prachera, John S. "Background Characteristics and Judicial Voting Behavior: An Examination." Paper presented at the Annual Meeting of the Western Political Science Association, Phoenix, March 31–April 2, 1977.

Price, Miles O., and Harry Bitner. *Effective Legal Research*. Student ed., rev. Boston: Little, Brown, 1962.

Pritchett, C. Herman. *Civil Liberties and the Vinson Court*. Chicago: Univ. of Chicago Press, 1954.

––––––. *The Roosevelt Court: A Study of Judicial Votes and Values, 1937–1947*. New York: Macmillan, 1948.

Rappaport, Leon, and David Summers, eds. *Human Judgment and Social Interaction*. New York: Holt, Rinehart, 1973.

Reynolds, H.T. *Analysis of Nominal Data*. Beverly Hills, Calif.: Sage, 1977.

Richardson, Richard J., and Kenneth N. Vines. *The Politics of Federal Courts: Lower Courts in the United States*. Boston: Little, Brown, 1970.

Ripley, Randall B. *Congress: Process and Policy*. 2d ed. New York: Norton, 1978.

Robinson, Glen O., and Ernest Gellhorn. *The Administrative Process*. St. Paul, Minn.: West, 1974.

Rodgers, Harrell R., Jr., and Charles S. Bullock, Ill. *Coercion to Compliance*. Lexington, Mass.: Heath, 1976.

Rowland, C.K., and Robert A. Carp. "A Longitudinal Study of Party Effects on Federal District Court Policy Propensities." *American Journal of Political Science* 24 (1980):291–305.

Schlesinger, Arthur M., Jr. *Robert Kennedy and His Times*. Boston: Houghton Mifflin, 1978.

Schnore, Leo F. "The Social and Economic Characteristics of American Suburbs." In B.T. Downes, ed., *Cities and Suburbs*. Belmont, Calif.: Wadsworth, 1971.

Schmidhauser, John R. *Constitutional Law in the Political Process.* Chicago: Rand McNally, 1963.

_____. "Judicial Behavior and the Sectional Crisis of 1837-1860." *Journal of Politics* 23 (1961):615-40.

_____. "The Justices of the Supreme Court: A Collective Portrait." *Midwest Journal of Political Science* 3 (1959):1-57.

_____. *The Supreme Court: Its Politics, Personalities, and Procedures.* New York: Holt, Rinehart, 1960.

Schubert, Glendon. *The Constitutional Polity.* Boston: Boston Univ. Press, 1970.

_____. *The Judicial Mind Revisited.* New York: Oxford, 1974.

_____. *Judicial Policy Making.* 2d ed. Glenview, Ill.: Scott, Foresman, 1974.

_____. *Quantitative Analysis of Judicial Behavior.* New York: Free Press, 1959.

Schubert, Glendon, ed. *Judicial Behavior: A Reader in Theory and Research.* Chicago: Rand McNally, 1964.

Shannon, W. Wayne. *Party, Constituency, and Congressional Voting.* Baton Rouge: Louisiana State Univ. Press, 1968.

Simon, Herbert. *Administrative Behavior.* 3d ed. New York: Free Press, 1976.

Simon, James F. *In His Own Image.* New York: David McKay, 1973.

Sinclair, Barbara D. "Determinants of Aggregate Party Cohesion in the U.S. House of Representatives, 1901-1956." *Legislative Studies Quarterly* 2 (1977):155-75.

_____. "Party Cohesion in the House of Representatives: Trends and Determinants." Paper presented at the Annual Meeting of the Southwestern Political Science Association, Houston, April 12-15, 1978.

_____. "The Policy Consequences of Realignment: Social Welfare Legislation in the House of Representatives, 1933-1959." *American Journal of Political Science* 22 (1978):82-105.

_____. "Who Wins in the House of Representatives: The Effect of Declining Party Cohesion on Policy Outputs, 1959-1970." *Social Science Quarterly* 58 (1977):121-28.

Slotnick, Elliot E. "The Carter Presidency and the U.S. Circuit Judge Nominating Commission." Paper presented at the Annual Meeting of the American Political Science Association, New York, Aug. 31-Sept. 3, 1978.

_____. "Reforms in Judicial Selection: Will They Affect the Senate's Role? (Part II)." *Judicature* 64 (1980):115-31.

Sorauf, Frank J. *Party Politics in America.* Boston: Little, Brown, 1976.

Stidham, Ronald. "An Exploration of Environmental Influences on

Judicial Policy-Making by Federal District Judges." Ph.D. diss., Univ. of Houston, 1979.

Stoner, J.A.F. "Comparison of Individual and Group Decisions Involving Risk." Master's thesis, Mass. Institute of Technology, School of Industrial Management, 1961.

Stouffer, Samuel A. *Communism, Conformity, and Civil Liberties.* New York: Doubleday, 1955.

Sutton, L. Paul. *Federal Sentencing Patterns: A Study of Geographical Variations.* Albany, N.Y.: Criminal Justice Research Center, 1978.

Tanenhaus, Joseph, and Walter F. Murphy. *The Study of Public Law.* New York: Random House, 1972.

Tate, C. Neal. "Personal Attribute Models of the Voting Behavior of U.S. Supreme Court Justices' Liberalism in Civil Liberties and Economics Decisions, 1946–1978." *American Political Science Review* 75 (1981):355–67.

Teger, Allen I., and Dean G. Pruitt. "Components of Group Risk Taking." *Journal of Experimental Social Psychology* 3 (1967): 189–205.

Turner, Frederick J. *The Significance of Sections in American History.* New York: Holt, 1932.

Ulmer, Sidney S. "The Political Party Variable in the Michigan Supreme Court." *Journal of Politics* 11 (1962):352–62.

_____. "Social Backgrounds as Indicators of the Votes of Supreme Court Justices in Criminal Cases: 1947–1956." *American Journal of Political Science* 17 (1973):622–30.

Vestal, Allan D. "Publishing District Court Opinions in the 1970's" *Loyola Law Review* 17 (1970–71):673–81.

_____. Reported Federal District Court Opinions: Fiscal 1962." *Houston Law Review* 4 (1966):185–220.

_____. "Reported Opinions of the Federal District Courts: Analysis and Suggestions." *Iowa Law Review* 52 (1966):379–405.

_____. "A Survey of Federal District Court Opinions: West Publishing Company Reports." *Southwestern Law Journal* 20 (1966): 63–96.

Vines, Kenneth N. "Federal District Judges and Race Relations Cases in the South." *Journal of Politics* 26 (1964):337–57.

_____. "The Role of Circuit Courts of Appeals in the Federal Judicial Process: A Case Study." *Midwest Journal of Political Science* 7 (1963):305–19.

Vose, Clement E. "Litigation as a Form of Pressure Group Activity." *The Annals of the American Academy of Political and Social Science* 391 (1958):20–31.

Wahlke, John, Heinz Eulau, William Buchanan, and LeRoy C. Ferguson. *The Legislative System.* New York: Wiley, 1962.

Walker, Darlene. "The Burger Court and Civil Liberties: The Problem of Moving the Law Backward." In T. Lowi and A. Stone, eds., *Nationalizing Government.* Beverly Hills, Calif.: Sage, 1978.

Walker, Thomas G. "Judges in Concert: The Influences of the Group on Judicial Decision-Making." Ph.D. diss., Univ. of Kentucky, 1970.

_____. "A Note Concerning Partisan Influences on Trial-Judge Decision Making." *Law and Society Review* 6 (1972):645-49.

Walker, Thomas G., and William E. Hulbary. "The Supreme Court Selection Process: Presidential Motivations and Judicial Performances." *Western Political Quarterly* 33 (1980):185-97.

Wallach, M.A., and N. Kogan. "The Roles of Information, Discussion, and Consensus in Group Risk Taking." *Journal of Experimental Social Psychology* 1 (1965):1-19.

Wallach, M.A., N. Kogan, and D.J. Bem. "Diffusion of Responsibility and Level of Risk Taking in Groups." *Journal of Abnormal and Social Psychology* 68 (1964):263-74.

Wallach, M.A., N. Kogan, and D.J. Bem. "Group Influence on Individual Risk Taking." *Journal of Abnormal and Social Psychology* 65 (1962):75-86.

Wasby, Stephen L. *Continuity and Change: From the Warren Court to the Burger Court.* Santa Monica, Calif.: Goodyear, 1975.

_____. *The Supreme Court in the Federal Judicial System.* New York: Holt, Rinehart, 1978.

Weiner, Norbert. *The Human Use of Human Beings: Cybernetics and Society.* Garden City, N.Y.: Doubleday, 1954.

Wirt, Frederick M., Benjamin Walter, Francine F. Rabinovitz, and Deborah R. Hensler. *On the City's Rim: Politics and Policy in Suburbia.* Lexington, Mass: D.C. Heath, 1972.

Wuebben, Paul L., Bruce C. Straits, and Gary I. Schulman. *The Experiment as a Social Occasion.* Berkeley, Calif.: Glendessary, 1974.

Zumwalt, William James. "The Anarchy of Sentencing in the Federal Courts." *Judicature* 57 (1973):96-105.

Index

Policymaking and Politics in the Federal District Courts has been composed on the Compugraphic phototypesetter in ten-point Palatino with one-point line spacing. Palatino was also selected for display. The book was designed by Jim Billingsley, set into type by Metricomp, Inc., printed offset by Thomson-Shore, Inc., and bound by John H. Dekker & Sons. The paper on which the book is printed bears the watermark of S. D. Warren and is designed for an effective life of at least 300 years.

THE UNIVERSITY OF TENNESSEE PRESS : KNOXVILLE